Multivariate Analysis: Engineering and Administrative Sciences

Multivariate Analysis: Engineering and Administrative Sciences

Edited by **Roland Chan**

LANRYE
INTERNATIONAL

New Jersey

Published by Clanrye International,
55 Van Reypen Street,
Jersey City, NJ 07306, USA
www.clanryeinternational.com

Multivariate Analysis: Engineering and Administrative Sciences
Edited by Roland Chan

© 2015 Clanrye International

International Standard Book Number: 978-1-63240-369-8 (Hardback)

Contents

Preface   VII

Section 1   Multivariate Analysis in Management   1

Chapter 1   Contributions of Multivariate Statistics
             in Oil and Gas Industry   3
             Leandro Valim de Freitas, Ana Paula Barbosa Rodrigues de Freitas,
             Fernando Augusto Silva Marins, Estéfano Vizconde Veraszto,
             José Tarcísio Franco de Camargo, J. Paulo Davim
             and Messias Borges Silva

Chapter 2   Technology and Society Public Perception.
             A Structural Equation Modeling Study of
             the Brazilian Undergraduate Students'
             Opinions and Attitudes from Sao Paulo State   15
             Estéfano Vizconde Veraszto, José Tarcísio Franco de Camargo,
             Dirceu da Silva and Leandro Valim de Freitas

Chapter 3   Application of Multivariate
             Data Analyses in Waste Management   37
             K. Böhm, E. Smidt and J. Tintner

Section 2   Multivariate Analysis in Engineering   61

Chapter 4   Multivariate Analysis in Advanced Oxidation Process   63
             Ana Paula Barbosa Rodrigues de Freitas, Leandro Valim de Freitas,
             Gisella Lamas Samanamud, Fernando Augusto Silva Marins,
             Carla Cristina Almeida Loures, Fatima Salman,
             Hilton Túlio Lima dos Santos and Messias Borges Silva

Chapter 5   Variable Selection and Feature Extraction
             Through Artificial Intelligence Techniques   81
             Silvia Cateni, Marco Vannucci, Marco Vannocci and Valentina Colla

Chapter 6   Itaipu Hydroelectric Power Plant Structural
             Geotechnical Instrumentation Temporal Data Under
             the Application of Multivariate Analysis –
             Grouping and Ranking Techniques   97
             Rosangela Villwock, Maria Teresinha Arns Steiner,
             Andrea Sell Dyminski and Anselmo Chaves Neto

Section 3   Multivariate Analysis in the Sciences:
             Chemometrics Approach   119

Chapter 7   Chemometrics: Theory and Application   121
             Hilton Túlio Lima dos Santos, André Maurício de Oliveira,
             Patrícia Gontijo de Melo, Wagner Freitas
             and Ana Paula Rodrigues de Freitas

Chapter 8   Multivariate Analysis in Vibrational Spectroscopy
             of Highly Energetic Materials and Chemical
             Warfare Agents Simulants   133
             John R. Castro-Suarez, William Ortiz-Rivera, Nataly Galan-Freyle,
             Amanda Figueroa-Navedo, Leonardo C. Pacheco-Londoño
             and Samuel P. Hernández-Rivera

Chapter 9   Classification and Ordination Methods as a Tool
             for Analyzing of Plant Communities   161
             Mohammad Ali Zare Chahouki

Chapter 10   Ageing and Deterioration of Materials in the Environment –
             Application of Multivariate Data Analysis   195
             E. Smidt, M. Schwanninger, J. Tintner and K. Böhm

Chapter 11   Multivariate Analysis for Fourier
             Transform Infrared Spectra of
             Complex Biological Systems and Processes   223
             Diletta Ami, Paolo Mereghetti and Silvia Maria Doglia

             Permissions

             List of Contributors

Preface

This book presents the state-of-the-art information of multivariate analysis and its application in various fields. Currently, statistical knowledge has become an essential need and holds a significant position in the exercise of various professions. The procedures have a huge volume of data in the real world, and are naturally multifarious and as such, need an appropriate treatment. For these conditions it is problematic or practically not possible to utilize methodologies of univariate statistics. The broad spectrum of applications of multivariate strategies and the necessity to spread them more significantly in academics and business justify the creation of this book. The aim of this book is to illustrate interdisciplinary applications to recognize trends, patterns, relations and dependencies, in the fields of engineering, sciences and management and to serve as a valuable source of reference for both veteran researchers and engaged professionals in the field.

Various studies have approached the subject by analyzing it with a single perspective, but the present book provides diverse methodologies and techniques to address this field. This book contains theories and applications needed for understanding the subject from different perspectives. The aim is to keep the readers informed about the progresses in the field; therefore, the contributions were carefully examined to compile novel researches by specialists from across the globe.

Indeed, the job of the editor is the most crucial and challenging in compiling all chapters into a single book. In the end, I would extend my sincere thanks to the chapter authors for their profound work. I am also thankful for the support provided by my family and colleagues during the compilation of this book.

Editor

Multivariate Analysis in Management

Chapter 1

Contributions of Multivariate Statistics in Oil and Gas Industry

Leandro Valim de Freitas, Ana Paula Barbosa Rodrigues de Freitas,
Fernando Augusto Silva Marins, Estéfano Vizconde Veraszto,
José Tarcísio Franco de Camargo, J. Paulo Davim and Messias Borges Silva

Additional information is available at the end of the chapter

1. Introduction

This study aims to develop and validate multivariate mathematical models in order to monitor in real time the quality processing of derivatives in an oil refinery.

Methods heavily based on statistical and artificial intelligence as multivariate or chemometric methods have been widely used in the oil industry (KIM; LEE, KIM, 2009). Several articles have been written about applications of multivariate analysis to predict properties of oil derivatives (Santos Junior et al., 2005; Chung, 2007).

Pasadakis, Sourligas and Foteinopoulos (2006) have used the first six principal components of Principal Component Analysis (PCA) as input variables in nonlinear modeling of oil properties.

Pasquini and Bueno (2007) have proposed a new approach to predict the true boiling point of oil and its degree API (American Petroleum Institute) - a measure of the relative density of liquids by Partial Least Squares (PLS) and Artificial Neural Networks (ANN). Samples of mixtures oil were obtained from various producing regions of Brazil and abroad. In this application, the models obtained by the PLS method were superior to neural networks. The short time required for prediction the properties justifies the proposed of characterization the oil quicker to monitor refining processes.

Teixeira et al. (2008) in work with Brazilian gasoline used the multivariate algorithm Soft Independent Modeling of Class Analogy (SIMCA) for clusters analysis. Aiming to quantify the amount of adulteration of gasoline by other hydrocarbons, the PLS method was applied. Finally, the models were validated internally by cross-validation algorithm and externally with an independent set of samples.

Bao and Dai (2009) studied different multivariate methods, including linear and nonlinear techniques in order to minimize the error of prediction by models developed for quality control of gasoline. Lira et al. (2010) applied the PLS method for inference of the quality parameters: density, sulfur concentration and distillation temperatures of the mixture diesel / bio-diesel, providing great savings in time compared with the traditional methods by laboratory equipment.

Aleme, Corgozinho and Barbeira (2010) have conducted a study of classification of samples using the PCA method for discrimination of diesel oil type and the prediction of their origin.

Paiva Ferreira and Balestrassi (2007) have combined the Response Surface Method (RSM) of Design of Experiments (DOE) with Principal Component Analysis in optimizing multiple correlated responses in a manufacturing process.

Huang, Hsu and Liu (2009) have used Mahalanobis-Taguchi integrated with Artificial Neural Networks in data mining to look for patterns and modeling in manufacturing. Pal and Maiti (2010) have adopted the Mahalanobis-Taguchi algorithm to reduce the dimensionality of multivariate data and for optimization with Metaheuristics in the sequence.

Liu et al. (2007) have made inferences about quality parameters of jet fuel using Multiple Linear Regression (MLR) and ANN. The work showed that the performance of modeling by ANN was superior.

In optimization of multivariate models, there are applications combined with Multivariate Analysis of Metaheuristics, such as simulated annealing (SAUNIER, et al., 2009), genetic algorithm (GA) (Roy, Roy, 2009) tabu search (QI; SHI; KONG, 2010), particle swarm (Pal; Mait, 2010), and ant colony (Goodarzi; Freitas; Jensen, 2009; Allegrini; Oliveri, 2011).

With the objective of optimizing the dimensionality of multivariate models and avoid the overfitting phenomenon in determining principal components, Xu and Liang (2001) have used the Monte Carlo Simulation on simulated data sets and two real cases. Gourvénec et al. (2003) compared Monte Carlo cross-validation with the traditional method of cross validation to determine the appropriate number of latent variables.

Adler e Yazhemsky (2010) have combined the Monte Carlo Simulation, PCA and Data Envelopment Analysis (DEA) in a context where there is a relatively large number of variables related to the number of observations for decision making. Llobet et al. (2005), by means a Multiple Criteria Decision-Making (MCDM) model, have used Fuzzy classification of samples of chips. For prediction oxidative and hydrolytic properties, was used an electronic nose based on PLS models, with prior selection of input variables by a GA Metaheuristic.

Wu, Feng and Wen (2011), in studies related to Botany, compared the performance of the growth of a tree species - Carya Cathayensis Sarg by PCA methods and Analytic Hierarchy Process (AHP), identifying the advantages and the disadvantages of each method, although the results obtained by both have been essentially identical.

Zhang et al. (2006) have combined the method Preference Ranking Organization Method for Enrichment Evaluations (PROMETHEE), from the Elimination et la Choix Traduisant Réalité (ELECTRE) and Geometrical Analysis for Interactive Assistance (GAIA) with PCA and PLS methods to classify 67 oils and determine an indicator of product quality. Purcell, O'Shea and Kokot (2007) also combined PROMETHEE and GAIA with PCA and PLS in studies related to cloning of sugarcane.

Regarding to the control charts designed to monitor the mean vector, Machado and Costa (2008) have studied the performance of T^2 charts based on principal components for monitoring multivariate processes. Lourenço et al. (2011) have used the principles of Process Analytical Technology (PAT) in the construction of control charts based on the scores of the first principal component versus time for the on-line monitoring of pharmaceutical processes.

Moreover, Multivariate Analysis is an important technique in various areas of knowledge such as Data Mining (Kettaneh; Berglund; Wold, 2005); Econometrics (Mackay, 2006); Marketing (Ahn; Choi; Han, 2007) and Supply Chain Management (Pozo et al., 2012).

2. Application: Oil refining

The first process in a refinery is atmospheric distillation or direct distillation, where components of crude oil are separated into different sections using different boiling points. The main products obtained in this process are: liquefied petroleum gas (LPG), naphtha - precursor of gasoline, jet fuel, diesel and fuel oil.

Additionally, refineries usually have a second tower, vacuum distillation, to produce diesel cuts. These intermediate streams feeding a chemical process called Fluid Catalytic Cracking (FCC). In this, two noble streams are generated: LPG, and gasoline. It is a refining scheme much more flexible, but though modern, may also present difficulties for framing products stricter specifications.

The production scheme level 3 is more flexible and cost effective than the previous one, because it uses the chemical process of Coking, which transforms a fraction of lower value - vacuum residue of distillation towers, in the noblest products like LPG, gasoline, naphtha and diesel oil.

This final refining scheme incorporates the process Hydrotreating of middle fractions generated in the Coker Unit, enabling increased supply of diesel with good quality. This scheme allows a more balanced supply of gasoline and diesel oil, producing more diesel and less gasoline than the previous settings.

Of course, there are other macro-processes and auxiliary processes such as water treatment plant, effluent disposal, sulfur recovery units, units of hydrogen generation and consequently other interconnections, details of which are not subject of this work (ANP, 2012).

3. Methods

3.1. Acquisition database: Infrared radiation

In the oil industry, signs of infrared radiation generated by sensors are associated with the prediction of the quality of distillates such as naphtha, gasoline, diesel and jet fuel (Kim, Cho; Park, 2000).

Freitas et al. (2012) and Pasquini (2003) explain this instrumentation (Figure 1): the polychromatic radiation emitted by the source has a wavelength selected by a Michelson interferometer. The beam splitter has a refractive index such that approximately half of the radiation is directed to the fixed mirror and the other half is reflected, reaching the movable mirror and is therefore reflected by them. The optical path differences occur due the movement of the movable mirror that promotes wave interference.

An interferogram is obtained as a result of a graph of the signal intensity received by the detector versus the difference in optical path traveled by the beams. By calculating the Fourier Transform (FT) the interferogram can be written as a sum of sines and cosines (Tarumi et al, 2005) and in this case, happens to be called transmittance spectra, T (Forato; Filho; Colnago, 1997). Finally, the spectrum of transmittance, T, is converted to absorbance spectra, A, by co-logarithm of T (Suarez et al. May 2011). The absorbance can be interpreted as the amount of radiation that the sample absorbs and the transmittance, the fraction of radiation that the sample does not absorb. These phenomena occur depending on their chemical composition (Kramer; Small, 2007).

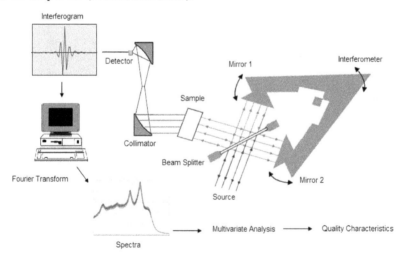

Figure 1. Scheme for technology acquisition database (Adapted from Pasquini, 2003)

The chemical bonds of the type carbon-hydrogen (CH), oxygen-hydrogen (OH) and nitrogen-hydrogen (NH), present in petroleum products (Pasquini; Bueno, 2007), are responsible for the absorption of infrared radiation, however, are not very intense and overlap. The broad spectral bands formed are difficult to interpret (Skoog; Holler; Crouch, 2007) due to the phenomenon of collinearity (Naes; Martens, 1984). The origin of this phenomenon is associated with the manner in which the infrared radiation interacts with matter and can be demonstrated by Quantum Mechanics at work Pasquini (2003).

These input variables (radiation absorbed), called X_i are correlated, so are said collinear or multicollinear (NAES et al., 2002). To illustrate the collinearity, X is a dummy matrix a_{ij} with i rows and j in terms columns, where a_{ij} is the radiation absorption of three samples i (i = 1, 2, 3) at two wavelengths j (j = 1, 2).

$$X = \begin{bmatrix} 1 & 4 \\ 2 & 5 \\ 3 & 6 \end{bmatrix}$$

The columns of X are linearly dependent, so the variables column j_1 and j_2 are colinear, that is, when increases j_1, j_2 increases proportionally. This causes the determinant of X'X to be zero, where X' is the transpose of matrix X.

$$X^T X = \begin{bmatrix} 14 & 28 \\ 28 & 56 \end{bmatrix}$$

Then, the det (X'X) = (14.56) - (28.28) = 0 and this according to Naes et. al (2002) means that there is a singular error matrix and that those erros are propagated when the dependent properties, Y, are determined by regression methods which are not based on the principal components, such as the MLR.

However, the multivariate approaches such as Principal Component Regression (PCR) and PLS have been quite appropriate due to dimensionality reduction, which creates a new set of variables called principal components (Rajalahti; Kvalheim, 2011). So with data mining for Multivariate Analysis, it is possible to relate the physicochemical properties (quality characteristics) of products with the chemical composition of the sample reflected by the absorption spectra. So once modeled a property, just a sample is subjected to infrared radiation to predict their properties.

3.1. Acquisition data base: Reference properties

In this work were modeled properties of gasoline, diesel and jet fuel. For gasoline, the octane number and for diesel oil and jet fuel, the kinematic viscosity property.

According to Freitas (2012), kinematic viscosity of the diesel oil and jet fuel products is an important property in terms of its effect on power system and in fuel injection. Both high and low viscosities are undesirable since they can cause, among others, problems in fuel atomization. The formation of large and small droplets (low viscosity), can lead to a poor distribution of fuel and compromise the mixture air – fuel resulting in an incomplete combustion followed by loss power and greater fuel consumption.

The octane number of a gasoline is an important characteristic which is related to their ability to burn in spark-ignition engines. It is determined by comparing its tendency to detonate with the reference fuel with octane known under standard operating conditions.

When it comes to defining the octane required by engines, many countries use anti-knock index (I), defined by Equation 1:

$$I = \frac{MON + RON}{2} \tag{1}$$

where MON is the Motor Octane Number and RON is the Research Octane Number. The method MON measures the resistance to detonation when gasoline is being burned in the most demanding operating conditions and at higher rotations. The test is done in motors CFR (Cooperative Fuel Research), single-cylinder with variable compression ratio equipped with the necessary instrumentation in a stationary base, as shown in Figure 2.

Figure 2. CFR engine for MON octane (WAUKESHA, 2012)

The RON method evaluates the resistance of the gasoline to detonation under milder conditions and work in less rotation than that measured by octane number MON. The test is done in similar engines to those used for testing in MON octane.

It takes two hours and half to run the test MON and it is spent the same time for the test RON.

4. Results and discussion

Samples of gasoline, diesel and jet fuel, collected during 1 year, were subjected to laboratory tests, to determine the input variables, X_i, which are the infrared radiation absorbed, and the response variables, Y_i, that are physicochemical properties. The physicochemical properties will be predicted by PLS models.

The Table 1 summarizes the validation results of each model for products gasoline, diesel and jet fuel, where RMSEP (Root Mean Square Error of Prediction) corresponds to the standard deviation of the residuals (differences between measured and predicted values by the model).

The Figures 3-6 illustrate that the residues of models follow normal distribution, since in all cases the p-value was greater than 0.05.

Product	Property	Number of samples	Latent Variables	RMSEP	Correlation
Diesel Oil	Viscosity (40ºC)	180	8	0.116 cSt	0.9368
Gasoline	MON	350	6	0.22	0.8723
Gasoline	RON	350	7	0.22	0.9891
Jet Fuel	Viscosity (-20ºC)	279	7	0.01 cSt	0.8836

Table 1. Summary of results of modeling and validation.

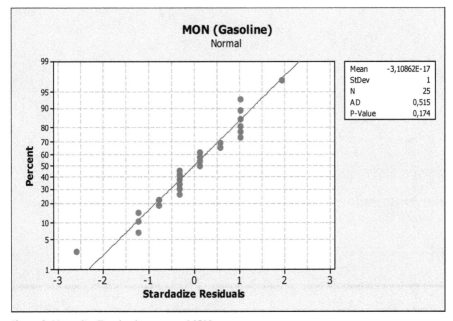

Figure 3. Normality Test for the property MON

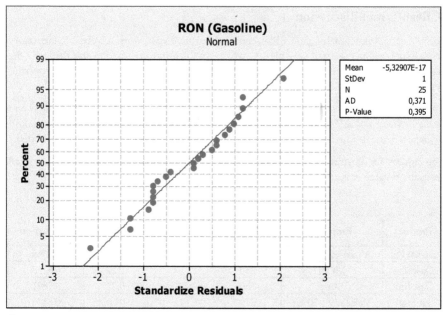

Figure 4. Normality Test for the property RON

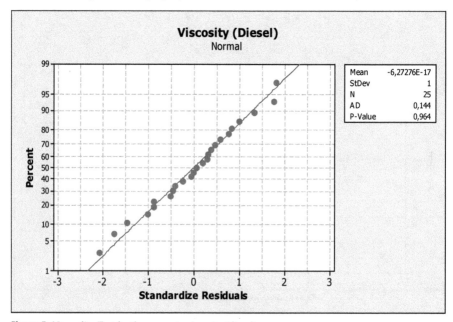

Figure 5. Normality Test for the property viscosity (diesel)

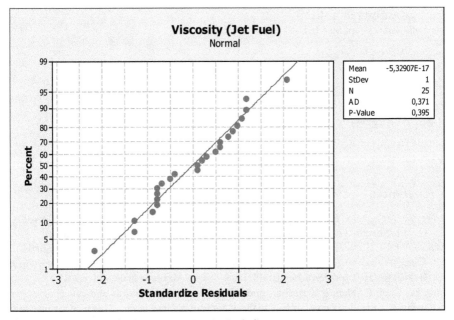

Figure 6. Normality Test for the property viscosity (jet fuel)

5. Conclusions

The following conclusions can be drawn from the results of this study:

It was possible to model mathematically the properties octane number and viscosity of the products gasoline, diesel and jet fuel.

The developed models were externally validated according to ASTM D-6122 and their predictions have precision equivalent to the reference methods.

The results were used in an oil refinery and contributed immensely to speed up the decision-making in blendings systems. Unlike the laboratory trials, the response time of a property along with the computational time does not exceed three minutes.

Author details

Leandro Valim de Freitas
Petróleo Brasileiro SA (PETROBRAS), Brazil
São Paulo State University (UNESP), Brazil

Ana Paula Barbosa Rodrigues de Freitas and Messias Borges Silva
São Paulo State University (UNESP), Brazil
University of São Paulo (USP), Brazil

Fernando Augusto Silva Marins
São Paulo State University (UNESP), Brazil

Estéfano Vizconde Veraszto
Municipal College Franco Montoro Professor (FMPFM), Brazil
Campinas State University (UNICAMP), Brazil

José Tarcísio Franco de Camargo
Municipal College Franco Montoro Professor (FMPFM), Brazil

J. Paulo Davim
Aveiro University (UA), Portugal

6. References

Adler, N.; Yazhemsky, E. Improving discrimination in data envelopment analysis: PCA–DEA or variable reduction. European Journal of Operational Research, 2010, 202, 273-284.

AGENCY OF OIL, NATURAL GAS AND BIOFUELS. Schemes Production in Oil Refining: <http://www.anp.gov.br/?pg=7854&m=esquema+de+refino&t1=&t2=esquema+de+refino &t3=&t4=&ar=0&ps=1&cachebust=1331008874709>. Accessed in 06 March 2012.

Ahn, H.; Choi, E.; Han, I. Extracting underlying meaningful features and canceling noise using independent component analysis for direct marketing. Expert Systems with Applications, 2007, 33, 181-191.

Aleme, H. G.; Corgozinho, C. N. C.; Barbeira, P. J. S. Diesel oil discrimination by origin and type using physicochemical properties and multivariate analysis. Fuel, 2010, 89, 3151-3156.

Bao, X.; Dai, L. Partial least squares with outlier detection in spectral analysis: A tool to predict gasoline properties. Fuel, 2009, 88, 1216-122.

Forato, L. A.; Filho, R. B.; Colnago, L. A. Estudos de métodos de aumento de resolução de espectros de FTIR para análises de estruturas secundárias de proteínas. Química Nova, 1997, 20, 146-150.

Freitas, L. V.; Freitas, A. P. B. R.; Marins, F. A. S.; Loures, C. C. A.; Silva, M. B. Multivariate modeling in quality control of viscosity in fuel: an application in oil industry. Fuel Injection in Automotive Engineering. Rijeka: InTech, 2012.

Goodarzi, M.; Freitas, M.; Jensen, R. Ant colony optimization as a feature selection method in the QSAR modeling of anti-HIV-1 activities of 3-(3,5-dimethylbenzyl) uracil derivatives using MLR, PLS and SVM regressions. Chemometrics and Intelligent Laboratory Systems, 2009, 98, 123-129.

Gourvénec, S.; Pierna, J. A. F.; Massart, D. L.; Rutledge. An evaluation of the PoLiSh smoothed regression and the Monte Carlo Cross-Validation for the determination of the complexity of a PLS model. Chemometrics and Intelligent Laboratory Systems, 2003 68, 48-51.

Huang, C. L.; Hsu, T. S.; Liu, C. M. The Mahalanobis–Taguchi system – Neural network algorithm for data-mining. Expert Systems with Applications, 2009, 36, 5475-5480.

Kettaneh, N.; Berglund, A.; WOLD, S. PCA and PLS with very large data sets. Computational Statistics & Data Analysis, 2005, 48, 69-85.

Kim, D.; Lee, J.; Kim, J. Application of near infrared diffuse reflectance spectroscopy for on-line measurement of coal properties. Korean Journal of Chemical Engineering, 2009; 26; 489-495.

Kim, K.; Cho, I.; Park, J. Use of real-time NIR (near infrared) spectroscopy for the on-line optimization of a crude distillation unit. In: NPRA, Computer Conference. Chicago, 2000.

Kramer, K. E.; Small, G. W. Robust absorbance computations in the analysis of glucose by near-infrared spectroscopy. Vibrational Spectroscopy, 2007, 43, 440-446.

Lira, L. F. B.; Vasconcelos, F. V. C.; Pereira, C. F.; Paim, A. P. S.; Stragevitch, L.; Pimentel M. F. Prediction of properties of diesel/biodiesel blends by infrared spectroscopy and multivariate calibration. Fuel, 2010, 89, 405-409.

Liu, H.; Yu, J.; Xu, J.; Fan, Y.; Bao, X. Identification of key oil refining technologies for China National Petroleum Co. (CNPC). Energy Police, 2007, 35, 2635 -2647.

Llobet, M. V. E.; Brezmes J.; Vilanova, X.; Correig, X. A fuzzy ARTMAP- and PLS-based MS e-nose for the qualitative and quantitative assessment of rancidity in crisps. Sensors and Actuators 2005, 106, 677-686.

Lourenço, V.; Herdling, T.; Reich, G.; Menezes, J. C.; Lochmann, D. Combining microwave resonance technology to multivariate data analysis as a novel PAT tool to improve process understanding in fluid bed granulation. European Journal of Pharmaceutics and Biopharmaceutics, 2011, 78, 513-521.

Machado, M. A. G.; Costa, A. F. B. The use of principal components and univariate charts to control multivariate processes. Operational Resarch, 2008, 28, 173-196.

Mackay, D. Chemometrics, econometrics, psychometrics - How best to handle hedonics? Expert Systems with Applications, 2006, 17, 529-535.

Naes, T.; Isaksson, T.; Fearn, T.; Davies, T. Partial Least Squares. In: Multivariate calibration and classification. Chichester. NIR Publications, 2002.

Naes, T.; Martens, H. Multivariate calibration II. Chemometric methods. Trends in analytical chemistry, 1984, 3, 266-271.

Paiva, A. P. Metodologia de superfície de resposta e análise de componentes principais em otimização de processos de manufatura com múltiplas respostas correlacionadas. PhD Thesis; Itajubá Federal University, 2006.

Pal, A.; Maiti, J. Development of a hybrid methodology for dimensionality reduction in Mahalanobis–Taguchi system using Mahalanobis distance and binary particle swarm optimization. Expert Systems with Applications, 2010, 37, 1286-1293.

Pal, A.; Maiti, J. Development of a hybrid methodology for dimensionality reduction in Mahalanobis–Taguchi system using Mahalanobis distance and binary particle swarm optimization. Expert Systems with Applications, 2010, 37, 1286-1293.

Pasadakis, N.; Sourligas, S.; Foteinopoulos, Ch. Prediction of the distillation profile and cold properties of diesel fuels using mid-IR spectroscopy and neural networks. Fuel, 2006, 85, 1131-1137.

Pasquini, C. Near Infrared Spectroscopy: Fundamentals, Practical Aspects and Analytical Applications. Journal of Chemical Brazilian Society, 2003, 14, 198-219.

Pasquini, C.; Bueno, A. F. Characterization of petroleum using near-infrared spectroscopy: Quantitative modeling for the true boiling point curve and specific gravity. Fuel, 2007, 86, 1927-1934.

Pasquini, C.; Bueno, A. F. Characterization of petroleum using near-infrared spectroscopy: Quantitative modeling for the true boiling point curve and specific gravity. Fuel, 2007, 86, 1927-1934.

Pozo, C.; Fermenia, R. R.; Caballero, J.; Gosa, G. G. Jiménez, L. On the use of Principal Component Analysis for reducing the number of environmental objectives in multi-objective optimization: Application to the design of chemical supply chains. Chemical Engineering Science, 2012, 69, 146-158.

Purcell, D. E.; O'shea, M. G.; Kokot, S. Role of chemometrics for at-field application of NIR spectroscopy to predict sugarcane clonal performance. Chemometrics and Intelligent Laboratory Systems, 2007, 87, 113-124.

Qi, S.; Shi, W. M.; Kong, W. Modified tabu search approach for variable selection in quantitative structure–activity relationship studies of toxicity of aromatic compounds. Artificial Intelligence in Medicine, 2010, 49, 61-66.

Rajalahti, T.; Kvalheim, O. M. Multivariate data analysis in pharmaceutics: A tutorial review. International Journal of Pharmaceutics, 2011, 417, 280-290.

Roy, K.; Roy, P. P. Comparative chemometric modeling of cytochrome 3A4 inhibitory activity of structurally diverse compounds using stepwise MLR, FA-MLR, PLS, GFA, G/PLS and ANN techniques. European Journal of Medicinal Chemistry, 2009, 44, 2913-2922.

Santos Jr V. O.; Oliveira F. C. C.; Lima, D. G.; Petry, A. C.; Garcia, E.; Suarez, P. A. Z.; Rubim, J. C. A comparative study of diesel analysis by FTIR, FTNIR and FT-Raman spectroscopy using PLS and artificial neural network analysis. Analytica Chimica ACTA, 2005, 547, 188-196.

Saunier, O.; Bocquet, M.; Mathieu, A.; Isnard, O. Model reduction via principal component truncation for the optimal design of atmospheric monitoring networks. Atmospheric Environment, 2009, 43, 4940-4950.

Skoog, D. A.; Holler, F. J.; Crouch, S. R. Principles of Instrumental Analysis, 6 ed. Porto Alegre: Bookman, 2007.

Suarez, J. R. C.; Londoño, L. C. P.; Reyes, M. V.; Diem, M.; Tague, T. J.; Rivera, S. P. H. Fourier Transforms - New Analytical Approaches and FTIR Strategies: Open-Path FTIR Detection of Explosives on Metallic Surfaces. Rijeka: InTech, 2011. 520p.

Tarumi, T.; Small, G. W.; Combs, R. J.; Kroutil, R. T. Infinite impulse response filters for direct analysis of interferogram data from airborne passive Fourier transform infrared spectrometry. Vibrational Spectroscopy, 2005, 37, 39-52.

Teixeira, L. S. G.; Oliveira, F. S.; Santos, H. C. S.; Cordeiro, P. W. L.; Almeida, S. Q. Multivariate calibration in Fourier transform infrared spectrometry as a tool to detect adulterations in Brazilian gasoline. Fuel, 2008, 87, 346-352.

WAUKESHA. Industrial Engine - Industrial Gas Engine: <http://www.dresserwaukesha.com/index.cfm/go/list-products/productline/CFR-F1-F2-octane-category/>. Accessed in 06 March 2012.

Wu, D. S.; Feng, X.; Wen, Q.Q. The Research of Evaluation for Growth Suitability of Carya Cathayensis Sarg. Based on PCA and AHP. Procedia Engineering, 2011, 15, 1879-1883.

Xu, Q. S.; Liang, Y. Z. Monte Carlo cross validation. Chemometrics and Intelligent Laboratory Systems, 2001, 56, 1-11.

Zhang, G.; Ni, Y.; Churchill, J.; Kokot, S. Authentication of vegetable oils on the basis of their physico-chemical properties with the aid of chemometrics. Talanta, 2006, 70, 293-300.

Technology and Society Public Perception: A Structural Equation Modeling Study of the Brazilian Undergraduate Students' Opinions and Attitudes from Sao Paulo State

Estéfano Vizconde Veraszto, José Tarcísio Franco de Camargo, Dirceu da Silva and Leandro Valim de Freitas

Additional information is available at the end of the chapter

1. Introduction

Humans has constantly changed the environment, requiring the design and the development of new technologies and these, in turn, eventually modify the man, his attitudes and society as a whole. This demand for innovations may be the result of well-intentioned ideas for a better life, or they may appear at the intention of ostentation of fetishes or even to perpetuate conditions of inequalities and hegemonic power [1-3]. Thus, different forms of relationship between society and technology are set out in pursuit of progress. A growing concern to integrate science and technology (S&T) for the welfare of society gets increasingly more space, especially since last century, when we felt a strong mixture of hope and fear on seeing the concretization of man's dream to conquer space at the same time in which the world feared for its end due to major advances in nuclear weapons [4-6].

In an attempt to discuss the results of progress, much has been said about the formation of citizens conscious and able to take decisions involving the welfare of the community, at the same time they get prepared to live in a technological and dynamic society [7-13].

To better understand the scene briefly discussed here, this work propose the creation and analysis of indicators of how society can influence people in their relationships with technology, reflecting their conceptions or their attitudes towards the technological development. The understanding of these relationships can generate foundations for many discussions, especially for the support of future questions of how public policies for science, technology and education will allow a more effective and active participation by the citizens in decisions involving technological aspects.

Thus, considering that the man, inserted in a society, conceives creates or enhances technologies, in this paper we will present hypotheses, futilely transformed in models that these social interactions also influence the conception that the individual has about the technology and these require different attitudes facing the technological development in the quest for sustainability.

2. Research problem

Considering the aspects mentioned in the introduction, here is formulated the research problem to be developed in this work: how the undergraduate students in the State of São Paulo perceive the relationship between technology and society and how they position themselves ahead of technological development.

3. Research goals

The main goal of this research is to analyze and test, using Structural Equations Modeling (SEM), the adhesion of different models that relate the interactions among man, society, environment and technology (conceptions and expectations and/or attitudes). To do so, we conducted a survey of the main aspects (or dimensions) of technological activities, such as: indicators of production and technology diffusion, the perception of the current model of society in our day by people from various sectors of our society and indicators of technological challenges in today's contemporary world scene. It will also be developed a scale capable of generate models that allow a better understanding of how individuals understand the technology and what they expect from it nowadays, taking into account the influence of social factors such as antecedent. Finally, we will present a theoretical hypothesis and the development of its respective model able to relate the points covered in previous sections.

4. Science, technology and society: Historical bases and sociological studies

The advancement of science and technology, often overblown, raised a concern to integrate science and technology for the welfare of society, especially since mankind, in the last century, felt a mixture of hope and fear when seeing realized man's dream to reach the space, at the same time that the world feared for their end because of major advances in nuclear weapons. The apathy of society regarding the decisions in science and technology at the beginning of last century was changing while new discoveries began to bring unpopular consequences and show disastrous prospects for the future of humanity. [14].

Especially in English-speaking countries, the economic crises turned on social alarms about some ecological aspects, such as, for example, the side effects of some bactericides and the war in Vietnam. These were some of the factors that led to the first anti-establishment actions, giving rise in the international arena to new positions and attitudes towards irrational advance of modern society. Due to strong political and economic crises that plagued the world, step by step, the belief in the neutrality of science and the naive view of technological development, which once dominated the social scene, was fading. A discussion of political and social implications of the production and application of scientific and technological knowledge was required, both in the social sphere as in the classroom [15, 16]. And so, as a way to consciously challenge the overblown advances that the world saw emerge, raised in some parts of the world in the mid-1970s, a movement that tried and still tries to establish a tripod: Science, Technology and Society (STS), searching for a stronger integration and a more critical training of future professionals, as well as seeking to obtain new theories about the implications and relations of science and technology in society [17].

Two traditions have been recognized within the scope of CTS: the North American, which emphasizes more the social consequences and prioritizes a greater emphasis on technology, marked by strong ethical and educational issues, and the European, which has the unmistakable mark to focus their investigations on issues which discuss more the science through anthropological, sociological and psychological referrals [18]. The power of the CTS movement took place through several curricular innovations around the world, either as a discipline, or even as changes in the way of inserting some topics in already existing and structured courses. Contents or the integral transformation of the curriculum, with the main objective to provide students a formation able to assist in the most different decision-making processes that occur in everyday life, having as reference the values considered as ethical and moral by society.

5. The facets of technology: Myths and realities

The diversity of ways in which technology was and is developed and studied over the years that man inhabits and modifies the world makes us realize that it is structured in its own field of knowledge, involving other aspects such as the culture of the society where it has been developed and its organization. In [19] it is shown that technology requires from their agents a deep knowledge of how and why your goals are achieved also are requiring a reformulation of structures and goals of the society where it is installed. Thus, technology can be seen as a set of human activities associated to an intricate system of symbols, machinery and instruments, always aiming the construction of works and artifacts, according methods and processes from modern science. Through the bibliographical survey presented, it is possible to see the diversity of opinions and studies that exist to try to better understand technology. Table 1 shows a summary of these conceptions.

CONCEPTION OF TECHNOLOGY	WAY OF UNDERSTANDING	REFERENCES
intellectualist	Understands the technology as a practical knowledge derived directly from the development of scientific knowledge through progressive and cumulative processes.	[20-26]
UTILITARIAN	Considers technology as being a synonym of technique. That is, the process involved in its development has not relationship with technology, just its purpose and use.	[7, 14, 24, 25]
TECHNOLOGY AS A SYNONYM OF SCIENCE	Faces technology as Natural Sciences and Mathematics, with the same logic and same patterns of production and design.	[16, 27-34]

CONCEPTION OF TECHNOLOGY	WAY OF UNDERSTANDING	REFERENCES
Instrumentalist (OR artifactual)	Considers technology as being simple tools, artifacts, or products, usually sophisticated.	[14, 22, 25, 35-38]
TECHNOLOGICAL NEUTRALITY	Understands that technology is neither good nor bad. Its use is that may be inappropriate, not the artifact itself.	[4, 22, 25, 39, 40, 41]
Determinism TECHNOLOGICAL (AUTONOMOUS TECHNOLOGY)	Considers technology as being autonomous, self-evolving, following naturally its own momentum and logic of evolution, lacking the control of human beings.	[4, 22, 25, 40, 41]
UNIVERSALITY OF TECHNOLOGY	Understands technology as something universal; the same product, service or artifact could arise in any location and, therefore, be useful in any context.	[9, 41]
TECHNOLOGICAL PESSIMISM	Considers technology as something harmful and hurtful to the sustainability of the planet, responsible for the degradation of the environment and the widening of social inequalities.	[7, 42-48]
TECHNOLOGICAL OPTIMISM	Understands technology as having mechanisms able to ensure the sustainable development and solve environmental, social and materials problems.	[2, 3, 7, 45, 49-60]
SOCIAL SYSTEM	Considers that technology is determined by the interaction of different groups through social, political, economic, environmental, cultural and others relationships.	[5, 17, 22, 24, 25, 27, 36, 61-71]

Source: [10]

Table 1. Referenced overview of the different conceptions of technology.

6. The challenges of technology in the contemporary world scene

It is known that sustainable development is volatile and requires a complex series of complementary policies, due to the uncertainty of the generation and distribution of knowledge of C & T [51]. In addition, there is the lack of appropriate instruments or the inability of scientific models to measure the environmental impacts. [72]. According to [73] the relationship between technology and the environment occurs in an uncertain way, being very difficult to predict which current and future impacts can be brought by technological innovation. The generation of new "clean technologies" becomes a challenge. At this point, the political factor should be relaxed, because the environmental goals of short and long term may not be compatible, as well as the policies in force, with innovative attitudes. From the literature reviewed, national and international papers and documents were analyzed, showing the main challenges identified by theorists, researchers and technicians, as being the current problems that the technological development faces worldwide. What we were able to check is that sustainability and environmental conservation are issues prioritized in the material analyzed ([2, 3, 7, 8, 34, 44, 45, 50, 56-60, 67, 74-89]).

7. Methodological procedures of the research

This work is characterized as a quantitative research. This option is based on the assertion in [90] that the structural equation model provides a direct method to simultaneously handle with multiple dependency relationships with statistical efficiency, exploring them in depth, generating confirmatory analysis, and allowing the representation of unobservable concepts in these relationships, verifying even possible measurement errors that occurred during the statistical process. By establishing an alternative to analyzing the relationship between society and its influence on conceptions and attitudes of undergraduate students facing the technological development, the structural equation modeling and the procedures for descriptive and multivariate analysis denote a precondition to the application of the technique.

7.1. Theoretical models and research hypotheses

In this way, evidences were pointed out that the literature, on numerous occasions, provides broad considerations that indicate that society generates demand for new technologies and these, in turn, change habits, relationships and forms of consumption of the individuals who make use thereof.

7.2. Introducing the model

We created a master model that relates the conceptions (CON) that individuals have about technology, their attitudes and expectations facing the technological development (ATI) and the influences of the social aspect (DSO). Due to the theoretical recommendations of the adopted method, four models were tested in the study. However, to simplify and make the research more objective, this paper will present only the original model, related to the null hypothesis of the research. Thus, starting from this model, the relations among the constructs with the lowest number of causal pathways will be defined, taking as fundamental change the antecedent factor (also treated as an independent variable or exogenous) in the causal relationships ([90, 91]). Initially, DSO1 model was chosen, which is characterized by having the social dimension (DSO) as an antecedent to the factors conception (CON) and attitude (ATI). Thus, the graphical representation of causal relationships among the constructs, known as path diagram, is shown in Diagram 1.

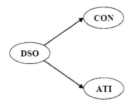

DSO: independent variable (exogenous). **CON e ATI**: dependent variables (endogenous).

Source: [10]

Diagram 1. Structural relationship Model - DSO1: Influence of Society.

In general, this model can be translated into the following hypothesis: the social dimension influences the conceptions of technology of the individuals within it, providing favorable attitudes in the face of a sustainable technological development.

This initial model formed the basis for other five variations, two of which were obtained by exchanging the places of the constructs in the model, and the remaining three were obtained from their respective inverse relationships.

7.3. Formulation of indicators and development of the research tool

All the literature review summarized in Figure 1 passed through a systematic process of analysis and classification for the construction of the research tool. The values obtained resulted from a process of content analysis which methodology will be described below. From papers, books, national and international documents, this study aimed to collect information provided in each text classifying all existing conceptions about technology as well as which are the challenges of technology in today's global scenario. It was also prioritized the provision of information that could classify the various sectors of society. Based on these categorizations, the indicators of this work were developed. All variables were grouped into categories and transformed into statements (indicators) and the end result, after a refinement based on the methodology of content analysis in [92], is presented in tables 2, 3 and 4.

DIMENSIONS	INDICATORS
CONCEPTIONS OF TECHNOLOGY	CON 01: Technology is the application of laws, theories and models of science.
	CON 02: The technology does not need theories; only needs to be practical and efficient.
	CON 03: Technology explains the world around us.
	CON 04: Today there are technologies that can be purchased at an affordable price for many, such as cell phones, stereos, computers, etc.
	CON 05: Technologies are tools (or artifacts) built to assist humans in solving different types of tasks.
	CON 06: The technology does not suffer influences from society.
	CON 07: The way we use technology is what determines whether it is good or bad.
	CON 8: The inventor loses control over the invention since it is available to the public.
	CON 9: A new technological discovery can be useful anywhere in the world.
	CON 10: Technology can destroy the planet.
	CON 11: Technology increases the socio-economic inequalities.
	CON 12: Technology threatens the privacy of individuals.
	CON 13: The benefits of technological development are greater than its negative effects.
	CON 14: Genetic engineering can help to cure diseases.
	CON 15: Different groups of interests determine the technological production from social, political, economic, environmental and cultural relationships.

Source: [10]

Table 2. Indicators proposed for Conceptions of Technology.

SOCIAL DIMENSION	DSO 01: The government must not influence in decisions of technological development.
	DSO 02: The technological research developed by companies is directed to hegemonic private interests aiming solely at profit.
	DSO 03: The decisions and technological choices have nothing to do with codes of ethics and conduct.
	DSO 04: The educational and research institutions, such as large universities must conduct research to develop new technologies.
	DSO 05: Non-governmental organizations (NGOs) should have an active voice in technological decisions.
	DSO 06: Environmental organizations can prevent or stop the technological development.
	DSO 07: Religious organizations can prevent or stop the technological development.
	DSO 08: It is important the effective participation of citizens in issues related to decision making in technology.
	DSO 09: Personal interests do not influence the process of technology creation.
	DSO 10: Religious beliefs do not affect the work of scientists and experts involved in the production of technology.
	DSO 11: Media influences the production of technology.
	DSO 12: Ethnic minorities have no guaranteed space to assist in choosing new technologies.

Source: [10]

Table 3. Proposed Indicators for the Social Dimension.

ATTITUDES TOWARD TECHNOLOGICAL DEVELOPMENT	ATI 01: I use technology to socialize information.
	ATI 02: I am not able to express an opinion about technology, because in decisions of this magnitude should be left to experts.
	ATI 03: I choose a technology by its efficiency.
	ATI 04: I choose a technology due to its practicality.
	ATI 05: At the time of purchase of a new technological product the price is the determining factor for my choice.
	ATI 06: Technology consolidates the democratization of relations among human beings.
	ATI 07: I am aware to the issues related to technology that appear in the media.
	ATI 08: I welcome the increase in investment in technology even if it means spending less on social programs.
	ATI 09: I would use nuclear power without questioning, because it is a plausible exit to solve future problems of the energy crisis.
	ATI 10: The concern about future generations should be a crucial point to drive technological choices.

	ATI 11: I am aware that my technological choices will help to overcome the water crisis in the twenty-first century.
	ATI 12: Having financial conditions, when buying a new phone, I choose the one which has more features and functions.
	ATI 13: With the safe use of technology it is possible to protect nature from human contamination.
	ATI 14: avoid using technological artifacts that cause environmental destruction.
	ATI 15: I know that genetically modified foods may be the solution to world hunger.
	ATI 16: I do not buy furniture that is not made from certified wood.
	ATI 17: I admit the exploitation of nature instead of the welfare of humanity.

Source: [10]

Table 4. Proposed Indicators for Attitudes toward technological development.

7.4. Sampling and data collection

In this research we adopted the technique of cross-section as it brings the advantage of allowing the acquisition of a picture of the variables of interest at a given moment in time and to emphasize the selection of a significant and representative sample of the target population ([93, 94]).

The four institutions that represented the sampling unit were selected considering the criteria of being institutions both public and private. The selected public university, located in Campinas/SP, has students from different regions of Sao Paulo State, as well as the other three private institutions. These private institutions were one university and one faculty of Sao Paulo/SP and one faculty of Campinas/SP. The two private faculties selected receive students from different regions in the state and were also chosen because the researcher had already served for a long period in one of them and is now starting activities in the other one. The diversity of courses that the four institutions have was also a decisive factor in their choices.

The data collection in the public institution was done directly with the students, from different courses, and the questionnaires were, in the most part, passed before the beginning of the classes in the days chosen for the data acquisition. Students were selected from the following courses: Environmental Engineering, Computer Science, Nutrition, Psychology, Business Administration with emphasis in International Business, Electrical Engineering, Production Engineering, Physics, Mathematics, Technology in Environmental Management, Administration and Education.

Initially, around 1006 questionnaires were returned, yielding a proportion of almost 23 interviewed by assertion. However, LISREL software was used in a procedure that made the disposal of questionnaires that were not fully answered. Thus, the amount passed to 600 valid questionnaires, representing a proportion of nearly 14 respondents per statement, which is a significant value considering [90] as basis, and taking into account that the model is not complete and it still gave a good fit in LISREL software.

8. Methodology of data analysis and results

Following guidelines from [90], at the end of the collect, the data recorded in the questionnaires were entered in an Excel spreadsheet to be later processed by specific statistical software's to aid in the treatment and analysis of quantitative data. The software *SPSS*® 13.0 was used to verify the reliability and constructs unidimensionality, as well as the system *LISREL*® *8.54*, one of the most traditional statistical structural equation modeling package that became popular in social science research, as shown in [95], and has adequate resources to the purposes of this research ([91, 95-102]). A The coding was made with the SIMPLIS™ command language, available in the system, which made possible the estimation of the parameters of the model through confirmatory factorial analysis, according to different estimation methods, and the verification of the respective measures of adjustment of the models.

8.1. Individual evaluation of the constructs

From the individual evaluation of each construct was then possible to conduct the validation of the models of measures of each of these (DSO, ATI and CON) and this validation was performed by applying the Confirmatory Factorial Analysis (*Confirmatory Factor Analysis - CFA*). This technique has the purpose to test the hypothesis of adjustment of empirical data to a theoretical model, where a relationship structure is imposed and confirmed by analysis. Nevertheless, the variables need not to be related to all common factors. In particular, as is the case of this investigation, each variable is related to only one factor.

8.2. Unidimensionality of the constructs

The constructs presented earlier had their dimensionalities tested since this action is an premise to the reliability of the construct. The observation of the unidimensionality was made observing if each value of the normalized residue matrix of the construct was lower than 2.58, in modulus, at a level of significance of 1%, indicating if the effect on the overall adjustment of the model was low. In each process the indices of fit were checked, supplemented by information generated by the option "Modification Index" programmed in LISREL ®, which points out how much is expected to decrease the chi-square if a given a re-estimation occurred, as in [98]. A detailed analysis of the standardized residuals of all dimensions was made and it was found that the overall quantity of residues which exceeds the value of 2.58 is very low and don't reaches 3% of the total. Thus, the unidimensionality of the constructs is not compromised.

8.3. Reliability of the constructs

Reliability is a measure of the internal consistency of the construct indicators and of the adequacy of the scales to measure it. According to the authors, a value commonly used for acceptance of reliability is 0.70, although this is not an absolute standard, and values below

0.70 have been accepted if the research is exploratory in its nature and this value was observed in the research. The results from each one of the dimensions are indicated in the following table (Table 5):

Constructs	Composite Reliability of the Construct
DSO Models	0,704161
CON Models	0,703772
ATI Models	0,716902

Source: Lisrel® Software

Table 5. Composite Reliability of the Constructs

As can be seen, the values are higher than the reference commonly established when calculated for each of the constructs. This indicates that the measures performed are suitable.

8.4. Adjustment measures of the constructs

In this step we evaluated all the models seeking to understand the structural relationships hypothesized. The most common procedure for the estimation of these parameters and which usually has higher efficiency, in accordance with [90], is the Maximum Likelihood method (*Maximum Likelihood Estimation – MLE*). The results achieved (Table 6) with the MLE method were well adjusted, considering the values given in the literature.

Main Indicators of the Adjustment of the Model	Values Obtained with the MLE Method						REF. VALUES
	DSO1	DSO2	CON1	CON2	ATI1	ATI2	
Degrees of freedom	144	143	144	143	144	143	X
Chi-square	218.865	218.131	218.865	218.131	218.16	218.131	X
Weighted Chi-square (χ^2/GL)	1,52	1,53	1,52	1,52	1,52	1,53	lower than 5,00
Root Mean Square Error of Approximation (RMSEA)	0.0308	0.0309	0.0308	0.0309	0.0306	0.0309	Between 0,05 and 0,08
Normed Fit Index (NFI)	0.817	0.818	0.817	0.818	0.818	0.818	Over than 0,90
Non-Normed Fit Index (NNFI)	0.913	0.912	0.913	0.912	0.914	0.912	Over than 0,90
Comparative Fit Index (CFI)	0.927	0.927	0.927	0.927	0.928	0.927	Over than 0,90
Goodness of Fit Index (GFI)	0.962	0.962	0.962	0.962	0.962	0.962	Over than 0,90
Adjusted Goodness of Fit Index (AGFI)	0.95	0.949	0.95	0.949	0.95	0.949	Over than 0,90

Source: [10]

Table 6. Comparison of the Measures of Adjustment of the Model with MLE.

These measures were used as a way to evaluate each construct and the integrated model, because an adjusted model provides a benchmark for the confirmation of the validity of the constructs and the relationships among them, with respect to the complete structural model.

8.5. Evaluation of the integrated model

Several indicators were excluded in an attempt to get the best fitted model resulting in a total of 44, 19 indicators on the scale validated following the guidelines of [90]. Applying the MLE technique to estimate the model with antecedents in the social dimension, we obtained the structural equations, t-values of the estimated parameters and their respective R2, as shown in Table 7 for the estimation of DSO1, the t-values are above to 1.96 for a level of significance of 5%. This demonstrates the significant contribution of the endogenous constructs (conceptions and attitudes) for the Social Dimension (DSO) predictor construct and we have this model as the most adequate, satisfying the theory and our initial hypothesis.

Models	METHOD OF ESTIMATION MLE		
	structural equations	t-values	R²
DSO1	ATI = 1.096*DSO	7.708	1.202
	CON = 1.016*DSO	6.220	1.033
DSO2	DSO = 0.116*ATI + 0.764*CON	0.188 e 0.906	0.795
CON1	ATI = 1.109*CON	7.896	1.231
	DSO = 0.880*CON	1.288	0.774
CON2	CON = 4.408*ATI - 3.386*DSO	0.271 e -0.208	1.908
ATI1	DSO = 0.889*ATI	1.354	0.791
	CON = 1.069*ATI	6.348	1.144
ATI2	ATI = - 0.145*DSO + 1.249*CON	-0.151 e 1.327	1.257

Source: LISREL® Software

Table 7. Complete model estimated according to the MLE method.

These results indicate that the model which predicts the other variables is the DSO1.

8.6. Presentation of the fitted model

From the observations presented in the previous sections, the best fitted model showed a number of constructs and indicators below the initial, as shown in Table 8 and graphically represented in Diagram 2.

CONSTRUCTS	VARIABLES
SOCIAL DIMENSIONS	DSO 01; DSO 02; DSO 04; DSO 06; DSO 08
CONCEPTIONS OF TECHNOLOGY	CON 01; CON 03; CON 05; CON 07
ATTITUDES TOWARDS THE TECHNOLOGICAL DEVELOPMENT	ATI 01; ATI 05; ATI 06; ATI07; ATI010; ATI 11; ATI 12; ATI 13; ATI 15; ATI 16

Source: [10]

Table 8. Adjusted Model of Measure.

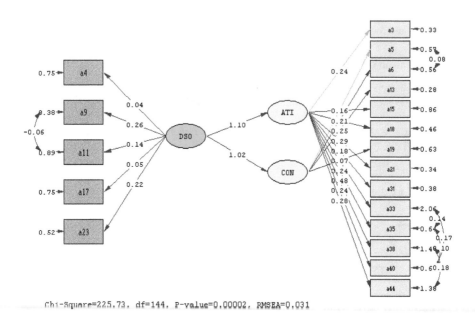

Chi-Square=225.73, df=144, P-value=0.00002, RMSEA=0.031

Source: LISREL® Software.

Diagram 2. Path Diagram of the Integrated Model.

In summary, it can be said that the final model proposed was adequate and the various factors, in turn, significant. Thus, it is clear that the social dimension, measured by the DSO construct, can be considered a predictor of the attitudes (ATI) and conceptions (CON) related to the technology and that, by the unadjusted models, the inverse relationships are not true for the sample consulted.

9. Concluding remarks

Seeking an understanding of how elements of society can influence the conceptions and attitudes of individuals concerning the technological development, this research developed a theoretical model from which a research tool was elaborated and applied with undergraduate students.

It was found that all models were adjusted, but only the model DSO1 attested the research hypotheses according to the results previously presented.

The society, in the created model, was represented by different variables which represented specific sectors. Among all possibilities, in a comprehensive manner, the adjusted model showed that the undergraduate students surveyed gave evidence that the government, the research and educational institutions, and also the citizens in general, are the components that best represent, or could represent, the society in processes of technological decision making. Either for the choice of new technologies as for the development of other, with these points in common it is possible to say that undergraduates expect a government position at the same time they feel able to participate in a more active form.

Complementing the scenery, the indifference presented regarding the environmental non-governmental institutions may not mean a lack of opinion, but tend to show that issues of sustainability and preservation of the planet must be taken into consideration. This will be evident in the analysis of the attitudes that will be made in future paragraphs.

Summarizing these statements we can say that government, people, academic and educational sectors should join forces for better choices and technological decisions. This statement shows that all the literature indicated in Section 4 is consistent with the fitted model. Thus, these considerations show the reflex of the society in the attitudes of people in their technology choices and it can also be said that this reflex is also present in the way they understand the technology.

In the case of the conceptions, for one of the dependent constructs, we can infer that the undergraduates surveyed show three basic aspects that commonly appear as indicators of common sense of the interpretation of technology. More generally, one can say that the research has shown that technology is understood by the great majority of undergraduates as being intellectualistic and synonymous of science, as well as neutral and instrumentalist.

This way, the research shows that understanding technology as a practical knowledge derived from scientific theoretical knowledge, or even mistakes it with science, is a strong indicator. This means that a deeper reflection about the production process of technology and all of its real reasons of conception are not present in the majority of respondents. The instrumentalist conception supports this conclusion significantly. If the process is not considered, there remains only the product. And the use of this product is sole responsibility of the person who acquires it, not reflecting, this way, the interests of the developers. This statement is supported by the neutral view of technology also present in the model.

In general, even the concept of technology can be somewhat limited, its direct dependence on social factors is a good indicator and raises good evidence that undergraduates expect that influential sectors of the society act jointly in the development process of technology.

Regarding the attitudes (ATI), the second construct dependent on the social background (DSO), three points are possible to identify in a more comprehensive way: the awareness of the need to ensure the sustainability of the planet, consuming appropriate technologies, the use of technologies to socialize information and keep informed, and the practical manifestation of the instrumentalist conception. By taking again as a starting point the social dimension, we can infer that the students surveyed believe that jointly, government, teaching and research institutions and the population in general, can combine efforts to the pursuit of sustainable development. Thus, progress is possible if, and only if, political, social and economical efforts, are gathered in the search of a growth able to preserve the natural and material resources to ensure the well being of people.

With a differentiated education, new educational public policies may be developed in order to point to a sustainable world, whose maintenance of the life forms and inanimate resources can only be achieved through the joint action of all sectors of society. With an efficient technological education it is possible to educate for the consumption in a conscious and not so materialistic way, as pointed by some attitudes of the model. With a conscious technological education and with the use of all socializing and educational potential of technology, it is possible to manage and generate gradually an educational system solid and participatory.

Finally, it is possible to establish a contrast with the idea of consumption that also appeared, which indicates that the economic sector of society, which aims at maintaining a competitive market structure, also exerts influence. Even so, the adjusted model showed that the attitudes (or intentions) of undergraduates show evidence of change of attitude in college students that, even in a subjective way, give evidence that it is necessary to create a social mechanism where the holders of the technical knowledge must meet with the representatives from all sectors of society to decide which new technological systems should be adopted, since it does not harm the environment.

We emphasize that it was found that undergraduate students surveyed have a limited conception of technology, and this, as showed in the survey, is a reflection of the society in which they are inserted. Another point to be considered is the social reflex in the attitudes of the individuals facing the technological development. The study showed that there is a sustainable awareness, but also showed that some key variables of technological advances presented in the research model does not appear so striking in the way the students surveyed are positioned. These two observations open up space for a last important point: society, in general, need a technological reeducation, so that the citizens within it start to understand the process of technological decision making in a more comprehensive way and become capable to reflect about the different aspects related to the social environment in which they belong.

Thus, speaking in rethink the public policies in education is to propose the use of technological knowledge in education. And that does not mean simply perform tasks for training or specialization in new technologies, but to ensure to the students a solid foundation that helps them to manage and generate, in the future, the demands placed on society. The integration means of the individual in society, as well as their formation, more critical and more human.

Author details

Estéfano Vizconde Veraszto and José Tarcísio Franco de Camargo
Faculdade Municipal "Professor Franco Montoro" (FMPFM), Mogi Guaçu, SP, Brazil

Estéfano Vizconde Veraszto and Dirceu da Silva
Universidade Estadual de Campinas (UNICAMP), Campinas/SP, Brazil

José Tarcísio Franco de Camargo
Centro Universitário Regional de Espírito Santo do Pinhal (UNIPINHAL), Esp. Sto do Pinhal, SP, Brazil

Leandro Valim de Freitas
Petróleo Brasileiro SA (Petrobrás), São José dos Campos, SP, Brazil
Universidade Estadual Paulista "Júlio de Mesquita Filho", (UNESP), Guaratinguetá, SP, Brazil

10. References

[1] Cardoso, T. F. L. (2001). Sociedade e Desenvolvimento Tecnológico: Uma Abordagem Histórica. In: Grinspun, M.P.S.Z. (org.). Educação Tecnológica: Desafios e Perspectivas. São Paulo. Cortez. p. 183-225.

[2] Miranda, N. A. et al. (2007a). New Tchnologies of the Information and Communication in Education: A pre-test analysis In: 4th International Conference on Information Systems and Technology Management, 2007, São Paulo/SP. Anais do 4th CONTECSI. São Paulo/SP. v.1. p.1590-1602.

[3] Miranda, N. A. et al. (2007b). Tecnologias da Informação e Comunicação na escola pública: realidade ou ilusão? In: II EIDE - Encontro Iberoamericano de Educação, Araraquara/SP. Anais do II EIDE.

[4] Dagnino, R. (2007). Um Debate sobre a Tecnociência: neutralidade da ciência e determinismo tecnológico. Disponível em < http://www.ige.unicamp.br/site/aulas/138/ UM_DEBATE_SOBRE_A_TECNOCIENCIA_DAGNINO.pdf >. Acesso em 8 Jan 2010.

[5] Echeverria, J. (1998). Teletecnologías, espacios de interacción y valores. Teorema – Revista Internacional de Filosofía. Vol.17/3.

[6] Liguori, L. M. (1997). As Novas Tecnologias da Informação e da Comunicação no Campo dos Velhos Problemas e Desafios Educacionais. In.: LITWIN, E. (org.). Tecnologia Educacional: política, histórias e propostas. (Trad.: ROSA, E.). Artes Médicas, Porto Alegre. pp. 78-97.

[7] Agazzi, E. (2002). El impacto de la tecnología. Biblioteca Digital da OEI. Disponível em: < http://www.argumentos.us.es/numero1/agazzi.htm >. Acesso em: 7 Jun 2009.

[8] Berne, R. W. (2003). Ethics, Technology, and the Future: Na Intergenerational Experience in Engineering Education. Bulletin of Science, Technology & Society. Vol. 23. N. 2. April 2003. pp. 88-94.

[9] Gordillo, M. M. & Galbarte J. C. G. (2002). Reflexiones Sobre la Educación Tecnológica desde el Enfoque CTS. Revista Iberoamericana de Educación. No. 28: 17-59.

[10] Veraszto, E. V. et al. Estudios CTS en Brasil: relación causal entre concepciones y actitudes de estudiantes universitarios del Estado de São Paulo frente al desarrollo

tecnológico. Icono 14 - Revista de Comunicación, Educación y TIC, v. 1, p. 407-424, 2009b.

[11] Veraszto, E. V. et al. El desarrollo tecnológico en la vida cotidiana: influencias sociales comprendidas por universitarios brasileños. Prisma Social. Revista de Ciencias Sociales, v. 1, p. 1-33, 2010.

[12] Veraszto, E. V. et al. Educación, tecnología y sociedad: relaciones de causalidad de la influencia social en los procesos de toma de decisiones tecnológicas. ETD : Educação Temática Digital, v. 12, p. 126-153, 2011a.

[13] Veraszto, E. V. et al. Influência da sociedade no desenvolvimento tecnológico: um estudo das concepções de graduandos brasileiros do Estado de São Paulo. Revista Iberoamericana de Ciencia, Tecnología y Sociedad, v. 6, p. 1-30, 2011b.

[14] Veraszto, E. V. (2004). Projeto Teckids: Educação Tecnológica no Ensino Fundamental. Dissertação de Mestrado. Campinas. Faculdade de Educação. UNICAMP.

[15] Brasil. (1996). Lei de Diretrizes e bases 9394/96. MEC (Ministério da Educação e do Desporto). Disponível em: < http://www.mec.gov.br/legis/default.shtm >. Acesso em: 23 Nov 2009.

[16] Gordillo, M. M. (2001). Ciencia, Tecnología e Sociedad. Projeto Argo. Materiales para la educación CTS. p. 7-12; 64-101. Grupo Norte.

[17] Silva, D., Barros Filho, J e Lacerda Neto, J. C. N. (2000). Atividades de Ciência, Tecnologia e Sociedade (CTS) para as disciplinas dos cursos de Administração de Empresas. Revista Álvares Penteado. Junho 2000. Nº 4: 47-67.

[18] Lacerda Neto, J. C. M. (2002). Ensino de Tecnologia: uma Investigação em sala de aula. Dissertação de Mestrado da Faculdade de Educação da UNICAMP. Campinas/SP. 2002.

[19] Vargas, M. Prefácio. (2001). In: Grinspun, M.P.S.Z.(org.). Educação Tecnológica - Desafios e Perspectivas. São Paulo: Cortez. pp. 7-23.

[20] Layton, D. (1998). Revaluing the T in STS. International Journal of Science Education. 10(4): 367-378.

[21] Acevedo, G. D. R. (1998). Ciencia, Tecnología y Sociedad: una mirada desde la Educación en Tecnología. Revista Iberoamericana de Educación. No. 18. p. 107-143.

[22] García, M. I. G. et al. (2000). Ciencia, Tecnologia y Sociedad: una introducción al estudio social de la ciencia y la tecnología. Tecnos. Madrid. 2000. p. 327.

[23] Acevedo Díaz, J. A. (2002a). ¿Qué puede aportar la Historia de la Tecnología a la Educación CTS? Biblioteca Digital da OEI (Organização de Estados Iberoamericanos para a Educação, a Ciência e a Cultura. Disponível em < http://www.campus-oei.org >. Acesso em 8 Dez 2009.

[24] Acevedo Díaz, J. A. Educación Tecnológica desde una perspectiva CTS. (2002b). Una breve revisión del tema. Biblioteca Digital da OEI. Disponível em: < http://www.oei.es/bibliotecadigital.htm > Acesso: 6 Fev 2010. pp. 1-8.

[25] Osorio M., C. (2002). Enfoques sobre la tecnología. Revista Iberoamericana de Ciencia, Tecnología, Sociedad e Innovación. N. 2. ISSN: 1681-5645.

[26] Osorio M., C. (2002). La Educación científica y tecnológica desde el enfoque en ciencia, tecnología y sociedad. Aproximaciones y experiencias para la educación secundaria. Revista Iberoamericana de Educación. N.28.

[27] Sancho, J. M. (org.). (1998). Para uma tecnologia educacional. (Trad.: Neves, B A.). Porto Alegre, Artmed. pp: 28-40.

[28] Jarvis, T. & Rennie, L. J. (1998). Factors that Influence Children's Developing Perception of Technology. Journal of Technology and Design Education. Vol. 8: 261-279. Netherlands. Kluwer Academic Publishers.

[29] Silva, D. & Barros Filho, J. (2001). Concepções de Alunos do Curso de Pedagogia sobre a Tecnologia e suas Relações Sociais: Análise de um pré-teste. Revista Educação e Ensino da Universidade São Francisco. Nº 6, V. 2.

[30] Valdés, P. Y Valdés R., Guisáosla, J. Santos, T. (2002). Implicaciones de la Relaciones Ciencia-Tecnología en la Educación Científica. Revista Iberoamericana de Educación. No. 28. p. 101-127.

[31] Hilst, V. L. S. (1994). A tecnologia necessária: uma nova pedagogia para os cursos de formação de nível superior. Piracicaba/SP: Editora da UNIMEP. p. 15-41.

[32] Acevedo Díaz, J. A. et al. (2002). Persistencia de las actitudes y creencias CTS en la profesión docente. Revista Electrónica de Enseñanza de las Ciencias. Vol. 1 Nº 1. pp. 1-28.

[33] Acevedo Díaz, J. A. (2002c). Tres criterios para diferenciar entre Ciencia y Tecnología. Biblioteca Digital da OEI. Disponível em: < http://www.oei.es/ bibliotecadigital.htm > Acesso: 6 Fev 2010. pp. 1-17.

[34] Acevedo Díaz, J. A. et al. (2002d). Persistencia de las actitudes y creencias CTS en la profesión docente. Revista Electrónica de Enseñanza de las Ciencias. Vol. 1 Nº 1.

[35] Silva, D. et. al. (1999). Ensino de Engenharias e Ensino de Ciências das Disciplinas Experimentais: Proposta de Ações Pedagógicas. Atas do XV Congresso Brasileiro de Engenharia Mecânica (COBEM). Águas de Lindóia/SP. ABCM e UNICAMP.

[36] Pacey, A. (1983). The Culture of Technology. Cambridge, MA: MIT Press.

[37] Acevedo Díaz, J. A. (2003a). Una breve revisión de las creencias CTS de los estudiantes. Biblioteca Digital da OEI (Organização de Estados Iberoamericanos para a Educação, a Ciência e a Cultura. Disponível em < http://www.campus-oei.org >. Acesso em 19 Jan 2010 (d).

[38] Acevedo Días, J. A., Alonso, A. V., Massanero Mas, M. A. (2003). El movimiento Ciencia-Tencología-Sociedad y la enseñanza de las Ciencias. Biblioteca Digital da OEI (Organização de Estados Iberoamericanos para a Educação, a Ciência e a Cultura. Disponível em < http://www.campus-oei.org >. Acesso em 19 Jan 2010.

[39] Winner, L. (2008). La Ballena y el Reactor: Una búsqueda de los límites en la era de la alta tecnología. Gedisa Editorial. 2ª. ed. Barcelona. España. 290p.

[40] Carrera, A. D. (2001). Nuevas tecnologías y viejos debates: algunas ideas sobre la participación social. Ingeniería sin fronteras - Revista de Cooperación. n. 14.

[41] Gómez, S. C. (2001). Los estudios Ciencia, Tecnología y Sociedad y la Educación para el Desarrollo. Ingenieria sin fronteras - Revista de Cooperación. n. 14.

[42] Meadows, D. H. et all. (1972). The limits to growth. Potomac, Washington D. C.

[43] Barnett, H. J. & Morse, C. (1977). Scarcity and Growth: the economics of natural resources availability. John Hopkins Press, Baltimore.

[44] Colombo, C. R. & Bazzo, W. A. (2002). Educação Tecnológica Contextualizada, ferramenta essencial para o Desenvolvimento Social Brasileiro. Biblioteca Digital da OEI. Disponível em: < http://www.oei.es/bibliotecadigital.htm > Acesso: 6 Fev 2010. pp. 1-10.

[45] Carranza, C. C. (2001). Nuevas tecnologías y sostenibilidad ambiental y humana. Ingenieria sin fronteras - Revista de Cooperación. n. 14.

[46] Corazza, R.I. (1996). A questão ambiental e a direção do progresso de inovação tecnológica na indústria de papel e celulose. Dissertação de Mestrado. Instituto de Geociências. Universidade Estadual de Campinas.

[47] Corazza, R. I. (2004). Políticas públicas para tecnologias mais limpas: uma analise das contribuições da economia do meio ambiente. Tese de doutorado. Instituto de Geociências. Universidade Estadual de Campinas.

[48] Corazza, R. I. (2005). Tecnologia e Meio Ambiente no Debate sobre os Limites do Crescimento: Notas à Luz de Contribuições Selecionadas de Georgescu-Roegen. Revista Economia. 1.

[49] Herrera, A. et al. (1994). Las Nuevas Tecnologías y el Futuro de América Latina. Siglo XXI. México.

[50] WCEAD – World Commission on Environment and Development. (1987). Our Common Future. Oxford University Press. Oxford and New York. Em português: Comissão Mundial sobre meio ambiente e desenvolvimento. Nosso futuro comum. Rio de Janeiro: Ed. da Fundação Getúlio Vargas. 430p.

[51] Foray, D. & Grübler, A. (1996). Technology and the environment: an overview. Technological Forecasting and Social Change, v. 53, n. 1, p. 3-13, Sep 1996.

[52] Freeman, C. (1996). The greening of technology and models of innovation. Technological Forecasting and Social Change, 53 (1), Sep 1996.

[53] Andrade, T. (2004). Inovação tecnológica e meio ambiente: a construção de novos enfoques. Ambiente & Sociedade - Vol. VII nº. 1 jan./jun. 2004.

[54] Bin, A. (2004). Agricultura e meio ambiente: contexto e iniciativas da pesquisa pública. Dissertação de Mestrado. Instituto de Geociências. Universidade Estadual de Campinas.

[55] Bin, A. & Paulino, S. R. (2004). Inovação e meio ambiente na pesquisa agrícola. ANNPAS. Indaiatuba/SP.

[56] Miranda, N. A. et. al. (2006a). Educação ambiental na óptica discente: análise de um pré-teste. In: SEGET - III SIMPÓSIO DE EXCELÊNCIA EM GESTÃO E TECNOLOGIA. Resende/RJ. III Simpósio de Excelência em Gestão e Tecnologia. v. 1. p. 1-10.

[57] Miranda, N. A. et al. (2006b). Educação ambiental na óptica discente: análise de um pré-teste In: 3º SEMINÁRIO INTERNACIONAL CIÊNCIA E TECNOLOGIA NA

AMÉRICA LATINA. Campinas/SP. Anais do 3º Seminário Internacional Ciência e Tecnologia na América Latina. v.1. p.1 – 10.

[58] Veraszto, E. V. et al. (2007a). Science, Technology and Environment: limits and possibilities In: 4th International Conference on Information Systems and Technology Management, 2007, São Paulo/SP. Anais do 4th CONTECSI. São Paulo/SP. v.1. p.3806-3820.

[59] Veraszto, E. V. et al. (2007d). O atual processo de globalização e as Novas Tecnologias da Informação e Comunicação. Santa Lúcia em Revista. v.1, p.21-27.

[60] Veraszto, E. V. et al. (2007e). Contribuições da ciência & tecnologia no panorama ambiental contemporâneo. Conexão IESF. v.1, p.6-14.

[61] Bosch, G. (2002). La peligrosa armonía de la tecnologia. Biblioteca Digital da OEI (Organização de Estados Iberoamericanos para a Educação, a Ciência e a Cultura. Disponível em < http://www.campus-oei.org >. Acesso em 8 Dez 2009.

[62] Grinspun, M. P. S. Z. (2001). Educação Tecnológica. In: Grinspun, M.P.S.Z. (org.). Educação Tecnológica - Desafios e Pespectivas. São Paulo: Cortez. p. 25-73.

[63] Barros Filho, J. et. al. (2003). Projetos Tecnológicos no Ensino Fundamental como Alternativa para o Futuro do Ensino de Física . In: Garcia, Nilson M. D. (org.). Atas do XV Simpósio Nacional de Ensino de Física. Curitiba: CEFET-PR. p. 2065-2074.

[64] Simon, F. O. et al. (2004). Uma Proposta de Alfabetização Tecnológica no Ensino Fundamental Usando Situações Práticas e Contextualizadas. Resúmenes: VI Congresso de Historia de las Ciencias y la Tecnología: "20 Años de Historiagrafia de la Ciencia y la Tecnología en América Latina", Sociedad Latinoamericana de Historia de las Ciencias e la Tecnología. Buenos Aires, Argentina.

[65] Veraszto, E. V.; Silva, Dirceu da. (2005a). Tecnologia e Sociedade: Criação de um modelo de percepção pública. In: VII ENCONTRO DE PESQUISA EM EDUCAÇÃO DA REGIÃO SUDESTE. Belo Horizonte.

[66] Veraszto, E. V. et al. (2005b). Tecnologia e Sociedade: Projeto Para Mapear Modelos de Percepção Pública. In: V Encontro Nacional de Pesquisa em Educação em Ciências.

[67] Veraszto, E. V. et. al. (2006). O papel e os desafios da Ciência e Tecnologia no cenário ambiental contemporâneo. In: III Simpósio de Excelência em Gestão e Tecnologia. Resende/RJ. Anais do SEGeT 2006. Resende/RJ: Associação Educacional Dom Bosco. v. 1. p. 1-11.

[68] Veraszto, E. V. & Silva, D. (2007b). Tecnologia e responsabilidade social: um modelo de percepção pública In: ANPED - VIII Encontro de Pesquisa em Educação da Região Sudeste. Vitória/ES. Desafios da Educação Básica a Pesquisa em Educação. Vitória/ES: Universidade Federal do Espírito Santo. v.1. p.1-7.

[69] Veraszto, E. V. et al. (2007c). As influências das Tecnologias da Informação e Comunicação no atual processo de globalização: uma breve reflexão a partir de perspectivas históricas In: II EIDE - Encontro Iberoamericano de Educação. Araraquara/SP. Anais do II EIDE.

[70] Veraszto, E. V. et. al. (2008a). Technology: looking for a definition for the concept In: 5th CONTECSI International Conference on Information Systems and Technology Management., 2008, São Paulo/SP. Anais do 5th CONTECSI. São Paulo. v.1. p.1567-1592

[71] Veraszto, E. V. et al. (2008b). Tecnologia: buscando uma definição para o conceito. Prisma.com. Revista de Ciências da Informação e da Comunicação do CETAC. 6 Ed. V. 1. p.60-85. Jul 2008.

[72] Benedick, R. E. (1999) Tomorrow's is global. Futures, vol 31, pp. 937-947.

[73] Lustosa, M. C. J. (1999). Evolução e Meio Ambiente no enfoque evolucionista: o caso das empresas paulistas. XXVII Encontro Nacional da ANPEC - Belém. Disponível em < http://www.ie.ufrj.br/gema/pdfs/inovacao_e_meio_ambiente.pdf > Acesso em 7 Jul 2009.

[74] Brasil. (2000). Ciência & Tecnologia para o Desenvolvimento Sustentável. Ministro do Meio Ambiente. Instituto Brasileiro do Meio Ambiente e dos Recursos Naturais Renováveis. Consórcio CDS/UnB – Abipti. Brasília. Disponível em < http://www.seplan.go.gov.br/download/cienctecn.pdf >. Acesso em 25 Jun 2009.

[75] Bursztyn, M. (2004). Meio ambiente e interdisciplinaridade: desafios ao mundo acadêmico. Desenvolvimento e Meio Ambiente. N. 10. Ed. UFPR. Curitiba/PR. ISSN: 1518-952X. p. 67-76.

[76] Cordeiro Netto, O. M. & Tucci, C. E. M. (2003). Os desafios em ciência, tecnologia & inovação: resultados alcançados com o fundo setorial de recursos hídricos. Cienc. Cult., Oct./Dec. 2003, vol.55, no.4, p.44-46.

[77] Costa Ferreira, L. (2004). Idéias para uma sociologia da questão ambiental - teoria social, sociologia ambiental e interdisciplinaridade. Desenvolvimento e Meio Ambiente. N. 10. Ed. UFPR. Curitiba/PR.

[78] Glenn, J. C. & Gordon, T. J. (2004). Future issues of science and tecnhology. Technological Forecasting and Social Change. N. 71. pp. 405-416.

[79] Grübler, A. & Gritsevskyi, A. (2002). A Model of EndogenousTechnological Change through Uncertain Returns on Innovation. In: Grübler, A; Nakicenovic, N & Nordhaus, W.D. (eds) Technological Change and the Environment. Washington DC: IIASA. Oct 2002: 464p.

[80] Knechtel, M. R. (2001). Educação Ambiental: uma prática interdisciplinar. Desenvolvimento e Meio Ambiente. N. 3. Ed. UFPR. Curitiba/PR. ISSN: 1518-952X. p. 125-139.

[81] Meadows, D. H. et all. (2002). Beyond the limits. Earthscan Publications Ltd. London.

[82] OEI. (2006). Declaración de Colón: Conclusiones del V Foro Iberoamericano de Ministros de Medio Ambiente. Revista iberoamericana de ciencia, tecnología, sociedad e innovación. n.7.

[83] ONU. (1998). Protocolo de Quioto. 1998. Disponível em < http://www.mct.gov.br/upd_blob/0012/12425.pdf >. Acesso em 24 Mar 2010.

[84] PNUD. (2001). Relatório do desenvolvimento humano 2001. Programa das Nações Unidas para o Desenvolvimento. New York. Disponível em <www.undp.org/hdr2001>. Acesso em 25 Jun 2009.

[85] PNUD. (2004). Relatório do desenvolvimento humano 2004. Programa das Nações Unidas para o Desenvolvimento. New York. Disponível em <http://www.undp.org/undp/hdro>. Acesso em 25 Jun 2009.

[86] PNUD. (2006). Relatório do desenvolvimento humano 2006 - A água para lá da escassez: poder, pobreza e a crise mundial da água. Programa das Nações Unidas para o Desenvolvimento. New York. Disponível em < http://hdr.undp.org >. Acesso em 25 Jun 2009.

[87] UNESCO. (1999). Declaración de Budapest. Proyecto de programa en pro de la ciencia: Marco general de acción Unesco - ICSU. Conferencia Mundial sobre la Ciencia para el Siglo XXI: Un nuevo compromiso. Budapeste. Biblioteca da OEI. Biblioteca Digital da OEI. Disponível em: < http://www.campus-oei.org > Acesso: 6 Fev 2010.

[88] Veraszto, E. V. et al. (2007f). Tecnologia e Sociedade: uma busca por relações da influência social nas concepções e atitudes frente ao desenvolvimento tecnológico In: VI Encontro Nacional de Pesquisa em Educação em Ciências (ENPEC). Florianópolis/SC. VI Encontro Nacional de Pesquisa em Educação em Ciências (ENPEC). Florianópolis/SC.

[89] Vilches, A. (2006). et al Tecnologías para la sostenibilidad. OEI. Biblioteca da OEI. Biblioteca Digital da OEI. Disponível em: < http://www.oei.es/decada/accion003.htm >. Acesso em 6 Fev 2010.

[90] Hair JR. J. F. et al. (2005). Análise multivariada de dados. Trad. Adonai Schlup Sant'Anna e Anselmo Chaves Neto. 5 ed. Porto Alegre-RS: Bookman.

[91] Maruyama, G.M. (1998). Basics of structural equation modeling. Thousand Oaks, Ca: Sage Publications, Inc..

[92] Bardin, L. (1991). Análise de Conteúdo. Trad.: RETO, L. A. e PINHEIRO, A. Primeira Edição. Edições 70, 1991, Lisboa, Portugal.

[93] MacCallum, R. C.; Austin, J. T. (2000). Applications of structural equation modeling in psychological research. Annual Review of Psychology, n. 51, p. 201-226.

[94] Malhotra, N.K. (2001). Pesquisa de marketing: uma orientação aplicada. 3 ed. Porto Alegre: Brookman.

[95] Garson, G.D. (2003). PA 765 Statnotes: an Online Textbook. Disponível em <http://www2.chass.ncsu.edu/garson/pa765/statnote.htm> Acesso em 21 Mar 2010.

[96] Hayduk, L. A. (1987). Structural Equation Modeling with Lisrel: Essentials and Advances. Baltimore: The Johns Hopkins University Press.

[97] Bollen, K. A. e Long, J. S. (eds). (1993). Testing Structural Equation Models. Newbury Park: Sage publications.

[98] Joreskog, K. & Sobom, D. (1993). Structural Equation Modeling with the SIMPLES Command Language. Lincolnwood: SSI, 1993.

[99] Jöreskog, K. & Söbom, D. (2001). LISREL 8: User's Reference Guide. Lincolnwood: SSI.

[100] Jöreskog, Karl; Sörbom, D. (2003). LISREL 8.54 Student Edition. Lincolnwood: Scientific Software International.

[101] Jöreskog, K.; Söbom, D.; Toit, M. e Toit, S. (2000). LISREL 8: New Statistical Features. Lincolnwood: SSI.

[102] Hancock, G. R.; Mueller (org). (2006). Structural Equation Modeling: a Segund Course. Greenwich: Information Age Publishing.

Chapter 3

Application of Multivariate Data Analyses in Waste Management

K. Böhm, E. Smidt and J. Tintner

Additional information is available at the end of the chapter

1. Introduction

First of all, what is multivariate data analysis and why is it useful in waste management?

Methods dealing with only one variable are called univariate methods. Methods dealing with more than one variable at once are called multivariate methods. Using univariate methods natural systems cannot be described satisfactorily. Nature is multivariate. That means that any particular phenomenon studied in detail usually depends on several factors. For example, the weather depends on the variables: wind, air pressure, temperature, dew point and seasonal variations. If these factors are collected every day a multivariate data matrix is generated. For interpretation of such data sets multivariate data analysis is useful. Multivariate data analysis can be used to process information in a meaningful fashion. These methods can afford hidden data structures. On the one hand the elements of measurements often do not contribute to the relevant property and on the other hand hidden phenomena are unwittingly recorded. Multivariate data analysis allows us to handle huge data sets in order to discover such hidden data structures which contributes to a better understanding and easier interpretation. There are many multivariate data analysis techniques available. It depends on the question to be answered which method to choose.

Due to the requirement of representative sampling number of samples and analyses in waste management lead to huge data sets to obtain reliable results. In many cases extensive data sets are generated by the analytical method itself. Spectroscopic or chromatographic methods for instance provide more than 1000 data points for one sample. Evaluation tools can be developed to support interpretation of such analytical methods for practical applications. For specific questions and problems different evaluation tools are necessary. Calculation and interpretation are carried out by the provided evaluation tool.

In this study an overview of multivariate data analysis methods and their application in waste management research and practice is given.

2. Multivariate data analysis in waste management

The main objectives of multivariate data analysis are exploratory data analysis, classification and parameter prediction. Many different multivariate data analysis methods exist in literature. Thus the following list is not exhaustive however subdivided into the mentioned superior categories. It only concentrates on the methods applied in waste management.

Table 1 gives an overview of the existing literature in waste management on multivariate data analysis applied by several authors. It can be summarised that PCA and PLS1 are the most popular multivariate data analysis methods applied in waste management. Details are given in the following sections 2.1 and 2.2. Due to easy traceability of the parameters investigated in the different papers parameter descriptions have been taken as they were mentioned in the original.

In practice there are many software packages available which include different multivariate data analysis methods. Some software tools are: SPSS (www.spss.com\de\statistics), Canoco (www.canoco.com), The Unscrambler (www.camo.com) and the Free Software R-project (www.cran.r-project.org).

	Pattern recognition						Calibration			
Method	PCA	FA	CCA	CA	DA	SIMCA	MLR	PLS1	PLS2	PSR
Chapter		2.1.1		2.1.2	2.1.3	2.1.3	2.2.1	2.2.2		
Compost science	[1-23]	[24]	[25]	[1, 4, 22, 24-31]	[3, 9]	[8, 12]	[29, 32, 33]	[2, 6, 8, 19, 21, 23, 34-47]	[8, 21, 48]	[49]
Municipal solid waste	[50-55]			[56]				[17, 53, 57, 58]		
Landfill research	[59-72]	[65]	[73, 74]	[72, 75]	[66, 71, 76, 77]	[78]	[79, 80]	[17, 61, 62, 66, 71, 78]		
Logistics	[81]	[82]		[82]			[83, 84]			

Table 1. Literature review of different multivariate data analysis methods applied in waste management; PCA – Principal Component Analysis, FA – Factor Analysis, CA – Cluster Analysis, CCA – Canonical Correspondence Analysis, DA – Discriminant Analysis, SIMCA – Soft Independent Modelling of Class Analogy, MLR – Multiple Linear Regression, PLS-R – Partial Least Squares Regression, PSR – Penalised Signal Regression

2.1. Pattern recognition

2.1.1. *Exploratory data analysis*

• Principal Componant Analysis (PCA)

PCA is mathematically defined as an orthogonal linear transformation that arranges the data to a new coordinate system in that the greatest variance by any projection of the data takes place along the first coordinate (called the first principal component), the second greatest variance along the second coordinate, and so on. Theoretically the PCA is the optimum transformation for a given data set in least square terms. That means PCA is used for dimensionality reduction of variables in a data set by retaining those characteristics of the data set that contribute most to its variance. The transformation to the new coordinate system is described by scores (T), loadings (P) and errors (E). In matrix terms, this can be written as $X = T * P + E$. Fig. 1 illustrates the mathematical transformation using PCA. The matrices can be displayed graphically. The scores matrix illustrates the data structure and the loading matrix displays the influence of the different variables on the data structure.

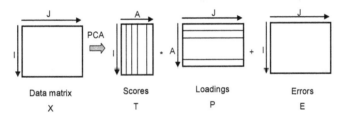

Figure 1. Principle of the PCA (according to Esbensen [85])

PCA displays hidden structures of huge data sets. PCA is applied in different fields of waste management to find out the relevant parameters of a large parameter set. So we can see which properties of a sample are significant and important to answer a particular question. Due to the results obtained time and money can be saved in further research activities.

Many applications can be found in compost science. Zbytniewski and Buszewski [1] applied PCA to reveal the significant parameters and possible groupings of chemical parameters, absorption band ratios and NMR data. Campitelli and Ceppi [3] investigated the quality of different composts and vermicomposts. The collected data were evaluated by means of PCA to extract the significant differences between the two compost types. Gil et al. [4] used PCA to show effects of cattle manure compost applied on different soils. Termorshuizen et al. [13] carried out a PCA based on disease suppression data determined by bioassays in different compost/peat mixtures and pure composts. PCA was applied by Planquart et al. [10] to examine the interactions between nutrients and trace metals in colza (Brassica napus) when sewage sludge compost was applied to soils. LaMontagne et al. [7] applied PCA on terminal restriction fragment length polymorphisms (TRFLP) patterns of different composts to reveal their characteristics with respect to microbial communities. Malley et al. [8] recorded near infrared spectra from cattle manure during composting. The collected spectral data were evaluated by PCA to show the relationships among samples and changes due to stockpiling and composting. Hansson et al. [6] observed the anaerobic treatment of municipal solid waste by using on-line near infrared spectroscopy. For spectral data interpretation PCA was carried out. Albrecht et al. [2] also performed a PCA for near infrared (NIR) spectra evaluation from an ongoing composting process. Smidt et al. [12] used PCA to show differences in spectral characteristics of different waste materials. Lillhonga et al. [23] used PCA to observe spectral characteristics of different composting processes. Vergnoux et al. [21] applied a PCA on NIR spectra as well as on physico-chemical and biochemical parameters to derive regularities from the data. Nicolas et al. [9] used PCA to evaluate data from an electronic nose. The correlations between the sensor of an electronic nose and chemical substances were determined by Romain et al. [11] using PCA. PCA was applied to observations of a composting process by means of analytical electrofocusing. The electrofocusing profiles were evaluated by Grigatti et al. [5]. PCA was also used by Biasioli et al. [19] to evaluate odour emissions and biofilter efficiency in composting plants using proton transfer reaction-mass spectrometry. Bianchi et al. [18] also used PCA to reduce the complex data set and to analyse the pattern of organic compounds emitted from a composting plant, a municipal solid waste landfill and ambient air. The effect of 14 different soil amendments on compost quality were evaluated using a PCA by Tognetti et al. [20]. Smidt et al. [16] applied PCA to illustrate the influence of input materials and composting operation on humification of organic matter. Böhm et al. [14] and Smidt et al. [15, 17] used PCA to illustrate spectral differences caused by different materials such as biowaste, manure, leftovers, straw and sewage sludge.

PCA was also applied to illustrate the alteration of municipal solid waste during the biological degradation process reaching stability limits for landfilling as well as to demonstrate similarities and differences of reactor and old landfills based on thermal data [53, 66]. Scaglia and Adani [52] focused on municipal solid waste treatment. They used PCA to create a stability index for quantifying the aerobic reactivity of municipal solid waste. Abouelwafa et al. [54, 55] investigated the degradation of sludge from the effluent of a vegetable oil processing plant mixed with household waste from landfill. Abouelwafa et al. [54] applied PCA on various parameters measured during composting (e.g. pH, electrical conductivity, moisture, C/N, NH_4/NO_3, ash, decomposition in percent, level of polyphenols, lignin, cellulose, hemicellulose, humic acid) to find the main parameters in the decomposition and restructuring phase [54]. Abouelwafa et al. [55] extracted fulvic acids from the samples mentioned above and extended the data set used for PCA by a series of absorption band ratios resulting from of FTIR spectra.

PCA has also been used in landfill research. Mikhailov et al. [62] applied PCA for monitoring data from different landfills. They included parameters such as depth, ash content, volumetric weight, humidity, amounts of refuse in summer and winter as well as the topsoil depth of landfill sections, sewage sludge lenses and the existence of a protection system. Kylefors [61] investigated data of leachate composition using PCA. The idea was to reduce the analytical monitoring program for further investigations. Durmusoglu and Yilmaz [60] used PCA to extract the significant independent variables of the collected data of raw and pre-treated leachate. A comparable work was done by De Rosa et al. [59]. They also investigated the leachate composition of an old waste dump connected to the groundwater. Olivero-Verbel et al. [63] investigated the relationships between physico-chemical parameters and the toxicity of leachates from a municipal solid waste landfill. PCA was used to find out which parameters were responsible for their toxicity. Jean and Fruget [72] used PCA to compare landfill leachates according to their toxicity and physico-chemical parameters. Ecke et al. [71] showed an example for PCA application in landfill monitoring of data from landfill test cells, leachate and gas data. Smidt et al. [64] investigated landfill materials by means of mid infrared spectroscopy, thermal analysis and PCA. They used PCA to support data interpretation. Van Praagh et al. [70] investigated the potential impacts on leachate emissions using pretreated and untreated refuse-derived material as a cover layer on the top of a municipal solid waste landfill. To interpret leachate characteristics they used PCA. Tintner and Klug [69] used PCA to illustrate how vegetation can indicate landfill cover features. Diener et al. [67] investigated the long-term stability of steel slags used as cover construction of a municipal solid waste landfill by means of a PCA. Smidt et al. [17] used PCA to display spectral characteristics of different landfill types.

Pablos et al. [68] used a PCA to evaluate toxicity bioassays for biological characterisation of hazardous wastes.

Other publications focus on the process monitoring of municipal solid waste incineration residues. Ecke [50] performed PCA on leaching parameters from municipal solid waste incineration fly ash to get an overview of the mobility of metals under certain conditions. Mostbauer et al. [51] carried out PCA to observe the long-term behaviour of municipal solid waste incineration (MSWI) residues.

In the field of waste management logistics PCA is rarely applied. Dahlén et al [81] used PCA to display the impact of waste costs on a weight basis in a specific municipality.

- Factor Analysis (FA)

FA is related to PCA but differs in its mathematical conception [86]. FA is also used to describe the variability of observed variables in terms of fewer variables called factors. That means factor analysis is a tool which reveals unobservable underlying features of a specific phenomenon by previous visible observations. The observed variables are modelled as linear combinations of the factors plus "error" terms. The information about interdependencies can be used to reduce the number of variables in a data set.

In waste management practice PCA is preferentially used. Differences between factor analysis and PCA are found to be small [86]. Srivastava and Ramanathan [65] investigated the groundwater quality of a landfill site in India by means of FA. They explained the observed relationship in simple terms expressed as factors. Bustamante et al. [24] used FA to identify the principal variables associated to the composting of agro-industrial wastes. Lin et al. [82] used FA for selecting the best food waste recycling method.

- Canonical Correspondence Analysis (CCA)

CCA is a multivariate method to explain the relationships between biological communities and their environment [87]. The method is designed to extract environmental gradients from ecological data sets. By means of the gradients an ordination diagram describing and visualising the diverse habitat preferences of taxa is calculated.

CCA is sometimes used in waste management if, for example, microbial communities or vegetation surveys are analysed. CCA was applied by Franke-Whittle et al. [25] and El-Sheikh et al. [73]. Franke-Whittle et al. [25] applied CCA to illustrate the similarities in microbial communities of three different composting processes. El-Sheikh et al. [73] investigated the ten-year primary succession on a newly created landfill at a lagoon of the Mediterranean Sea. Vegetation surveys where the basis for CCA. Kim et al. [74] applied CCA to investigate the vegetation and the soil of a not properly maintained landfill to suggest restoration alternatives by comparing the vegetation of the landfill to the nearby forests.

2.1.2. Unsupervised pattern recognition

* Cluster analysis (CA)

Clustering is the classification of objects into groups called clusters. Objects from the same cluster are more similar to one another than objects from different clusters. The difference of clusters is based on measured distances without any unit. Cluster analysis can be illustrated graphically in a dendrogram as shown in Fig. 2. The samples 2, 3 and 5 are clustered due to the high degree of similarity as well as the samples 1 and 4. The two clusters show little similarity.

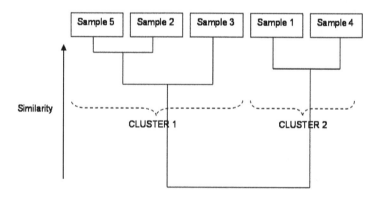

Figure 2. Example of a cluster analysis visualised by a dendrogram

CA was applied in compost science by Zybtniewskie and Buszewski [1]. They applied CA to conventional compost parameters and NMR data to find out the grouping depending on the composting time. He et al. [56] used a hierarchical cluster analysis to show the similarities and differences of UV-Vis and fluorescence spectra of water extractable organic matter, originating from municipal solid waste that had been subjected to different composting times. A hierarchical cluster analysis was also used by He et al. [22] to investigate water-extractable organic matter during cattle manure composting. Gil et al. [4] displayed dendrograms to illustrate the similarities or differences by application of cattle manure compost to different soils. Bustamante et al. [24] studied physico-chemical, chemical and microbiological parameters of different composts. The evaluation of the composts was conducted by a hierarchical cluster analysis [24].

Lin et al. [82] applied a CA for the selection of optimal recycling methods for food waste.

A stepwise cluster analysis (SCA) was used to describe the nonlinear relationships among state variables and microbial activities of composts by Sun et al. [29]. Sun et al. [30] developed a genetic algorithm aided stepwise cluster analysis (GASCA) to describe the relationships between selected state variables and the C/N ratio in food waste composting.

Furthermore CA has often been used to evaluate microbiological data, especially in compost science [25-28, 31]. Innerebner et al. [26] and Ros et al. [27, 28] used CA to identify related samples and similar groups of microorganisms. Franke-Whittle et al. [25] used CA to show the similarities of Denaturing Gradient Gel Electrophoresis (DGGE) data of three different compost types with proceeding compost maturity. Xiao et al. [31] used a hierarchical cluster analysis of DGGE data to estimate the succession of bacterial communities during the active composting process.

Tesar et al. [75] applied CA to spectral data to illustrate the effect of in-situ aeration of a landfill. Jean and Fruget [72] used CA to compare landfill leachates on the basis of their toxicity and physico-chemical parameters.

2.1.3. Supervised pattern recognition

All supervised methods are classifications. Classification can be considered as a predictive method where the response is a category variable. Different classification methods exist. There are types of "hard" and "soft" modelling. Hard modelling means that a non-relocatable line between the defined groups exists. One object can only belong to one group. Soft modelling allows an overlapping of the defined classes. An object can belong to both groups [88]. With regard to waste management practice two different classification methods are described in detail.

- Discriminant analysis (DA)

DA is a classification method of hard modelling. Campitelli and Ceppi [3] carried out a DA to distinguish between compost and vermicompost on the basis of parameters such as total organic carbon (TOC), germination index (GI), pH, total nitrogen (TN), and water soluble carbon (WSC). Nicolas et al. [9] performed a DA to classify data of an electric nose according to defined exceeded levels of odour. Ecke et al. [71] investigated samples from three different landfill sites by the biochemical methane potential and used DA for data evaluation. Huber-Humer et al. [77] applied DA to determine methane oxidation efficiency of different materials based on chemical and physical variables. Smidt et al. [66, 76] used DA to differentiate the infrared spectral [76] and thermal patterns [66] of municipal solid waste incinerator (MSWI) bottom ash before and after CO_2 uptake. A DA on the CO_2 ion current recorded during combustion was applied to illustrate the effect of CO_2 treatment of MSWI bottom ash [66]. DA was also used to illustrate the spectral characteristics of leachate from landfill simulation reactors under aerobic and anaerobic conditions [17].

- Soft independent modelling of class analogy (SIMCA)

SIMCA is a special method of soft modelling recommended by Wold in the 1970s [88]. Objects can belong to one of the defined class, to both classes or to none. Whether SIMCA can be applied on the data set depends on the question to be answered. According to Brereton [88] it is often legitimate in chemistry that an object belongs to more than one class For example a compound may have an ester and an alkene group which are both reflected by an infrared spectrum. Thus they fit in both classes. In natural science it is allowed in most cases for an object to be in line with more than one class simultaneously.

Contrarily in other cases an object can belong only to one class and the application of SIMCA is inappropriate. Brereton [88] gives a good example where the concept of SIMCA is not applicable: A banknote is either forged or not. In many cases there is only one true answer. For such problems SIMCA is not the adequate method.

In compost science Malley et al. [8] and Smidt et al. [12] carried out a SIMCA. Malley et al. [8] classified different decomposition stages of manures by means of near infrared spectroscopy and SIMCA. Smidt et al. [12] carried out a SIMCA to classify different waste materials such as biowaste compost, mechanically-biologically pretreated waste and landfill materials based on their spectroscopic pattern. Smidt et al. [78] used the SIMCA model developed by Smidt et al. [12] to identify different landfill types such as reactor landfill and industrial landfill samples.

2.2. Calibration

2.2.1. Multiple Linear Regression (MLR)

MLR is directed at modelling the relationship between two or more explanatory variables and a response variable by fitting a linear equation to observed data. Every value of the independent variable X is associated with a value of the dependent variable Y, with explanatory or predictive purposes. A direct correlation between Y and X-matrix is performed.

In waste management MLR was applied by Chikae et al. [32] to predict the germination index which was adopted as a marker for compost maturity. Thirty-two parameters of 159 samples were measured. MLR was carried out to reduce this huge parameter set to some significant parameters. Lawrence and Boutwell [79] used MLR for predicting the stratigraphy of landfill sites using an electromagnetic method. Moreno-Santini et al. [80] applied MLR to determine arsenic and lead levels in the hair of residents in a municipality constructed on a former landfill.

Noori et al. [84] compared two different statistical methods (artificial neural networks and MLR based on a PCA) to predict the solid waste generation in Tehran. Cheng et al. [83] used

MLR to predict the factors associated with medical waste generation at hospitals. Sun et al. [29] used MLR to predict mesophilic and thermopilic bacteria in food waste composts. Suehara and Yano [33] applied MLR to predict conventional compost parameters by NIR spectral data.

2.2.2. Partial Least Squares Regression (PLS-R)

- PLS1

PLS-R is used to find out the fundamental relations between two matrices. PLS-R is a bilinear modelling method. The main idea behind it is to calculate the principal components of the X and the Y matrix separately (external correlation) and to develop a regression model between the scores of the principal components (inner correlation). The concept of PLS-R is demonstrated in Fig. 3.

PLS1 is often used to predict time consuming or expensive parameters using an alternative analytical method. Modern analytical tools such as spectroscopic, chromatographic and thermo analytical methods generate data with inherent information on different parameters. With the development of an evaluated prediction model conventional analytical methods can be replaced by easier and/ or faster handling and robust methods.

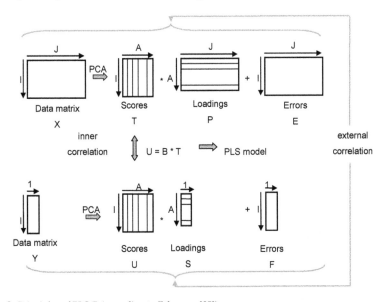

Figure 3. Principles of PLS-R (according to Esbensen [85])

Many authors have developed such prediction models in compost science. Zvomuya et al. [44] predicted phosphorus availability in soils, amended with composted and non-composted cattle manure by means of cumulative phosphorus analysis. Fujiwara and

Murakami [35] applied near infrared spectroscopy to estimate available nitrogen in poultry manure compost. Huang et al. [36] also used near infrared spectroscopy to estimate pH, electric conductivity, volatile solids, TOC, total N, the C:N ratio and the total phosphorus content. Furthermore they determined nutrient contents such as K, Ca, Mg, Fe and Zn of animal manure compost using near infrared spectroscopy and PLS1 [37]. Malley et al. [8] developed prediction models for total C, organic C, total N, C:N ratio, K, S and P by means of near infrared spectroscopy and PLS1. Morimoto et al. [43] carried out carbon quantification of green grass tissue using near infrared spectroscopy. Hansson et al. [6] predicted the concentration of propionate in an anaerobic process by near infrared spectra. Albrecht et al. [2] developed calibration models between spectral data and C, N, C:N ratio and composting time. Michel et al. [42] predicted chemical and biological properties of composts such as organic C (C_{org}), total N, C:N ratio, age, microbial biomass (C_{mic}), C_{mic}:C_{org}, basal respiration, enzymatic activity and plant suppression using near infrared spectroscopy. Ludwig et al. [39] also used near infrared spectroscopy to predict pH, electric conductivity, P, K, NO_3^- and NH_4^+ and phytotoxicity. Ko et al. [38] predicted heavy metal contents of Cr, As, Cd, Cu, Zn and Pb by means of near infrared spectroscopy and PLS1. They hypothesised that heavy metals are detectable by NIR when they are complexed with organic matter. Capriel et al. [34] found out that mid infrared spectroscopy is a rapid method to estimate the effect of nitrogen and relevant parameters such as total C, total N, the C:N ratio and the pH of biowaste compost. Meissl et al. [40] used PLS1 and the mid infrared region to predict humic acid contents in biowaste composts. Furthermore they determined humic acid contents by near infrared spectroscopy [41]. Sharma et al. [47] developed prediction models for conventional compost parameters, especially ammonia, pH, conductivity, dry matter, nitrogen and ash using NIR and Vis-NIR spectroscopy. Lillhonga et al. [23] used PLS-R for compost parameter prediction based on NIR spectra. They developed models for the parameters: time, pH, temperature, NH_3/NH_4^+, energy (calorific value) and moisture content. Galvez-Sola et al. [45] used PLS1 to predict different compost quality parameters such as pH, electric conductivity, total organic matter, total organic carbon, total N, C/N ratio as well as nutrients contents (N, P, K) and potentially pollutant element concentrations (Fe, Cu, Mn and Zn) from near infrared spectra. Vergnoux et al. [21] applied a PLS1 to predict physico-chemical and biochemical parameters from NIR spectra. Physico-chemical parameters comprised age, organic carbon, organic nitrogen, C/N, total N, fulvic acids (FA), humic acids (HA) and HA/FA. The soluble fraction, lignin and biological maturity index were summarised as biochemical parameters. Mikhailov et al. [62] used PLS1 to predict maturity and stability based on conventionally measured data. Kylefors [61] developed prediction models for leachate concentrations of specific organic substances in leachate by means of conventional leachate analysis and PLS1. Biasioli et al. [19] used PLS1 to predict odour concentrations in composting plants by proton transfer reaction-mass spectrometry (PTR-MS). Mohajer et al. [46] used a PLS1 to generate a model to predict the microbial oxygen uptake in sludge based on different physical compost parameters.

Böhm et al. [57] used PLS1 to predict the respiration activity (RA4) based on FT-IR spectra of mechanically-biologically pretreated (MBT) waste. The potential of thermal data of MBT waste was shown by Smidt et al. [53]. They applied PLS1 to predict the calorific value, total organic carbon (TOC) and respiration activity (RA4). Smidt et al. [17] also developed a prediction model for the calorific value based on spectral data. Biasioli et al. [58] used PLS1 to predict odour concentration from MSW composting plants based on PTR-MS.

Ecke et al. [71] performed detoxification of hexavalent chromium to less toxic trivalent chromium in industrial waste and applied a PLS model to identify the relevant factors. Smidt et al. [78] predicted the biological oxygen demand and the dissolved organic carbon (DOC) of old landfill materials from spectral data. They also used PLS-R to predict the total organic carbon and total nitrogen based on thermal data [78]. Furthermore PLS-R was used to predict respiration activity (RA4) from MS data of old landfill materials [66]. Smidt et al. [17] developed a prediction model for the DOC and the TOC from spectral data of landfill materials.

- PLS2

PLS2 is a variant of the PLS-R method where several Y-variables are modelled simultaneously. An advantage of this method is to find possible correlations or co-linearity between the Y-variables.

Malley et al. [8] developed prediction models for pH, total N, nitrate and nitrite, total C, organic C, C:N ratio, P, available P, S, K and Na by means of near Infrared spectroscopy and PLS2. Suehara et al. [48] used PLS2 for simultaneous measurement of carbon and nitrogen content of composts using near infrared spectroscopy. Vergnoux et al. [21] applied PLS2 to predict physico-chemical (moisture, temperature, pH, NH4-N) and biochemical parameters (hemicellulose and cellulose) from NIR spectra.

- Penalised signal regression (PSR)

This special regression method is described in Galvez-Sola et al. [49]. Galves Sola et al. [49] used this method to predict the phosphorus content in composts.

3. Selected examples from literature using multivariate data analysis in waste management

In the following chapter four selected examples using multivariate data analysis in waste management are described in detail. To illustrate the application of principal component analysis (PCA) the study by Mikhailov et al. [62] is presented. He carried out multivariate data analysis for the ecological assessment of landfills. The second example illustrates the application of partial least squares regression (PLS-R). Michel et al. [42] applied PLS-R to predict conventional parameters by spectroscopic data. Ros et al. [27] applied a cluster analysis to data of polymerase chain reaction coupled with denaturing gradient gel electrophoresis (PCR-DGGE) to observe the long-term effects of compost amendment on soil microbial activity. A soft independent model of class analogy (SIMCA) was applied by Malley et al. [8]. They used SIMCA to classify different composts according to their spectroscopic characteristic.

3.1. Principal component analysis (PCA)

3.1.1. Objective of the study

The objective of the study by Mikhailov et al. [62] was to evaluate the stability of landfills based on many conventional parameters such as ash content, temperature, volume weight, pH, humidity and depth. They supposed that a multivariate approach could provide a more efficient data interpretation. Therefore they compared conventional and multivariate data analysis methods.

3.1.2. Method of evaluation and results

In a first step Mikhailov et al. [62] collected conventional data to describe landfill stability. They investigated 3 different landfills in Russia, one illegal dump, an old poorly-run dump and a modern well-run landfill. They focused on geodesic surveys to obtain the overall object properties such as size, volume and different layers. Furthermore they investigated the physical and chemical properties of the samples collected in different depths of the landfill. The physical and chemical properties include ash content, humidity, and acidity. Using the conventional collected data they carried out a PCA for each landfill site. They included the ash content, temperature, volume weight, pH, humidity and depth. The PCA for the two landfills in Bezenchuk and Kinel are presented in the study [62]. Based on the data pool Mikhailov et al. [62] could identify two important sources of waste around Bezenchuk, a poultry farm and a granary. In addition to regular domestic refuse, the agricultural and industrial wastes were disposed illegally in this dump. Kinel on the other hand is a modern, well operated landfill, in which both domestic and industrial wastes are disposed. These assumptions were confirmed by chemometric investigations based on PCA. The mentioned PCAs show clustering of the different classes. The results of the PCA of the third investigated landfill are not shown in their study. Otradny was shown to be a poorly maintained landfill. Clear separation of layers by means of the scores plot was not possible. They found out that the information by the landfill manager and the results obtained did not correspond.

3.1.3. Conclusion

Mikhailov et al. [62] concluded that multivariate data analysis is an appropriate tool for ecological monitoring. They pointed out that chemometric methods provide the possibility to explore the structure of waste disposal by identification of specific areas.

3.2. Partial Least Square Regression (PLS1)

3.2.1. Objective of the study

The verification of compost quality has to be monitored consistently. However this is time-consuming and laborious. Due to the fact that NIR is a simple, accurate and fast technique used for routine analysis Michel et al. [42] hypothesised that NIR could be used for parameter prediction. The objective of the study was to use NIR spectroscopy to determine chemical and biological properties.

3.2.2. Method of evaluation and results

The first step was to define compost quality. Michel et al. [42] defined compost quality by C and N contents, suppression of pathogens, stability/ maturity and biological parameters, especially organic carbon (C_{org}), total N (N_t), C:N ratio, age, microbial biomass (C_{mic}), $C_{mic}:C_{org}$, basal respiration, enzymatic activity and suppression of plant disease. Spectroscopic data from 98 composts samples as well as the mentioned conventional parameters were collected. Fundamental relations between two matrices can be found by means of PLS1. Michel et al. [42] applied a PLS1 to express conventional parameters by spectral data. They designed for each conventional parameter a PLS1. Table 2 summarises the collected data and results obtained by Michel et al. [42]. The standard error of cross-validation (SECV) and the coefficient of determination (r^2) indicate the quality of prediction. The SECV provides information on the prediction error, r^2 demonstrates the quality of correlation. Composting age and basal respiration show the highest r^2. The specific enzymatic activity and the suppressive effect show the lowest r^2. It should be emphasised that biological tests that are carried out with the original wet compost are more susceptible to interferences due to the heterogeneity of the material. Michel et al. [42] concluded that especially compost age and basal respiration are clearly reflected by the NIR spectrum and feature the best results. By contrast, the specific enzyme activity and suppressive effects show the worst prediction results. The assigned correlations are illustrated in the paper [42].

	n	Mean	Range	Outliers removed	SECV	r^2
Age [d]	98	183.6	82.0 - 268.0	6	16.7	0.82
C_{org} content [%]	97	26.0	16.4 - 41.5	5	2.32	0.77
N_t content [%]	97	1.4	1.0 - 2.1	4	0.11	0.67
C:N ratio	97	18.2	12.2 - 29.1	4	1.51	0.71
C_{mic} [$\mu g\ g^{-1}$]	98	4986	774 - 8587	5	954	0.68
$C_{mic}:C_{org}$ [$mgCmicgCorg^{-1}$]	97	18.6	4.0 - 29.4	4	4.00	0.63
Basal respiration [$\mu g\ C\ g^{-1}\ d^{-1}$]	47	574.8	252.0 - 966.0	2	49.2	0.88
qCO_2 [μgCO_2-C mg $C_{mic}^{-1}\ d^{-1}$]	47	9.7	4.2 - 17.1	1	1.98	0.83
Hydrolysis of fluorescein diacetate (FDA-HR) [$\mu g\ g^{-1}h^{-1}$]	98	517.9	256.0 - 879.0	5	74.7	0.75
Specific enzyme activity [$\mu gFDA\ mgC_{mic}^{-1}h^{-1}$]	98	118.7	48.6 - 370.9	6	48.6	0.49
Suppression 5‰ (rating) [%]	98	57.3	8.0 - 101.0	2	19.3	0.71
Suppression 5‰ (fresh weight) [%]	98	59.1	14.0 - 103.0	3	18.7	0.47

Table 2. Excerpt of table 1 and 2 by Michel et al. [42], SECV = standard error of cross-validation, r^2 = the coefficient of determination

3.2.3. Conclusion

Michel et al. [42] concluded that NIR spectroscopy was a capable method to predict various chemical and biological parameters using PLS regression. They believe NIR spectroscopy to be capable of monitoring compost quality.

3.3. Cluster analysis (CA)

3.3.1. Objective of the study

The objective of the study by Ros et al. [27] was to find out the long-term effects of composts on soil microbial communities. Different types of compost were applied over a period of 12 years. DNA was extracted by Ros et al. [27] from differently treated soils. The microbial community was described by polymerase chain reaction coupled with denaturing gradient gel electrophoresis (PCR-DGGE). They used multivariate data analysis to show the differences or similarities of microbial communities using DGGE data.

3.3.2. Method of evaluation and results

A polymerase chain reaction coupled with denaturing gradient gel electrophoresis (PCR-DGGE) was performed to characterize the microbial community. In Fig. 4 a DGGE fingerprint is shown. For the interpretation of such fingerprints statistical tools are necessary. DGGE data were converted into a binary system for cluster analysis (Fig. 4). As mentioned above, cluster analysis visualises the similarity between the samples in a dendrogram.

Ros et al. [27] show the cluster analysis of the DGGE profiles of 16S rDNA from the whole bacterial community. The cluster analysis illustrates the segregation of two soil groups. The clusters are caused by two different amendments. One cluster comprises the soil with compost and nitrogen application, the second cluster represents the soil with amendment of different composts (compost + nitrogen as mineral fertiliser).

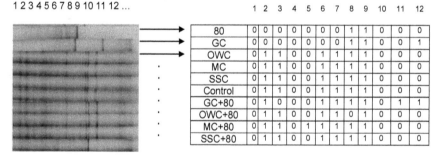

1 2 3 4 5 6 7 8 9 10 11 12 …

	1	2	3	4	5	6	7	8	9	10	11	12
80	0	0	0	0	0	0	0	1	1	0	0	0
GC	0	0	0	0	0	0	0	1	1	0	0	1
OWC	0	1	1	0	0	1	1	1	1	0	0	0
MC	0	1	1	0	0	1	1	1	1	0	0	0
SSC	0	1	1	0	0	1	1	1	1	0	0	0
Control	0	1	1	0	0	1	1	1	1	0	0	0
GC+80	0	1	0	0	0	1	1	1	1	0	1	1
OWC+80	0	1	1	0	0	1	1	0	1	0	0	0
MC+80	0	1	1	0	1	1	1	1	1	0	0	0
SSC+80	0	1	1	0	0	1	1	1	1	0	0	0

Figure 4. DGGE fingerprint and an example of a binary DGGE data matrix

3.3.3. Conclusion

Ros et al. [27] concluded that the differences between soils with compost with additional nitrogen fertiliser, and the second cluster comprising compost, control and mineral fertiliser soils are stronger than the influence of the different compost types. Furthermore they hypothesised that a certain microbial community inherent to the different composts is irrelevant after 12 years of compost application. Based on the cluster analyses of the PCR-

DGGE data, they concluded that the combined application of compost and nitrogen affected soil properties regarding microbial communities much more.

3.4. Soft independent modelling of class analogy (SIMCA)

3.4.1. Objective of the study

Malley et al. [8] used a portable near infrared (NIR) spectrometer to investigate changes of biogenic waste materials during composting. The idea of this study was to observe the composting process continuously in an easy and inexpensive way using NIR spectroscopy.

3.4.2. Method of evaluation and results

First of all many spectra were collected by Malley et al. [8]. The interpretation of spectral data requires experience in spectral interpretation. To provide rapid interpretation of the measured infrared spectra Malley et al. [8] applied the classification method SIMCA. The SIMCA model allows the assignment of a new sample to a defined class. A SIMCA model is always based on the PCAs of the various defined classes. Malley et al. [8] defined 3 different classes: raw manure (M), stockpiled manure (S) and manure compost (C). In the study 2 years of composting were observed (2000 and 2001). Figure 2 by Malley et al. [8] shows the scores plot of the PCA based on the spectral data of the three different classes in the year 2001. The PCA demonstrates a clear grouping of the 3 classes manure, stockpiled manure and manure compost.

Malley et al. [8] illustrated the results of the SIMCA by means of a Coomans plot. In figure 3 by Malley et al. [8] they show the Coomans plot for the investigations of 2001. The vertical and horizontal lines in the Coomans plot mark the 5 % level of significance. That means that 95 % of the samples that truly belong to this group are found within the line. Due to the fact that compost lies on the opposite side of the vertical line from the raw and stockpiled samples Malley et al. [8] concluded that compost is significantly different from the other two classes. The groups of raw manure and stockpiled manure are overlapping. Thus Malley et al. [8] concluded that they did not differ significantly. Nevertheless some raw samples were different. With these results Malley et al. [8] demonstrated that spectroscopic data and multivariate data analysis, especially SIMCA provides a sensitive analysis to differentiate between the products of stockpiles and compost.

3.4.3. Conclusion

Malley et al. [8] concluded that NIR spectroscopy and the multivariate data analysis method SIMCA can be a rapid, inexpensive method for assessing a composting process.

4. Critical discussion of multivariate statistical methods

In fact there are some statistical restrictions, which cannot be solved easily. The simple situation starts with the general linear model. This model usually has a character variable y depending on one or more predictor variables $x_1, x_2, ..., x_k$:

In case of cross-classified two-way analysis of variance (equal subclass numbers):

$$y_{ijk} = \mu + a_i + b_j + w_{ij} + e_{ijk}, \ (i = 1, \quad , a; j = 1, \ldots, b; k = 1, \ldots, n) \tag{1}$$

μ is the general mean, a_i are the main effects of factor A, b_j are the main effects of factor B, w_{ij} are the interactions between A_i and B_j, e_{ijk} are the random error terms.

In case of multiple linear regression:

$$y_j = \beta_0 + \beta_1 x_{1j} + \beta_2 x_{2j} + \ldots + \beta_k x_{kj} + e_j, \ (j = 1, \ldots, n), \tag{2}$$

y_j is the j-th value of y depending on the j-th values $x_{1j}, \ldots x_{kj}$;

e_j are error terms with $E(e_j) = 0$, $var(e_j) = \sigma^2$ (for all j), $cov(e_{j'}, e_j) = 0$ for $j' \neq j$

The simple case assumes a linear dependency. The statistical parameters (the model coefficients) of the model can be estimated, y can be estimated for given values $x_1, \ldots x_k$. Assuming that the e_j are normally distributed, confidence intervals can be calculated for each model coefficient and finally tests of hypotheses about the model coefficients can be performed. By this procedure each variable can be tested whether its influence on the variable y is significantly different from 0 or not. The type I and type II error can be stated. Furthermore optimal designs for the experiments and surveys can be calculated [89]. Several assumptions are typically made regarding the distribution of the populations and regarding homoscedasticity. Furthermore the problem of extreme values and outliers respectively is critical, especially in environmental measurements. Increasing the number of regressors and factors respectively also increases the error terms.

For some univariate models robust and powerful alternatives regarding the distribution assumptions and regarding homoscedasticity [90-92] already exist. In the case of cross classification there is still no satisfying, powerful alternative. Many multiple regressors methods (multiple regression models, logistic regression models, discriminant analysis, cross classification models) need independent variables.

In chemometrics some of these problems are highly relevant. Usually the number of regressor variables exceeds the number of samples, which excludes most of the common oligovariate models. Many of the regressor variables are highly collinear. Due to these reasons dimension reduction methods are used such as correspondence analysis or factor analysis. The new factors in the latter are strictly independent from one another and can therefore be used in conventional models. There are several possibilities to extract these factors, like Principal Components or Maximum Likelihood. A possibility to model discrete variables is the classification by means of cluster analysis. These clusters can be tested later by contingency tables. Both steps (factor analysis and cluster analysis) lead to descriptive variables of the data set. Just as all descriptive methods in statistics they do not serve as tests against hypothesis of pure chance. There is no risk assessment of the results. Testing of the new descriptive variables implies the understanding of these new variables. By loading the original variables onto the new variables sometimes the interpretation can be done easily. Then models with these variables can be established (PCR or PLS-R) with several quality parameters (e.g. correlation coefficient). A test of significance for the cross-validated r^2 was performed by Wakeling and Morris [93]. In this paper critical values of r^2 occurring just by chance alone are tabulated for one to three dimensional models at a significance level of 5 % based on Monte Carlo simulations. A comparable method was used by Stahle and Wold [94] to develop a polynomial approximation of the test statistic for the two-class problem and the number of objects, the number of variables, the percentage variance explained by the first component in X and the percentage of missing values.

$$cvd/sd = \sqrt{PRESS/RSS} \qquad (3)$$

cvd: cross-validated deviances
sd: standard deviation
PRESS: prediction error sum of squares
RSS: residual sum of squares

Unfortunately the definition of hypothesis regarding the regression coefficients still refers to the new components and provides no results regarding the original variables. There is no statistical possibility to prove whether the extraction method is optimal. Other methods of dimension reduction are already in use (e.g. Boosting, Random forest). Robust alternatives for PLS-R are also available [95].

As long as there are no satisfying testing routines, the results of the presented multivariate methods have to be interpreted very carefully. There is an inherent risk of over-interpretation, especially when using descriptive methods such as PCA or cluster analysis. There is no definition of the error probability of the results. That means whatever interpretation of the picture is done, it could be just pure coincidence and there is no information about the risk. The only possibility to overcome these problems would be to analyse a large number of samples and in case of regression models to validate these models.

5. Summary

In waste management research and practice often huge data sets for statistical evaluation are required to verify the findings. This request concerns both the natural scientific and the logistic field of waste management. Huge data sets can be generated on the one hand by vast numbers of investigated parameters and samples and on the other hand by modern analytical methods such as spectroscopic, chromatographic methods or thermal analysis.

Multivariate data analysis can help to explore data structures of the investigated samples. Another advantage is that the results can be displayed graphically. Furthermore, validated models can serve as adequate evaluation tools for practical application. Different software types are offered to develop such evaluation tools.

In this study the most important multivariate data analysis methods applied in waste management were described in detail and documented by a literature review. It could be demonstrated that Principal Component Analysis (PCA) and Partial Least Square

Regression (PLS-R) are the most applied methods in waste management. PCA was used to find hidden data structures, groupings and interrelationships of data. In most cases PLS-R was applied to predict parameters using new analytical instruments that allow faster and cheaper analyses.

In general it can be stated that multivariate data analysis was successfully applied in all experiments. Several authors compared different multivariate methods to determine which one provided the best results. Depending on the data set and the question to be answered the appropriate method must be identified.

Author details

K. Böhm*
Institute of Waste Management, Department of Water, Atmosphere and Environment, University of Natural Resources and Life Sciences, Vienna, Austria

E. Smidt and J. Tintner
Institute of Wood Science and Technology, Department of Material Sciences and Process Engineering, University of Natural Resources and Life Sciences, Vienna, Austria

6. References

[1] Zbytniewski R, Buszewski B (2005) Characterization of natural organic matter (NOM) derived from sewage sludge compost. Part 2: Multivariate techniques in the study of compost maturation. Bioresour. Technol. 96: 479-484.

[2] Albrecht R, Joffre R, Gros R, Le Petit J, Terrom G, Périssol C (2008) Efficiency of near-infrared reflectance spectroscopy to assess and predict the stage of transformation of organic matter in the composting process. Bioresour. Technol. 99: 448-455.

[3] Campitelli P, Ceppi S (2008) Chemical, physical and biological compost and vermicompost characterization: A chemometric study. Chemometrics Intell. Lab. Syst. 90: 64-71.

[4] Gil MV, Calvo LF, Blanco D, Sánchez ME (2008) Assessing the agronomic and environmental effects of the application of cattle manure compost on soil by multivariate methods. Bioresour. Technol. 99: 5763-5772.

[5] Grigatti M, Cavani L, Ciavatta C (2007) A multivariate approach to the study of the composting process by means of analytical electrofocusing. Waste Manage. 27: 1072-1082.

[6] Hansson M, Nordberg A, Mathisen B (2003) On-line NIR monitoring during anaerobic treatment of municipal solid waste. Water Sci. Technol. 48: 9-13.

[7] LaMontagne MG, Michel Jr FC, Holden PA, Reddy CA (2002) Evaluation of extraction and purification methods for obtaining PCR-amplifiable DNA from compost for microbial community analysis. J. Microbiol. Meth. 49: 255-264.

---

* Corresponding Author

[8]   Malley DF, McClure C, Martin PD, Buckley K, McCaughey WP (2005) Compositional analysis of cattle manure during composting using a field-portable near-infrared spectrometer. Communications in Soil Science and Plant Analysis 36: 455-475.

[9]   Nicolas J, Romain AC, Wiertz V, Maternova J, Andre P (2000) Using the classification model of an electronic nose to assign unknown malodours to environmental sources and to monitor them continuously. Sensors and Actuators, B: Chemical 69: 366-371.

[10] Planquart P, Bonin G, Prone A, Massiani C (1999) Distribution, movement and plant availability of trace metals in soils amended with sewage sludge composts: Application to low metal loadings. Sci. Total Environ. 241: 161-179.

[11] Romain AC, Godefroid D, Kuske M, Nicolas J (2005) Monitoring the exhaust air of a compost pile as a process variable with an e-nose. Sensors and Actuators, B: Chemical 106: 29-35.

[12] Smidt E, Meissl K, Schwanninger M, Lechner P (2008) Classification of waste materials using Fourier transform infrared spectroscopy and soft independent modeling of class analogy. Waste Manage. 28: 1699-1710.

[13] Termorshuizen AJ, van Rijn E, van der Gaag DJ, Alabouvette C, Chen Y, Lagerlöf J, et al. (2006) Suppressiveness of 18 composts against 7 pathosystems: Variability in pathogen response. Soil Biol. Biochem. 38: 2461-2477.

[14] Böhm K, Smidt E, Tintner J (2011) Modelled on Nature - Biological Processes in Waste Management. In: Kumar S, editor. Integrated Waste Management. Rijeka, Croatia: InTech. p. 153-178.

[15] Smidt E, Tintner J, Böhm K, Binner E (2011) Transformation of biogenic waste materials through anaerobic digestion and subsequent composting of the residues – A case study. Dyn. Soil Dyn. Plant 5: 63-69.

[16] Smidt E, Meissl K, Tintner J, Binner E (2008) Influence of Input Materials and Composting Operation on Humification of Organic Matter. In: Hao X, editor. Dyn. Soil Dyn. Plant. Special Issue 1: p. 50-59.

[17] Smidt E, Böhm K, Schwanninger M (2011) The Application of FT-IR Spectroscopy in Waste Management. In: G.S. N, editor. Fourier Transforms - New Analytical Approaches and FTIR Strategies. Rijeka, Croatia: InTech. p. 405-430.

[18] Bianchi G, Celeste G, Palmiotto M, Davoli E (2010) Source identification of odours and VOCs from a composting plant by multivariate analysis of trace volatile organic compounds. Chemical Engineering Transactions 23: 279-284.

[19] Biasioli F, Aprea E, Gasperi F, Mark TD (2009) Measuring odour emission and biofilter efficiency in composting plants by proton transfer reaction-mass spectrometry. Water Sci. Technol. 59: 1263-1269.

[20] Tognetti C, Mazzarino MJ, Laos F (2011) Comprehensive quality assessment of municipal organic waste composts produced by different preparation methods. Waste Manage. 31: 1146-1152.

[21] Vergnoux A, Guiliano M, Le Dréau Y, Kister J, Dupuy N, Doumenq P (2009) Monitoring of the evolution of an industrial compost and prediction of some compost properties by NIR spectroscopy. Sci. Total Environ. 407: 2390-2403.

[22] He XS, Xi BD, Jiang YH, He LS, Li D, Pan HW, et al. (2012) Structural transformation study of water-extractable organic matter during the industrial composting of cattle manure. Microchem. J. in press: DOI: 10.1016/j.microc.2012.1006.1004.

[23] Geladi P, Sethson B, Nystro?m J, Lillhonga T, Lestander T, Burger J (2004) Chemometrics in spectroscopy: Part 2. Examples. Spectrochimica Acta - Part B Atomic Spectroscopy 59: 1347-1357.

[24] Bustamante MA, Suarez-Estrella F, Torrecillas C, Paredes C, Moral R, Moreno J (2010) Use of chemometrics in the chemical and microbiological characterization of composts from agroindustrial wastes. Bioresour. Technol. 101: 4068-4074.

[25] Franke-Whittle IH, Knapp BA, Fuchs J, Kaufmann R, Insam H (2009) Application of COMPOCHIP Microarray to Investigate the Bacterial Communities of Different Composts. Microbial Ecol. 57: 510-521.

[26] Innerebner G, Knapp B, Vasara T, Romantschuk M, Insam H (2006) Traceability of ammonia-oxidizing bacteria in compost-treated soils. Soil Biol. Biochem. 38: 1092-1100.

[27] Ros M, Klammer S, Knapp B, Aichberger K, Insam H (2006) Long-term effects of compost amendment of soil on functional and structural diversity and microbial activity. Soil Use Manage. 22: 209-218.

[28] Ros M, Pascual JA, Garcia C, Hernandez MT, Insam H (2006) Hydrolase activities, microbial biomass and bacterial community in a soil after long-term amendment with different composts. Soil Biol. Biochem. 38: 3443-3452.

[29] Sun W, Huang GH, Zeng GM, Qin XS, Sun XL (2009) A stepwise-cluster microbial biomass inference model in food waste composting. Waste Manage. 29: 2956-2968.

[30] Sun W, Huang GH, Zeng GM, Qin XS, Yu H (2011) Quantitative effects of composting state variables on C/N ratio through GA-aided multivariate analysis. Sci. Total Environ. 409: 1243-1254.

[31] Xiao Y, Zeng GM, Yang ZH, Ma YH, Huang C, Shi WJ, et al. (2011) Effects of Continuous Thermophilic Composting (CTC) on Bacterial Community in the Active Composting Process. Microbial Ecol. 62: 599-608.

[32] Chikae M, Ikeda R, Kerman K, Morita Y, Tamiya E (2006) Estimation of maturity of compost from food wastes and agro-residues by multiple regression analysis. Bioresour. Technol. 97: 1979-1985.

[33] Suehara K, Yano T (2004) Bioprocess monitoring using near-infrared spectroscopy. Advances in biochemical engineering/biotechnology 90: 173-198.

[34] Capriel P, Ebertseder T, Popp L, Gutser R (1999) IR-spectroscopy: A rapid method to estimate the nitrogen effect and relevant parameters of biocomposts. IR-Spektroskopie: Eine Schnellmethode zur Prognose der N-Wirkung und relevanten Parameter von Biokomposten 162: 149-153.

[35] Fujiwara T, Murakami K (2007) Application of near infrared spectroscopy for estimating available nitrogen in poultry manure compost. Soil Science and Plant Nutrition 53: 102-107.

[36] Huang G, Han L, Liu X (2007) Rapid estimation of the composition of animal manure compost by near infrared reflectance spectroscopy. J. Near Infrared Spectrosc. 15: 387-394.

[37] Huang G, Han L, Yang Z, Wang X (2008) Evaluation of the nutrient metal content in Chinese animal manure compost using near infrared spectroscopy (NIRS). Bioresour. Technol. 99: 8164-8169.

[38] Ko HJ, Choi HL, Park HS, Lee HW (2004) Prediction of heavy metal content in compost using near-infrared reflectance spectroscopy. Asian-Australasian Journal of Animal Sciences 17: 1736-1740.

[39] Ludwig B, Schmilewski G, Terhoeven-Urselmans T (2006) Use of near infrared spectroscopy to predict chemical parameters and phytotoxicity of peats and growing media. Scientia Horticulturae 109: 86-91.

[40] Meissl K, Smidt E, Schwanninger M (2007) Prediction of humic acid content and respiration activity of biogenic waste by means of Fourier transform infrared (FTIR) spectra and partial least squares regression (PLS-R) models. Talanta 72: 791-799.

[41] Meissl K, Smidt E, Schwanninger M, Tintner J (2008) Determination of humic acids content in composts by means of near- And mid-infrared spectroscopy and partial least squares regression models. Appl. Spectrosc. 62: 873-880.

[42] Michel K, Bruns C, Terhoeven-Urselmans T, Kleikamp B, Ludwig B (2006) Determination of chemical and biological properties of composts using near infrared spectroscopy. J. Near Infrared Spectrosc. 14: 251-259.

[43] Morimoto S, McClure WF, Crowell B, Stanfield DL (2003) Near infrared technology for precision environmental measurements: Part 2. Determination of carbon in green grass tissue. J. Near Infrared Spectrosc. 11: 257-267.

[44] Zvomuya F, Helgason BL, Larney FJ, Janzen HH, Akinremi OO, Olson BM (2006) Predicting phosphorus availability from soil-applied composted and non-composted cattle feedlot manure. Journal of Environmental Quality 35: 928-937.

[45] Galvez-Sola L, Moral R, Perez-Murcia MD, Perez-Espinosa A, Bustamante MA, Martinez-Sabater E, et al. (2010) The potential of near infrared reflectance spectroscopy (NIRS) for the estimation of agroindustrial compost quality. Sci. Total Environ. 408: 1414-1421.

[46] Mohajer A, Tremier A, Barrington S, Martinez J, Teglia C, Carone M (2009) Microbial oxygen uptake in sludge as influenced by compost physical parameters. Waste Manage. 29: 2257-2264.

[47] Sharma HSS, Kilpatrick M, Lyons G, Sturgeon S, Archer J, Moore S, et al. (2005) Visible and near-infrared calibrations for quality assessment of fresh phase I and II mushroom (Agaricus bisporus) compost. Appl. Spectrosc. 59: 1399-1405.

[48] Suehara KI, Nakano Y, Yano T (2001) Simultaneous measurement of carbon and nitrogen content of compost using near infrared spectroscopy. J. Near Infrared Spectrosc. 9: 35-41.

[49] Galvez-Sola L, Morales J, Mayoral AM, Marhuenda-Egea FC, Martinez-Sabater E, Perez-Murcia MD, et al. (2010) Estimation of phosphorus content and dynamics during composting: Use of near infrared spectroscopy. Chemosphere 78: 13-21.

[50] Ecke H (2003) Sequestration of metals in carbonated municipal solid waste incineration (MSWI) fly ash. Waste Manage. 23: 631-640.

[51] Mostbauer P, Lechner P, Meissl K (2007) Langzeitverhalten von MVA-Reststoffen - Evaluierung von Testmethoden. Vienna: facultas.wuv. 158 p.

[52] Scaglia B, Adani F (2008) An index for quantifying the aerobic reactivity of municipal solid wastes and derived waste products. Science of the Total Environment 394: 183-191.

[53] Smidt E, Böhm K, Tintner J (2010) Application of various statistical methods to evaluate thermo-analytical data of mechanically-biologically treated municipal solid waste. Thermochim. Acta 501: 91-97.

[54] Abouelwafa R, Ait Baddi G, Souabi S, Winterton P, Cegarra J, Hafidi M (2008) Aerobic biodegradation of sludge from the effluent of a vegetable oil processing plant mixed with household waste: Physical-chemical, microbiological, and spectroscopic analysis. Bioresour. Technol. 99: 8571-8577.

[55] Abouelwafa R, Amir S, Souabi S, Winterton P, Ndira V, Revel JC, et al. (2008) The fulvic acid fraction as it changes in the mature phase of vegetable oil-mill sludge and domestic waste composting. Bioresour. Technol. 99: 6112-6118.

[56] He XS, Xi BD, Wei ZM, Guo XJ, Li MX, An D, et al. (2011) Spectroscopic characterization of water extractable organic matter during composting of municipal solid waste. Chemosphere 82: 541-548.

[57] Böhm K, Smidt E, Binner E, Schwanninger M, Tintner J, Lechner P (2010) Determination of MBT-waste reactivity - An infrared spectroscopic and multivariate statistical approach to identify and avoid failures of biological tests. Waste Manage. 30: 583-590.

[58] Biasioli F, Gasperi F, Odorizzi G, Aprea E, Mott D, Marini F, et al. (2004) PTR-MS monitoring of odour emissions from composting plants. Int. J. Mass Spectrom. 239: 103-109.

[59] De Rosa E, Rubel D, Tudino M, Viale A, Lombardo RJ (1996) The leachate composition of an old waste dump connected to groundwater: Influence of the reclamation works. Environmental Monitoring and Assessment 40: 239-252.

[60] Durmusoglu E, Yilmaz C (2006) Evaluation and temporal variation of raw and pre-treated leachate quality from an active solid waste landfill. Water, Air, and Soil Pollution 171: 359-382.

[61] Kylefors K (2003) Evaluation of leachate composition by multivariate data analysis (MVDA). J. Environ. Manage. 68: 367-376.

[62] Mikhailov EV, Tupicina OV, Bykov DE, Chertes KL, Rodionova OY, Pomerantsev AL (2007) Ecological assessment of landfills with multivariate analysis - A feasibility study. Chemometrics Intell. Lab. Syst. 87: 147-154.

[63] Olivero-Verbel J, Padilla-Bottet C, De la Rosa O (2008) Relationships between physicochemical parameters and the toxicity of leachates from a municipal solid waste landfill. Ecotox. Environ. Safe. 70: 294-299.

[64] Smidt E, Tintner J, Meissl K (2007) New approaches in landfill assessment. In: Velinni AA, editor. Landfill Research Trends. New York: Nova Science Publisher, Inc. p. 291.

[65] Srivastava SK, Ramanathan AL (2008) Geochemical assessment of groundwater quality in vicinity of Bhalswa landfill, Delhi, India, using graphical and multivariate statistical methods. Environmental Geology 53: 1509-1528.

[66] Smidt E, Böhm K, Tintner J (2011) Monitoring and assessment of landfills using simultaneous thermal analysis. Sustain. Environ. Res. 21: 247-252.

[67] Diener S, Andreas L, Herrmann I, Ecke H, Lagerkvist A (2010) Accelerated carbonation of steel slags in a landfill cover construction. Waste Manage. 30: 132-139.

[68] Pablos MV, Fernandez C, Babin MD, Navas JM, Carbonell G, Martini F, et al. (2009) Use of a novel battery of bioassays for the biological characterisation of hazardous wastes. Ecotox. Environ. Safe. 72: 1594-1600.

[69] Tintner J, Klug B (2011) Can vegetation indicate landfill cover features? Flora 206: 559-566.

[70] van Praagh M, Persson KM, Karlsson P (2009) Potential environmental impacts of using refuse derived material for landfill capping. Waste Manage. Res. 27: 471-488.

[71] Ecke H, Bergman A, Lagerkvist A (1998) Multivariate data analysis (MVDA) in landfill research. Journal of Solid Waste Technology and Management 25: 33-39.

[72] Jean G, Fruget JF (1994) Comparison of ecotoxicological and physico-chemical data by use of multivariate analyses and graphical displays. Chemosphere 28: 2249-2267.

[73] El-Sheikh MA, Al-Sodany YM, Eid EM, Shaltout KH (2012) Ten years primary succession on a newly created landfill at a lagoon of the Mediterranean Sea (Lake Burullus RAMSAR site). Flora 207: 459-468.

[74] Kim KD, Lee EJ, Cho KH (2004) The plant community of Nanjido, a representative nonsanitary landfill in South Korea: Implications for restoration alternatives. Water, Air, and Soil Pollution 154: 167-185.

[75] Tesar M, Prantl R, Lechner P (2007) Application of FT-IR for assessment of the biological stability of landfilled municipal solid waste (MSW) during in situ aeration. Journal of Environmental Monitoring 9: 110-118.

[76] Smidt E, Meissl K, Tintner J, Ottner F (2010) Interferences of carbonate quantification in municipal solid waste incinerator bottom ash: Evaluation of different methods. Environ. Chem. Lett. 8: 217-222.

[77] Huber-Humer M, Tintner J, Bohm K, Lechner P (2011) Scrutinizing compost properties and their impact on methane oxidation efficiency. Waste Manage. 31: 871-883.

[78] Smidt E, Böhm K, Tintner J (2010) Evaluation of old landfills - A thermoanalytical and spectroscopic approach. J. Environ. Monitor. 13: 362-369.

[79] Lawrence TA, Boutwell GP (1990) Predicting stratigraphy at landfill sites using electromagnetics. In: Landva A, Knowles DG, editors. Geotechnics of Waste Fills-Theory and Practice; 10-13. September 1989; Pittsburgh, PA, USA: ASTM Special Technical Publication; p. 31-40.

[80] Moreno-Santini V, Mansilla-Rivera I, García-Rodríguez O, Rodríguez-Sierra CJ (2012) A Pilot Study Determining Hair Arsenic and Lead Levels in Residents of a Community Established on a Former Landfill in Puerto Rico. B. Environ. Contam. Tox.: 1-5.

[81] Dahlén L, Vukicevic S, Meijer JE, Lagerkvist A (2007) Comparison of different collection systems for sorted household waste in Sweden. Waste Manage. 27: 1298-1305.

[82] Lin C, Wu EMY, Lee CN, Kuo SL (2011) Multivariate Statistical Factor and Cluster Analyses for Selecting Food Waste Optimal Recycling Methods. Environ. Eng. Sci. 28: 349-356.

[83] Cheng YW, Sung FC, Yang Y, Lo YH, Chung YT, Li KC (2009) Medical waste production at hospitals and associated factors. Waste Manage. 29: 440-444.

[84] Noori R, Abdoli MA, Ghazizade MJ, Samieifard R (2009) Comparison of Neural Network and Principal Component-Regression Analysis to Predict the Solid Waste Generation in Tehran. Iran. J. Public Health 38: 74-84.

[85] Esbensen K (2002) Multivariate Data Analysis - in practice. Esbjerg: Alborg University. 598 p.

[86] Velicer WF, Jackson DN (1990) Component Analysis versus Common Factor Analysis: Some issues in Selecting an Appropriate Procedure. Multivar. Behav. Res. 25: 1-28.

[87] ter Braak CJE, Verdonschot PEM (1995) Canonical correspondence analysis and related multivariate methods in aquatic ecology. Aquat. Sci. 57: 255-289.

[88] Brereton RG (2002) Chemometrics: Data analysis for the laboratory and chemical plant. Chichester, England: John Wiley & Sons Ltd. 489 p.

[89] Rasch D, Verdooren LR, Gowers JI (1999) Fundamentals in Design and Analysis of Experiments and Surveys. Munich, Vienna: Oldenbourg Wissenschaftsverlag GmbH. 253 p.

[90] Moder K (2007) How to keep the Type I Error Rate in ANOVA if Variances are Heteroscedastic. Austrian Journal of Statistics 36: 179-188.

[91] Moder K (2010) Alternatives to F-Test in One Way ANOVA in case of heterogeneity of variances (a simulation study). Psychological Test and Assessment Modeling 52: 343-353.

[92] Rasch D, Kubinger K, Moder K (2011) The two-sample t test: Pre-testing its assumptions does not pay off. Stat. Pap. 52: 219-231.

[93] Wakeling IN, Morris J (1993) A test of significance for partial least squares regression. J. Chemometr. 7: 291-304.

[94] Ståhle L, Wold S (1987) Partial least squares analysis with cross-validation for the two-class problem: a Monte Carlo study. J. Chemometr. 1: 185-196.

[95] Wakeling IN, Macfie HJH (1992) A robust PLS procedure. J. Chemometr. 6: 189-198.

Multivariate Analysis in Engineering

Chapter 4

Multivariate Analysis in Advanced Oxidation Process

Ana Paula Barbosa Rodrigues de Freitas, Leandro Valim de Freitas,
Gisella Lamas Samanamud, Fernando Augusto Silva Marins,
Carla Cristina Almeida Loures, Fatima Salman,
Hilton Túlio Lima dos Santos and Messias Borges Silva

Additional information is available at the end of the chapter

1. Introduction

Environmental degradation is attributable to improper industrial wastewater disposal, a situation that has caused serious contamination problems in many countries worldwide. Global consumption of potable water doubles every twenty years due to an exponential increase in world population (Han et al., 2009).

Industrial processes can create a wide variety of chemicals that pollute the air and water, with adverse impacts to ecosystems and humans. These impacts are caused by the polluting compounds that have toxic, carcinogenic, and also mutagenic properties (Busca et al., 2008). The treatment of wastewater containing phenolic compounds can be accomplished using applied principles of chemical oxidation, settling, membrane filtration, osmosis, ion, precipitation, and coagulation among other methods (Lin; Juang, 2009).

The treatment of hazardous wastes and reducing the presence of aqueous organic pollutants have placed focus on the use of alternatives to the standard environmental practices, such as the use of Advanced Oxidation Processes (AOPs), especially for the wastewater treatment (Segura et al., 2009).

AOPs are considered a highly effective means of water treatment contributing to the effective removal of organic pollutants that, otherwise, are untreatable whether are adopted the traditional methods (Oller; Malato; Sanchez-Pérez, 2011).

The study of riverine water quality by countries has recently become problematic due to the progressive scarcity of resources (Ongley, 1998). The monitoring water quality and making-decisions based on qualitative data is a challenge for field researchers engaged in sample collection, storage, analysis, and the interpretations of results (Lermontov et al., 2008).

This study demonstrates the application of Multivariate Analysis (MA) in effluent treatment of polyester resin by using advanced oxidation processes (heterogeneous photocatalysis - UV/TiO$_2$). Exploring the relationship between methodologies and computational chemistry, the use of MA can modify the industrial processes and simplify experimental conditions, with a consequent improvement of processes, products, and the resolution of environmental issues.

2. Polyester resin

Polyesters and alkyd resins represent a class of polymers used in the manufacture of solvent-based paints due to the reduced cost and its versatility. These resins are the condensation products of polyols (e.g., glycerol, pentaerythritol), polybasic acids or their anhydrides (most phthalic anhydride) and monobasic fatty acids or oils. The term is typically restricted to polyester resins with acid or hydroxyl functional groups, which are relatively free of oil mixtures. The alkyd resins, a type of polyester resin, can be synthesized from renewable resources, i.e., vegetable oils as soybean oil, but most oils are coming from non-renewable sources (Abrafati, 1995; Weiss, 1997).

3. Dye industry

Effluents from industries are highly complex dyes so they are not treated by conventional methods. Alternative matrices; AOPs; have been used to minimize the environmental impact of these industries on ecosystems (Nedhi; Sumner, 2003).

Industrial waste is classified into three main categories: wastewater, solid waste and air pollutants. Greater attention is given to wastewater since studies revealed content of significant amount of solvents (Metcalf; Eddy, 1991).

4. Advanced oxidation process

Advanced oxidation processes UV/TiO$_2$, UV/H$_2$O$_2$, UV/H$_2$O$_2$/Fe, O$_3$, O$_3$/Fe, O$_3$/TiO$_2$, UV-O$_3$/H$_2$O$_2$/Fe, are widely used in the degradation of effluents. These processes are characterized by the generation of free radicals in the organic matter degraded, and so are the polluting compounds mineralized or they are converted into a lower-chain or a less harmful process, in order to be subjected to a biological treatment subsequently (Thiruvenkatachari et al., 2007).

Oxidation processes are based on the generation of reactive species such as hydroxyl radical (OH). These radicals are highly reactive, non selective and may be used to degrade a wide range of organic pollutants. The OH radical is unstable and must be continuously generated *in situ*, by chemical or photochemical (Oliver; Hyunook; Pen-Chi, 2000). Table 1 shows reduction potential of various chemicals, and it can be observed that after fluorine, the hydroxyl radical is the one with higher oxidation potential (Domènech et al., 2001).

The treatment of hazardous waste and the presence of organic pollutants in water have increased the use of alternatives to environmental matrices such as the use of advanced oxidation processes (AOPs) in the treatment of wastewater (Segura et al., 2009).

According to Kusic, and Koppivanac Srsan (2007), the high standard reduction potential of the hydroxyl radical enables the oxidation of a wide variety of organic compounds to CO2, H2O and inorganic ions from heteroatoms.

According to Domenech et al. (2001), hydroxyl radicals can be produced by various advanced oxidation processes and heterogeneous and homogeneous systems, divided into two groups: non-photochemical and photochemical processes. Table 2 shows the procedures described above for the production of the hydroxyl radical.

Compound	E^0 Reduction (V, 25 ºC)[1]
Fluorine(F_2)	3,03
Hydroxyl Radical ($\bullet OH$)	2,80
Atomic Oxygen (O_2)	2,42
Ozone(O_3)	2,07
Hydrogen peroxide (H_2O_2)	1,78
Radical Perhydroxyl ($HO_2^\bullet$)	1,70
Chlorine dioxide	1,57
Hypochlorous acid (HCLO)	1,49
Chlorine (Cl_2)	1,36
Bromine (Br_2)	1,09
Iodine (I_2)	0,54

[1] Potential refers to the standard hydrogen electrode.
Source: Domenech et al. (2001)

Table 1. Reduction potential of some compounds

	With Irradiation	Without Irradiation
Homogeneous Systems	O_3/UV H_2O_2/UV H_2O_2/Fe^{2+}/UV	O_3/H_2O_2 O_3/OH^- H_2O_2/Fe^{2+}
Heterogeneous Systems	*Sc/O_3/UV *Sc/H_2O_2/UV *Sc/UV	Eletro-Fenton - -

*Sc: semiconductor (ZnO, TiO2, etc.)
Source: Morais (2005)

Table 2. Exploited systems to produce hydroxyl radical

4.1. Advantages of advanced oxidation processes

AOPs have a number of advantages when compared to conventional oxidation processes (Gabardo Filho, 2005; Domènech et al., 2001):

- Able to assimilate large variety of organic compounds;
- Full Mineralization of pollutants;
- Employed in the destruction of refractory compounds resistant to other treatments, such as the biologic;
- Can be integrated with other processes such as pre or post treatment;
- Used in high toxicity wastewater that can cause some difficulty in the treatment of biological process;
- Allow *in situ* treatment;
- Develop byproducts reaction intermediates that submitted to a post treatment may be mineralized;
- Improve organoleptic properties of treated water;
- Present high power with high oxidizing reaction kinetics.

4.2. Disadvantages of advanced oxidation processes

AOPs can be applied to certain types of waste under some restrictions, as follows (Domenech et al., 2001; Moral, 2005):

- Some processes are not available at appropriate scales;
- Costs can be high due to energy consumption;
- Some types do not apply to wastewater with high organic capability, turbidity, optical or color.

5. Heterogeneous photocatalysis

The heterogeneous photocatalysis is a process based on the absorption of UV-visible by a solid semiconductor. In the interface area between the solution and the electrically excited solid, a degradation reaction or transformation of pollutants may occur, without changing the chemical structure of the semiconductor (Custo et al., 2006).

According to Nogueira and Jardim (1998), a semiconductor is characterized by:

- Valence bands, where vacancies are generated;
- Driving Bands that are generating electrons;
- A region between bands called bandgap;
- Semiconductor particles, when irradiated, absorb photons that may excite electrons from the valence band to the conduction band;

This generates vacancy electrons. The electron / vacancy pair migrates to the surface of the particle resulting in oxidation and reduction sites (Carp et al. 2004). Figure 1 illustrates schematically the behavior described above.

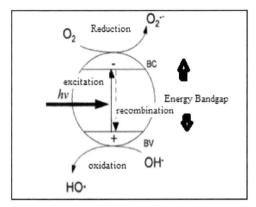

Figure 1. Electronic scheme of a photochemical process for heterogeneous photocatalysis (Ciola, 1981)

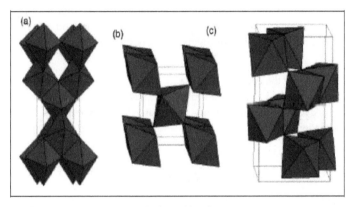

Figure 2. Crystal structures: anatase (a), rutile (b) and brookita (c)

TiO2 is a solid with a melting point of 1800 °C, and the ninth most abundant element corresponding to 0.63% of crust. The element described features 4 crystalline forms of anatase (tetragonal), brookita (orthorhombic), rutile (tetragonal) and TiO2 (B) monoclinic, as shown in Figure 2 (Carp et al., 2004).

6. Design of experiments

Design of Experiments (DOE) has been widely used in the optimization of process parameters and improving of quality products by the application of engineering concepts and Statistics (Wang, Huang, 2007).

Design of Experiments is defined as a set of statistical techniques applied to planning, conduction, analysis and interpretation of controlled tests, in order to find define factors that influence the values of a parameter or group of parameters (Bruns; Neto; Scarmínio, 2010).

According to Franceschini and Macchietto (2008), DOE is a statistical tool used to maximize the value of variable responses obtained on each experiment and also to minimize cost and time by reducing the number of experimental conditions.

Interactions between variables are considered in the experimental design and can be used for optimizing the operating parameters in multivariable systems (Ay; Catalkaya; Kargi, 2009).

According to Salazar (2009), the experimental has been studied as an important mathematical tool in the area of Advanced Oxidation Processes (Heterogeneous Photocatalysis). In this study, fractionated schedules for the degradation of organic matter and COD percentage of dairy effluent were used to obtain 93.70% of the treatment.

7. Taguchi orthogonal array

Taguchi method uses orthogonal arrays to study various factors with a small number of experiments (Sharma et al., 2005). Furthermore, the method provides other benefits, such as the reduction of process variability, low operating costs and expected results. (Barros; Bruns; Scarminio, 1995).

Rosa et al. (2009) define the Analysis of Variance (ANOVA) in the application of statistical analysis of Taguchi method in order to evaluate the significance of the parameters used in the process. A ANOVA table determines the most relevant parameters for the process according to equations 1, 2, 3 and 4:

-SS: Quadratic sum of the factors

$$SS= \sum_{i=1}^{n} (y_i - \bar{y})^2 \tag{1}$$

- df: Degrees of freedom for each factor

$$df=N-1$$

Where N means number of level for each factor

- MS: Mean square

$$MQ=\frac{SS}{df} \tag{3}$$

- F Test: Assessment of the significance of each factor

$$F = \frac{MS_{effect}}{MS_{error}} \tag{4}$$

8. Multivariate analysis

The Multivariate Analysis represents a set of statistical method in which most of variables of a data set are comprise information for decision-making (Rajalahti; Kvalheim, 2011), such as

Multiple Linear Regression (MLR), Principal Component Analysis (PCA), Principal Component Regression (PCR) and Partial Least Squares Regression (PLS) (Otto, 2007).

The manufacturing processes can generally have correlated variables depending on the process quality that involves a large number of characteristics (Paiva, 2006).

The field of chemometrics is a multivariate analysis defined as the application of designs and mathematical and statistical methods to solve chemical problems. It is utilized to improve data collection and to allow extraction of useful and obtained data information (Hopke, 2003).

Paiva, Ferreira and Balestrassi (2007) combined DOE with Multivariate Analysis when optimizing multiple correlated responses in a manufacturing process.

8.1. Multiple linear regression

The Multiple linear regression is a determining method of combinations of variables to achieve an optimal process or product. (Beebe; Pell; Seasholtz, 1998).

MLR property of interest relates to a linear combination of independent measurements. The modeling MRL can be represented by equation 5, where a set with n samples, $i = 1$ to n, Y is the response variable, X is the independent variable and i is the error estimation (Steiner et al., 2008)

$$y_i = \beta_0 + \sum_{j=1}^{k} \beta_i X_{ij} + e_i \tag{5}$$

According to Montgomery (2001), the method of Ordinary Least Squares (OLS - Ordinary Least Squares) to determine βi, minimize the sum of squared errors:

$$L = \sum_{i=0}^{n} \varepsilon_i^2$$

$$= \sum_{i=1}^{n} \left(y_i - \beta_0 - \sum_{j=1}^{k} \beta_i x_{ji} \right)^2$$

Function L must be minimized in terms of $\beta_0, \beta_1, ..., \beta_k$.

$$\frac{\partial L}{\partial \beta_j} = -2 \sum_{i=1}^{n} \left(y_i - \beta_0 - \sum_{j=1}^{k} \hat{\beta}_i x_{ji} \right)$$

Simply stated, there is equality:

$$\hat{\beta}_0 \sum_{i=1}^{n} x_{ik} + \hat{\beta}_1 \sum_{i=1}^{n} x_{ik}x_{i1} + \hat{\beta}_2 \sum_{i=1}^{n} x_{ik}x_{i2} + ... + \hat{\beta}_k \sum_{i=1}^{n} x_{ik}^2 = \sum_{i=1}^{n} x_{ik} y_i$$

In matrix notation, there is $Y = \beta X + \varepsilon$, where:

$$y = \begin{bmatrix} y_1 \\ y_2 \\ \vdots \\ y_n \end{bmatrix}, X = \begin{bmatrix} 1 & x_{11} & x_{11} & \cdots & x_{1k} \\ 1 & x_{21} & x_{22} & \cdots & x_{2k} \\ \vdots & \vdots & \vdots & \vdots & \vdots \\ 1 & x_{n1} & x_{n2} & \cdots & x_{nk} \end{bmatrix}, \beta = \begin{bmatrix} \beta_1 \\ \beta_2 \\ \vdots \\ \beta_k \end{bmatrix} e\ \varepsilon = \begin{bmatrix} \varepsilon_1 \\ \varepsilon_2 \\ \vdots \\ \varepsilon_n \end{bmatrix}$$

Then:

$$L = \sum_{i=0}^{n} \varepsilon_i^2 = \varepsilon^T \varepsilon = (y - X\beta)^T (y - X\beta)$$

$$L = y^T y - \beta^T X^T y - y^T X\beta + \beta^T X^T X\beta$$

$$L = y^T y - 2\beta^T X^T y + \beta^T X^T X\beta$$

Minimizing the function:

$$\frac{\partial L}{\partial \beta} = -2X^T y + 2X^T X\hat{\beta} = 0$$

Hence, is obtained:

$$X^T X\hat{\beta} = X^T y$$

and consequently, the coefficients are determined by Equation 6:

$$\hat{\beta} = (X^T X)^{-1} X^T y \tag{6}$$

9. Materials and methods

This work was performed at the Laboratory of the Environmental Engineering Department of the Chemical Engineering of School of Lorena EEL-USP. Polyester resin effluent was supplied by Valspar industry, located in São Bernardo do Campo, State of São Paulo. Statistical analyses were performed by Statistica version 2.0, available at the College.

Samples were stored cold chamber at EEL-USP at 4ºC. The effluent from the oxidation reaction was conducted into a Germetec tubular reactor, model FPG-463/1, with a nominal volume of approximately 1 L, receiving irradiation from a GPH-463T5L mercury lamp of low pressure, which emits a UV radiation at 254 nm with a power of 15 W and 21 W and protected by a quartz tube. The manufactured reactor model is shown in Figure 3.

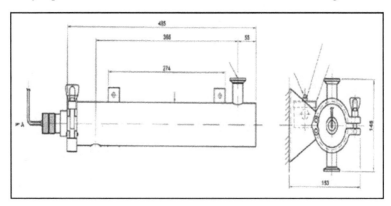

Figure 3. Tubular reactor used for photochemical treatment

Experimental design Taguchi L9 with advanced oxidation process and heterogeneous photocatalysis were used for 1.0 liters of fresh effluent and 2 liters of distilled water, previously homogenized and conditioned at room temperature. Semiconductor titanium dioxide (TiO2), and the amount of H2O2 (30% w / v) were added during the initial 50 minutes of 1-hour total reaction, using burettes of 25 and 50 ml. The temperature of the medium reaction during the whole period of the photocatalytic process was controlled at 25 °C by using an Ophterm DC1 thermostatic bath. pH reaction was performed using a combined glass electrode adapted to the shell. This was connected to the potentiostat digital Digimed. A centrifugal pump was used for conducting the effluent from the tubular reactor to the storage tank. Ultraviolet lamps of 15 and 21 watts were used. Figure 4 presents the detailed scheme for treatment with AOP showing the experimental procedure.

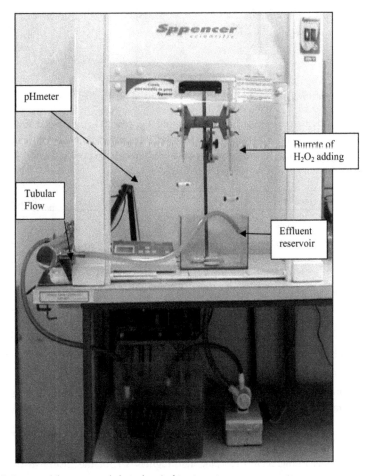

Figure 4. Layout of the process of photochemical treatment

10. Results and discussion

TOC (Total Organic Carbon) analysis of the effluent was conducted according to relevant physical-chemical aspects; that is, parameters monitored by environmental agencies (Morais, 2005). Figure 5 illustrates the appearance of the effluent polyester resin *in natura*.

Figure 5. Effluent polyester resin *in natura*

The statistical planning performed is represented by Taguchi L9 orthogonal array to which the response variable was TOC and independent variables as factors proposed for this stage were: pH, titanium dioxide, hydrogen peroxide and UV radiation power. Table 3 shows the variables with treatment of levels with selected AOP.

Control variables (factors)	Level 1	Level 2	Level 3
A- pH	3,0	5,0	7,0
B- TiO2 [g/L]	0,083	0,167	0,250
C- H2O2*[g]	120,0	151,0	182,0
D- UV [W]	Sem	15	21

* [H_2O_2] = 30 % m/m

Table 3. Control variables and their levels

Initially, the mass of H_2O_2 (30% w / w) is calculated by a stoichiometric ratio that depended on the organic load of the effluent. This obtained a mass of H2O2 of 50 g per liter of effluent.

The amount of TOC of the effluent *in natura* had a mean value of 7920mg / L that was subjected to pre-treatment. For each experiment amount of TOC, a sample in a 60-minute reaction was determined. The percent reduction of TOC is calculated by equation 7.

$$\% \text{ reduction of TOC} = \frac{TOC_{\text{in natura}} - TOC_{t=60 \text{ min}}}{TOC_{\text{in natura}}} \tag{7}$$

Table 4 shows the arrangement of orthogonal Taguchi L9 for the treatment of effluent polyester resin using AOP.

Experiment	pH Factor A	TiO2 Factor B	H_2O_2 Factor C	UV Factor D
1	1	1	1	1
2	1	2	2	2
3	1	3	3	3
4	2	1	2	3
5	2	2	3	1
6	2	3	1	2
7	3	1	3	2
8	3	2	1	3
9	3	3	2	1

Table 4. L_9 Taguchi Orthogonal Array with 4 factors and 3 levels each

Table 5 shows the percentage change in COT response to experiments using experimental design L9. Experiments 3 and 4 had a higher percentage of TOC removal for the advanced oxidation process (Heterogeneous Photocatalysis).

Experiment	pH Factor A	TiO2 Factor B	H2O2 Factor C	UV Factor D	Replica 1: reduction of total organic carbon (%)
1	1	1	1	1	31,970
2	1	2	2	2	34,981
3	1	3	3	3	39,489
4	2	1	2	3	37,216
5	2	2	3	1	29,962
6	2	3	1	2	30,095
7	3	1	3	2	30,549
8	3	2	1	3	33,504
9	3	3	2	1	28,182

Table 5. Results of the first replica of the percentage reduction obtained in experiments for an initial TOC of 7920mg / l.

Table 6 shows a replica of the experiment and the experimental conditions 3 and 4 that achieved significant values again.

Statistical analysis of Taguchi L9, on Figure 6, showed the most significant parameters for the degradation of organic matter in the wastewater, the latter reflecting of pH = 3, adjusted at a low level and factors set at a maximum level of: 182 g hydrogen peroxide and ultraviolet lamp power of 21 W. According to the plan performed, the level of titanium dioxide added to the process can be adjusted at low or medium level, i.e. with values 0.083g / L and 0.167g / L. According to Malik and Saha (2003), the influence of peroxide with temperature is related to the efficiency of ratio by using this compound and its rapid decomposition in the reaction.

Experiment	pH Factor A	TiO2 Factor B	H2O2 Factor C	UV Factor D	Replica 2: reduction of total organic carbon (%)
1	1	1	1	1	31,269
2	1	2	2	2	34,498
3	1	3	3	3	36,443
4	2	1	2	3	35,720
5	2	2	3	1	31,648
6	2	3	1	2	30,019
7	3	1	3	2	30,739
8	3	2	1	3	33,011
9	3	3	2	1	27,481

Table 6. Results of replica 2 of the percentage reduction percentage obtained in experiments, initial TOC of 7920mg / l.

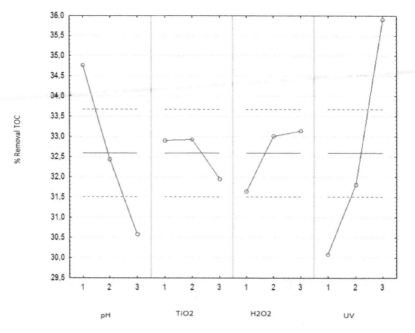

Figure 6. Main Effects in TOC percentage variation measurements in the effluent treatment of L9 planning

Statistical analysis at a level of 95%, showed the most significant factors for the removal of organic load. According to the distribution F whose critical value is 4.26 and a p-value less than 5%, the most important factors for the degradation of organic matter in the effluent were phenolic H_2O_2, pH, UV. The most significant factor was the ultraviolet lamp power with F of 60.65201 and a p-value less than 0.001%, and then the remaining factors are the pH (F = 30.11586; p-value = 0.10 %) and H₂O₂ (F = 4.67497; p-value = 4.053%). The values obtained by analysis of variance confirmed the significance shown in the graph of main effects.

The analysis of variance (ANOVA) with F> 2 demonstrated that the factor TiO2 is significant for TOC removal. According to Phadke (1989), an F value statistically greater than 2 is considered as a significant effect (factor). The statistical significance factor in TOC reduction in the effluent treatment was confirmed by ANOVA, as shown in Table7.

Source of Variation	SQ	GL	SMQ	F	P-Value
pH	53,0700	2,00	26,53499	30,11586	0,00010
TiO2	3,7711	2,00	1,88554	2,13999	0,17366
H2O2	8,2382	2,00	4,11909	4,67497	0,04053
UV	106,8806	2,00	53,44030	60,65201	<0,00001
Error	7,9299	9,00	0,88110		

Table 7. Analysis of variance Taguchi L₁₆ orthogonal array obtained for TOC (%) removal

Multiple linear regressions provide another statistical approach to evaluate variables in a quantitative approach. Significant parameters to the regression analysis are shown in Table 8, where pH, UV and H₂O₂ are relevant for the degradation process of the organic load of the polyester resin effluent.

Factor	Coefficient	t-value	Coef. Beta	Probability
pH	-1,04933	-4,573584	-0,542040	0,0003
TIO2	-5,73042	-1,042771	-0,123584	0,1580
H2O2	0,0266726	1,627560	0,192891	0,0638
UV	0,245688	5,791488	0,686380	0,0000
Constant	32,2247			

Table 8. Regression parameters

Multiple linear regression showed a coefficient of determination (R^2) of 0.817404, which demonstrates the efficiency of the degradation of effluent using the polyester resin of the experimental design. An ANOVA (Table 9) was performed in order to validate the multiple linear regression equation. The significance of equation shown is for a level of significance equal to 0.0001 at 95% confidence degree.

Sources of Variation	GL	SQ	SMQ	F	P-Value
Due to Regression	4	147,0425	36,76063	14,55	0,0001
Independent	13	32,84718	2,526706		

Table 9. ANOVA of multiple linear regression

The most influential factors in the process show the percentage removal of Total Organic Carbon in Figure 7. An increasing degradation of the organic load is observed on the surface. This is achieved by independent variables: pH and potency of the ultraviolet lamp. The percentage of the increased removal of organic load occurs when there is an increase of the power of the lamp and a decrease of the pH. The greatest percentage reduction of the organic load is equal to 39.489%, whose parameters used in this experimental condition = H2O2 were 182 g, pH = 3, TiO2 = 0.250 g / L and the lamp power of 21 W. The response variable was significant for the degradation of organic matter in the effluent.

$$\text{\% Removal TOC} = 34,7662 - 2,5704{}^{*}x - 1,3448{}^{*}y + 0,2301{}^{*}x{}^{*}y + 1,1778{}^{*}y{}^{*}y$$

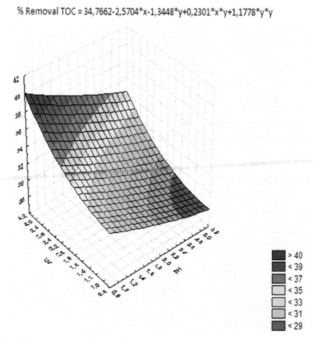

Figure 7. Graph of the two most influential factors in the process

11. Conclusions

Taguchi planning was applied to the degradation of effluent organic load. The experimental design showed that further reduction of TOC (%) is related to an increase in pH and ultraviolet intensity. The results obtained were significant for the removal of TOC (%) from polyester resin effluent treated with advanced oxidation processes, and heterogeneous photocatalysis.

In our Taguchi orthogonal array the removal-percentage achieved was COT = 39.489%, which corresponds to experimental condition number three. This condition is inclusive of the weight ratio of hydrogen peroxide at 183g, pH = 3, TiO 2 = 0.250 g/L and the lamp intensity = 21 W. We conclude that the process of heterogeneous photocatalysis is optimally suitable for treatment of the effluent studied in this work.

Author details

Leandro Valim de Freitas
Petróleo Brasileiro SA (PETROBRAS), Brazil

Ana Paula Barbosa Rodrigues de Freitas, Leandro Valim de Freitas,
Fernando Augusto Silva Marins, Carla Cristina Almeida Loures and Messias Borges Silva
São Paulo State University (UNESP), Brazil

Ana Paula Barbosa Rodrigues de Freitas, Carla Cristina Almeida Loures,
Fatima Salman, Hilton Túlio Lima dos Santos and Messias Borges Silva
University of São Paulo (USP), Brazil

Gisella Lamas Samanamud
University of Texas at San Antonio (UTSA), USA

12. References

Abrafati. Paints & Coatings: Science and Technology. 2nd ed. São Paulo. New text Publisher And Editorial Services Ltd, 1995.

Ay F, Catalkaya E C, Kargi F. A Statistical Experiment Design Approach for Advanced Oxidation of Direct Red Azo Dye by Photo-Fenton Treatment. Journal of Hazardous Materials 2009;162(1) 230-236.
http://www.ncbi.nlm.nih.gov/pubmed/18555599 (accessed 03 July 2012).

Barros N, Bruns R E, Scarminio I S. Optimization and Planning of Experiments. Campinas: Publisher of Unicamp;1995.

Beebe K R, Pell R J, SEASHOLTZ M B. Chemometrics: A Pratical Guide. New York: John Wiley and Sons; 1998.

Bruns R E, Neto B B, Scarminio I S. How Experiments. Porto Alegre: Publisher Artmed; 2010.

Busca G, Berardinelli S, Resini C, Arrighi, L. Technologies for the removal of phenol from fluid streams: A short review of recent developments. Journal of Hazardous Materials 2008;160 (2-3) 265-288.
http://www.sciencedirect.com/science/article/pii/S0304389408004172 (accessed 03 July 2012)

Carp O, Huisnab C L, Reller A. Photoinduced reactivity of titanium dioxide-progress in solid state chemistry. Progress in Solid State chemistry 2004; 32(1-2) 33-177.
http://www.sciencedirect.com/science/article/pii/S0079678604000123 (03 accessed July 2012).

Ciola, R. Foundations of Catalysis. São Paulo: University of São Paulo; 1981.

Custo G, Litter M I, Rodríguez D, Vàsquez C. Total reflection X-ray fluorescence trace Mercury determination by trapping Complexation: Application Technologies in Adavanced oxidation. Spectrochimica Acta Part B 2006;1119-1123.

Domenèch X, Garden W F, Litter M. I. Avanzados Oxidation Processes for La eliminación contaminants. In: Contaminant Eliminacion. La Plata: Network CYTED, 2001.

Franceschini G, Macchietto S. Model-based design of experiments for parameter precision: State of the art. Chemical Engineering Science 2008, 68(19) 4846-4872. http://www.sciencedirect.com/science/article/pii/S0009250907008871 (accessed 03 July 2012).

Gabardo S H. Study and design of photochemical reactors for wastewater treatment chemicals. Dissertation (Masters in Chemical Engineering) School of Chemical Engineering, State University of Campinas, Campinas; 2005.

Han F, Kambala R S V, Srinivasan M, Rajarathan D, Naidu R. Tailored titanium dioxide photocatalysts for the degradation of organic dyes in wastewater treatment: A review. Applied Catalysis A: General 2009, 359 (1-2) 25-40. http://www.sciencedirect.com/science/article/pii/S0926860X09001756 (accssed 04 July 2012).

Hopke P K. The evolution of Chemometrics. Analytical Chemica Acta, p. 365-377, 2003 (Review).

Kusic H, Koprivanac N, Srsan L. Azo dye degradation using Fenton type processes assisted by UV irradiation: A kinetic study. Journal of Photochemistry and photobiology A: Chemistry 2007, 181 (2-3) 195-202.

Lermontov A, Yokoyama L, Lermontov M, Machado B U T. Application of fuzzy logic in the parameterization of a new index of water quality. Directory of Open Access Journals 2008, 10(2).

Lin S H, Juang R S. Adsorption of phenol and its derivates from water using synthetic resins and low-cost natural adsorbents: A review. Journal of Environmental Management 2009, 90(3) 1336-1349.

Malik P K., Saha S K. Oxidation of direct dyes with hydrogen peroxide using ferrous ion the catalyst. Separation and Purification Technology 2003, 31(3) 241-250.

Metcalf L, Eddy H P. Wastewater Engineering: Treatment, Disposal and Reuse. São Paulo: McGraw-Hill, 1991.

Montgomery D C. Design and Analysis of Experiments. 5th ed. New York: John Wiley and Sons, 2001.

Morais J L. Study of the potential of advanced oxidation processes, isolated and integrated with traditional biological processes, for tratmento landfill leachate. 229 f. Thesis (Ph.D. in Chemical Engineering) - Department of Chemistry, Federal University of Paraná, Curitiba, 2005.

Nehdi M, Sumner J. Recycling waste latex paint in concrete. Cement and Concrete Research 2003, 33(6) 857-863.

Nogueira R F P, Jardim W F. The heterogeneous photocatalysis and environmental applications. New Chemistry 1998, 21(1).

Oliver J H, Hynook K., Pen-Chien C. Decolorization of wastewater, Crit. Rev. Environmental Science Technology 2000, 30(4) 499-505.

Oller I, Malate S, Sanchez-Perez J A. Combination of the advanced oxidation process and treatments for biological waste water decontamination: A review. Science of the total environment 2011, 409 (20) 4141-4166.

Ongley E. Modernization of water quality programs in Developing coutries: issues of relevancy and costefficiency. Water Quality International Sep / Oct 1998, p. 37-42.

Otto M. Modeling. In: Chemometrics: Statistics and computer application in analytical chemistry. New York: Wiley, 2007.

Paiva A P. Response surface methodology and principal component analysis for optimization of manufacturing processes with multiple correlated responses. 129 f. Thesis (PhD in Mechanical Engineering) - Institute of Mechanical Engineering, Federal University of Itajubá, Itajubá, 2006.

Paiva A P, Ferreira J R, Balestrassi P P. A hybrid multivariate approach applied to AISI 52100 hardened steel turning optimization. Journal of Materials Processing Technology 2007, 189(1-3) 26-35.

Phadke, M. S., Quality engineering using robust design. Publisher Prentice Hall. 1989.

Rajalahti I, Kvallielm, O. M. Multivariate data analysis in pharmaceutics: A tutorial review. International Journal of Pharmaceutics 2011, 417(1-2) 280-290.

Rosa J L, Robin A, Silva M B, Baldan C A, Peres M P. Electrodeposition of copper on titanium wires: Taguchi Experimental Design Approach. Journal of Materials Processing Technology 2009, 209 (3) p. 1181-1188.

Salazar R F S. Application of advanced oxidation processes and pre-treatment of dairy effluent for subsequent biological treatment. 210 f. Dissertation (Masters in Chemical Engineering) - Engineering School of Lorena, University of São Paulo, Lorena 2009.

Segura Y, Molina R, Martínez F, Melero J A. Integrated sleep heterogeneous photo-Fenton processes for the degradation of phenolic aqueous solutions. Ultrasonics Sonochemistry 2009, 16 417-424.

Sharma P, Verma A, Sidhu R K., Pandey O P. Process parameter selection for strontium ferrite sintered magnets using Taguchi L9 orthogonal design. Journal of Materials Processing Technology 2005, 168 (1) p.147-151.

Steiner M T A, Neto A C, Braulio S N, Alves V. Multivariate statistical methods applied to engineering evaluations. Management & Production, San Carlos 2008, 15 (1).

Thiruvenkatachari R, Kwon T O, Jun J C, Balaji S, Matheswaran M, Moon IS. Aplication of Several advanced oxidation process for the destruction of terephthalic acid (TPA). Journal of Hazardous Materials, v.142, p.308-314, 2007.

Wang T Y, Huang C Y. Improving forecasting performance by Employing the Taguchi method. European Journal of Operational Research 2007, 176 (2) 1052-1065.

Weiss K D. Paint and Coatings: a mature industry in transition. Prog. Polym. Sci, v. 22, p. 203-245, 1997.

Chapter 5

Variable Selection and Feature Extraction Through Artificial Intelligence Techniques

Silvia Cateni, Marco Vannucci,
Marco Vannocci and Valentina Colla

Additional information is available at the end of the chapter

1. Introduction

The issue of variable selection has been widely investigated for different purposes, such as clustering, classification or function approximation becoming the focus of many research works where datasets can contain hundreds or thousands variables. The subset of the potential input variables can be defined through two different approaches: feature selection and feature extraction. Feature selection reduces dimensionality by selecting a subset of original input variables, while feature extraction performs a transformation of the original variables to generate other features which are more significant. When the considered data have a large number of features it is useful to reduce them in order to improve the data analysis. In extreme situations the number of variables can exceed the number of available samples causing the so-called problem of *curse of dimensionality* [1], which leads to a decrease in terms of accuracy of the considered learning algorithm when the number of features increases. The main reason for seeking for data reduction include the need to reduce calculation time of a given learning algorithm, to improve its accuracy [2] but also to deepen the knowledge of the considered problem, by discovering which factors actually affect it. A high number of contributions based on artificial intelligence, genetic algorithms, statistical approaches have been proposed in order to develop novel efficient variable selection methods that are suitable in many application areas. Section 1 and Section 2 provide a preliminary review of traditional and Artificial Intelligence–based feature extraction techniques and variable selection in order to demonstrate that Artificial Intelligence are often capable to outperform the widely adopted traditional methods, due to their flexibility and to their possibility of self-adapting to the characteristics of the available dataset. Finally in Section 4 some concluding remarks are provided.

2. Feature extraction

Feature extraction is a process that transforms high dimensional data into a lower dimensional feature space through the application of some mapping. Brian Ripley [3] gives the following definition of the feature extraction problem:

> "*Feature extraction is generally used to mean the construction of linear combinations a^Tx of continuous features which have good discriminatory power between classes*".

In Neural Network research, as well as in other disciplines included in the Artificial Intelligence area, an important problem is finding a suitable representation of multivariate data. Feature extraction is used in this context in order to reduce the complexity and to give a simpler representation of data representing each component in the feature space as a linear combination of the original input variables. If the extracted features are suitably selected, then it is possible to work with the relevant information from the input data using a reduced dataset. The most popular feature extraction technique is the Principal Component Analysis (PCA) but many alternatives in the last years are been proposed. In the following sub-paragraphs several feature extraction approaches are proposed.

2.1. Principal Component Analysis

The Principal Component Analysis (PCA) was introduced by Karl Pearson in 1901 [4]. PCA consists into an orthogonal transformation to convert samples belonging to correlated variables into samples of linearly uncorrelated features. The new features are called *principal components* and they are less or equal to the initial variables. If data are normally distributed, then the principal components are independent. PCA mathematically transforms data by referring them to a different coordinate system in order to obtain on the first coordinate the first greatest variance and so on for the other coordinates [5]. Figure 1 shows an example of PCA in 2D. The original coordinate system (x,y) is transformed into the feature space (x', y') in order to have the maximum variance in the x' direction.

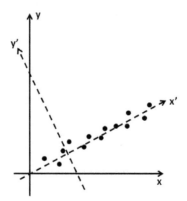

Figure 1. Example of PCA in 2D.

The main reason for the use of PCA concerns the fact that PCA is a simple non-parametric method used to extract the most relevant information from a set of redundant or noisy data. This method reduces the number of available variables by eliminating the last principal components that do not significantly contribute to the observed variability. Also, PCA is a linear transformation of data that minimizes the redundancy (which is measured through the covariance) and maximizes the information (which is measured through the variance). The principal components are new variables with the following properties:

1.   each principal component is a linear combination of the original variables;
2.   the principal components are uncorrelated to each other and also the redundant information is removed.

2.2. Linear Discriminant Analysis

While the PCA is unsupervised (i.e. it does not take into account class labels), the Linear Discriminant Analysis (LDA) is a popular supervised technique which is widely used in computer-vision, pattern recognition, machine learning and other related fields [6]. LDA performs an optimal projection by maximizing the distance between classes and minimizing the distance between samples within each class at the same time [7]. This approach reduces the dimensionality preserving as much of the class discriminatory information as possible. The main limitation of this approach lies in the fact that it can produce a limited number of feature projections (that is equal to the number of classes minus one). If more features are needed some other method should be employed. Moreover LDA is a parametric method and it fails if the discriminatory information lies not in the mean values but in the variance of data. When the dimensionality of data overcomes the number of samples, which is known as *singularity problem*, Linear Discriminant Analysis is not an appropriate method. In these cases the data dimensionality can be reduced by applying the PCA technique before LDA. This approach is called PCA+LDA [8, 9]. Other solutions dealing with the singularity problem include regularized LDA (RLDA) [10], null space LDA (NLDA) [11], orthogonal centroid method (OCM) [12], uncorrelated LDA (ULDA) [13].

2.3. Latent Semantic Analysis

Latent Semantic Analysis (LSA) was introduced by Deerwester et al. in 1990 [14] as a variant of the PCA concept. Firstly LSA was presented as a text analysis method when the features are represented by terms occurring in the considered text [2]. Subsequently LDA has been employed on image analysis [15], video data [16] and music or audio analysis [17]. The main objective of the LSA process is to produce a mapping into a "latent semantic space" also called *Latent Topic Space*. LSA finds co-occurrences of terms in documents to provide a mapping into the latent topic space where documents can be connected if they contain few terms in common respect to the original space. Recently Chen et al. [18] proposed a new method called Sparse Latent Semantic Analysis which selects only few relevant words for each topic giving a compact representation of topic-word relationships. The main advantage of this approach lies in the computational efficiency and in the low memory required for storing the projection matrix. In [18] the authors compare the Sparse Latent Semantic Analysis with LSA and LDA through experiments on different real world datasets. The obtained results demonstrate that Sparse LSA has similar performance with respect to LSA but it is more efficient in the projection computation, storage and it better explains the topic-world relashionships.

2.4. Independent Component Analysis

Independent Component Analysis (ICA) is an approach where the objective is to find a linear representation of non-gaussian data and the calculated components are statistically independent [19]. In literature at least three definitions of ICA has been given [20-22]:

i.   General definition. ICA of the random vector consists of finding a linear transform $s=Wx$ so that the components s_i are as independent as possible, in the sense of maximizing some functions $F(s_i, ... s_n)$ that measures independence.
ii. Noisy ICA model. ICA of a random vector x consists of estimating the following generative model for the data $x=As+n$ where the latent variables (components) s_i in the vector $s = (s_1, ..., s_n)^T$ are assumed independent. The matrix A is a constant mxn mixing matrix, and n is a m-dimensional random noise vector.
iii. Noise-free ICA model. ICA of a random vector x consists of estimating the following generative model for the data: $x=As$ where A and s are as in Definition 2.

The first definition is the most general one, as no a priori assumptions on the data are made. However it is an imprecise definition, as it is necessary to define a measure of independence for s_i. The second definition reduces the ICA problem to an estimation of a latent variable method, but this estimate can be quite difficult; definition 3 is actually the most used one.

The possibility to identify a noise-free ICA approach is ensured by adding the following assumptions [22]:

1.   All the independent components s_i must be non-gaussian (only one gaussian component should be accepted).
2.   The number of observed mixtures must be greater or equal to the number of independent components.

ICA can be used to extract features finding independent directions in the input space. This objective is more difficult than using PCA approach, as in PCA the variance of data along a direction can be immediately calculated and it is maximised by PCA itself, while there is not straightforward metric for quantifying the independence of directions belonging to the input space [23]. Recently, in order to extract independent components, neural network algorithms have been adopted [24].

3. Variable selection

Variable selection approach reduces the dimension of a dataset of variables potentially relevant with respect to a given phenomenon by finding the best minimum subset without transform data into a new set. Variable selection points out all the inputs affecting the phenomenon under consideration and it is an important data pre-processing step in different fields such as machine learning [25-26], pattern recognition [27, 28], data mining [29], medical data [30] and many others. Variable Selection has been widely performed in applications such as function approximation [31], classification [32-34] and clustering [35]. The difficulty of extracting the most relevant variables is due mainly to the large dimension of the original variables set, the correlations between inputs which cause redundancy and finally the presence of variables which do not affect the considered phenomenon and thus, for instance in the case of the development of a model predicting the output of a give system, do not have any predictive power [36]. In order to select the optimal subset of input variables the following key considerations should be taken into account:

- **Relevance.** The number of selected variables must be checked in order to avoid the possibility to have too few variables which do not convey relevant information.
- **Computational efficiency.** If the number of selected input variables is too high, then the computational burden increases. This is evident when an artificial neural network is performed. Moreover including redundant and irrelevant variables the task of training an artificial neural network is more difficult because irrelevant variables add noise and slow down the training of the network.
- **Knowledge improvement.** The optimal selection of input variables contributes to a deeper understanding of the process behaviour.

To sum up, the optimal set of input variables will contain the fewest number of variables needed to describe the behaviour of the considered system or phenomenon with the minimum redundancy and with informative variables.

If the optimal set of input variables is identified, then a more accurate efficient, inexpensive and more easy interpretable model can be built.

In literature variable selection methods are classified into three categories: filter, wrapper and embedded methods.

3.1. Filter approach

Filter approach is a pre-processing phase which is independent of the learning algorithm that is adopted to tune and/or build the system (e.g. a predictive model) that exploits the selected variables as inputs. Filters are computationally convenient but they can be affected by overfitting problems. Figure 2 shows a generic scheme of the approach.

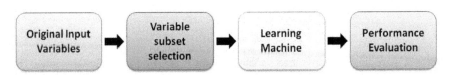

Figure 2. Generic scheme of filter methods.

The subset of relevant variables is extracted by evaluating the relation between input and output of the considered system. All input variables are classified on the basis of their pertinence to the target considering statistical tests [37, 38]. The main advantage of filter approach regards the low computational complexity ensuring speed to the model. On the other hand the main disadvantage of filter approach is that, being independent of the algorithm that is used to tune or build the model which is fed with the selected variables as inputs, this method cannot optimize the adopted model in the learning machine [39]. In the following subparagraphs some of the popular filter approaches presented in literature are described.

3.1.1. Chi-square approach

The chi-square approach [40] evaluates variables individually by measuring their chi-squared statistic. The test provides a score that follows a chi-square distribution with the objective to rank the set of input features. This approach is widely used but it does not take into account features interaction. If we assume that the class variable is binary the chi-squared value for scoring the belonging of variable v to the class k is evaluated as follows:

$$X^2(D,k,v) = \sum_{i=1}^{N}\left[\frac{(n_{i+}-\mu_{i+})^2}{\mu_{i+}} + \frac{(n_{i-}-\mu_{i-})^2}{\mu_{i-}}\right] \tag{1}$$

where D is the considered dataset, N is the number of the input variables, n_{i+} is the number of samples that have positive class for the variable i and finally μ_{i+} represents the expected value if there are any relationship between v and k.

In statistic the chi-squared test is used to verify if two events are independent. In feature selection chi-squared statistic performs a hypothesis test on the distribution of the class, as it relates to the measure of the variable under consideration; the null hypothesis represents an absence of correlation.

3.1.2. Correlation method

The correlation approach, used in feature selection, consists in calculating the correlation coefficient between the features and the target (or the class in the case of classification problems). A feature is selected if it is highly correlated with the class but not correlated with the remaining features [44]. There are two different approaches which evaluate the correlation between two variables: the classical linear correlation and the correlation based on information theory. Regard to the linear correlation coefficient, it is calculated by following equation:

$$c = \frac{\sum_i(x_i-\mu_{xi})(y_i-\mu_{yi})}{\sqrt{\sum_i(x_i-\mu_{xi})^2}\sqrt{\sum_i(y_i-\mu_{yi})^2}} \tag{2}$$

where x, y are the two considered variables, while μ_x and μ_y are their mean values. The linear correlation coefficient c lies in the range [-1, 1]. If the two variables are linearly correlated then $|c|=1$, while if they are independent c assumes a null value. This approach has two main advantages: it removes features having a very low correlation coefficient and it reduces redundancy. On the other hand, the linear correlation approach does not adequately outline non linear correlations, which often occur when treating with real world datasets.

3.1.3. Information Gain

Information Gain (IG) is widely used on high dimensional data, such as text classification [41]. It calculates the amount of information in bits concerning the class prediction when the only information available is the presence of a variable and the corresponding target (or class) distribution [42]. Also, it measures the expected decrease in entropy in order to decide how important a given feature is. An entropy function increases when the class distribution becomes more sparse and it can be recursively applied to find the subsets entropy. The following equation provides an entropy function which satisfies the two requirements.

$$H(D) = -\sum_{i=1}^{C} \frac{n_i}{n} \log(^{n_i}/n) \qquad (3)$$

where D is the dataset, n is the number of instances included in D, n_i represents the members in class i and C is the number of classes. Moreover the following equation represents the entropy of the subsets.

$$H(D|X) - \sum_j \left(\frac{|x_j|}{n}\right) H(D|x - r_j) \qquad (4)$$

where $H(D|x=x_j)$ represents the entropy correlated to the subset of instances which assumes a value of x_j for the feature x. For example, when x provides a good description of the class, the value which is associated to that feature assumes a low value of entropy in its class distribution. Finally the Information Gain is defined as the reduction in entropy as follows:

$$IG(X)=H(D)-H(D|X) \qquad (5)$$

High value of the IG indicates that X is a significant feature for the considered phenomenon [43].

3.2. Wrapper approach

While filter methods select the subset of variables in a pre-processing phase independently from the machine learning method that is used to build the model that should be fed with the selected variables, wrapper approaches consider the machine learning as a black box in order to select subsets of variables on the basis of their predictive power. The wrapper approach was introduced by Kohavi and John in 1997 [45] and the basic idea is to use the prediction performance (or the classification accuracy) of a given learning machine to evaluate the effectiveness of the selected subset of features. A generic scheme concerning wrapper approach is shown in Figure 3. Wrapper method is computationally more expensive than filter approach and it could be seen as a brute force approach. On the other hand, considering the learning machine as a black box, wrapper methods are simple and universal. The exhaustive search becomes unaffordable if the number of variables is too large. In fact, if the dataset contains k variables, 2^k possible subsets need to be evaluated, i.e 2^k learning processes to run. The following sub paragraphs treat some wrapper strategies commonly used.

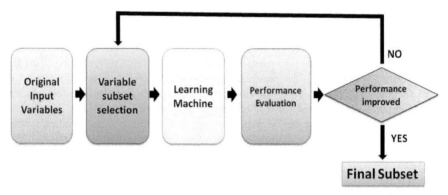

Figure 3. Generic diagram of wrapper approach.

3.2.1. Greedy search strategy

The Greedy search strategies can be divided into two different directions: Sequential Forward Selection (SFS) and Sequential Backward Selection (SBS). SFS approach starts with an empty set of features. The other variables are iteratively added into a larger subset until stopping criterion is reached. In general the adopted criterion is the improvement in accuracy. The proposed approach is computationally efficient and tests increasingly large sets in order to reach the optimal one. On the other hand SFS does not take into account all possible combinations but only selects the smallest subset: the risk arises to get trapped into a locally optimal point if the procedure prematurely ends [46]. SBS is the inverse of the forward selection approach. The process starts including all available features and then the less important variables are deleted one by one. In this case the importance of an input variable is determined by removing an input and evaluating the performance of the learning machine without it. If k is the number of the available input variables, the greedy search strategies needs, at maximum, $k(k+1)/2$ training procedures. When the SFS stops early it is less expensive than the SBS approach [47].

3.2.2. Genetic algorithm approach

Genetic algorithms (GAs) are efficient approaches for function minimization [43]. The genetic algorithm is a general adaptive optimization search technique and it is based on the Darwin Theory obtaining the optimal solution after iterative calculations. GAs create several populations of different possible solutions representing the so-called *chromosome* until an acceptable result is reached. A fitness function evaluates the goodness of a solution in evolution step. The crossover and mutation are operators that randomly affect the fitness score. In literature many wrapper approaches based on GA are proposed. Huang and Wang [48] present a genetic algorithm approach for feature selection and parameters optimization in order to improve the Support Vector Machine (SVM) classification accuracy [49]. Cateni et al. [50] present a method based on GAs that selects the best set of variables to be fed as input to a neural network. This approach is applied to a function approximation problem. The GA chromosomes are binary and their length corresponds to the number of available variables, also each gene is associated to an input. If the gene assumes unitary value it means that the corresponding input variable has been selected. The fitness function is represented by a feed-forward neural network [51] and the prediction performance is evaluated in terms of Normalized Square Root Mean Square Error (NSRMSE) [52]. The fitness function is computed for each chromosome of the population and crossover and mutation operators are applied. The crossover operator generates the son chromosome by randomly taking the genes values from the two parents, while mutation operation creates new individuals by randomly select a gene of the considered chromosome and switches it from 1 to 0 or vice-versa. The stop conditions include a fixed number of iterations or the achievement of a plateau for the fitness function. The generic scheme of the proposed approach is depicted in figure 4.

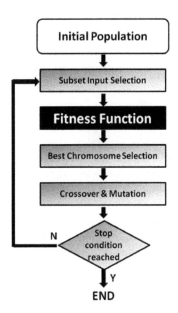

Figure 4. Genetic algorithm based approach.

The proposed approach has been tested on a synthetic database where three different targets (as non-linear combinations of variables) have been adopted. Moreover random noise, with gaussian distribution, has been added to each target variable in order to evaluate the effectiveness of the method. The obtained results demonstrate that the proposed approach selects all involved variables and the prediction error in terms of NSRMSE is about 4%. In [34] and [47] GAs are used not only for the selection of involved variables to be fed as inputs to the learning machine but also to optimize some important parameters of the learning algorithm used in a classification purpose. In particular in [34] a decision tree-based classifier [53] is adopted and the pruning level is optimized. Pruning [54] is used to increase the performance of the classifier by cutting unnecessary branches of the tree, by also improving the generalization capabilities of the decision tree. This approach has been tested on an industrial problem concerning the classification of the metal products quality on the basis on the product variables and process parameters. The results demonstrate the effectiveness of the proposed method obtaining a rate of misclassified products in the range 4%-6%. In [47] authors propose an automatic variable selection method which combines genetic algorithm and Labelled Self Organized Maps (LSOM) [55] for classification purpose. GAs are explored in order to find the best performing combination of variables in terms of accuracy concerning the classifier and for setting some important parameters of the SOM such as dimension of the net, topology function, distance function and others. The GA explores and computes the classification performance of different combinations of input features and Som Organized Map (SOM) parameters providing the optimal solution. The method has been tested on several databases belonging to the UCI repository [56]. The proposed approaches provide a satisfied classification accuracy given also comprehensions of the phenomenon under consideration by selecting the input variables which mainly affect the final classification.

3.3. Embedded approach

Unlike previous methods, embedded approach performs the variable selection in the learning machine. The variables are selected during the training phase, by thus reducing the computational cost and improving the efficiency during the phase of variables selection. The difference between embedded approach and wrapper approach is not always obvious but the main ones lies in the fact that embedded method requires iterative updates and the evolution of the model parameters are based on the performance of the considered model. Moreover wrapper approach considers only the model performance of the selected set of variables [57]. Figure 5 illustrates a generic scheme concerning the embedded approach.

As in embedded methods the learning machine and the variable selection should be incorporated the structure of the considered functions plays an important role [58]. For instance, in [59] the importance of a variable is measured through a bound that has a logic sense only for SVM-based classifiers. In [60] a novel neural network model is proposed called Multi-Layer Perceptrons using embedded feature selection (MLPs-EFS). Being an embedded approach, the feature selection part is incorporated into the training procedure.

With respect to the traditional MLPs this approach adds a pre-processing phase where each variable is multiplied by a scaling factor [61-62]. When the scaling factor is small then the features are considered redundant or irrelevant, while when it is large the features are relevant. Moreover another main advantage is that all optimization algoritms used for the MLPs are also suitable for MLPs-EFS. The authors demonstrate the effectiveness of the proposed approach compared to other existing methods such us Fisher Discriminant Ratio (FDR) associated to MLPs or SVM with Recursive Feature Elimination (RFE). Results demonstrate that MLPs-EFS outperform the other considered methods. Another good result of this approach lies in its generality, which allows to apply it to other type of neural networks.

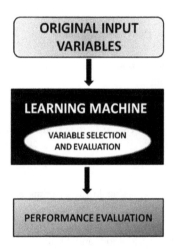

Figure 5. Generic scheme of embedded approach.

4. Conclusion

A survey about feature extraction and feature selection is proposed. The objective of both approaches concern the reduction of variables space in order to improve data analysis. This aspect becomes more important when real world datasets are considered, which can contain hundreds or thousands variables. The main difference between feature extraction and feature selection is that the first reduces dimensionality by computing a transformation of the original features to create other features that should be more significant, while feature selection performs the reduction by selecting a subset of variables without transforming them. Both traditional methods and their recent enhancements as well as some interesting applications concerning feature extraction and selection are presented and discussed. Feature selection improves the knowledge of the process under consideration, as it points out the variables that mostly affect the considered phenomenon. Moreover the computation time of the adopted learning machine and its accuracy need to be considered as they are crucial in machine learning and data mining applications.

Author details

Silvia Cateni, Marco Vannucci, Marco Vannocci and Valentina Colla
Scuola Superiore S.Anna,
TECIP - PERCRO Ghezzano, Pisa, Italy

5. References

[1] Bellman R. Adaptive Control Processes: A guided tour. Princeton University Press, 1961.

[2] Cunningham P. Dimension Reduction. Technical Report UCI-CSI-2007-7, August 8th, 2007. University College Dublin.

[3] Ripley B.D. Pattern Recognition and Neural Networks. Cambridge University Press, 1996.

[4] Pearson K. On lines and planes of closest fit to systems of points in space. Phisophical magazine 2, 1901, pp.559-572.

[5] Jolliffe I.T. Principal Component Analysis, Springer Series in Statistics, 2nd ed. Springer, NY 2002.

[6] Zhao J., Yu P. Shi, L., Li S. Separable linear discriminant analysis. Computational Statistics anda Data Analysis, 2012.

[7] Ye J., Ji S. Discriminant analysis for dimensionality reduction: an overview of recent developments. Biometrics Theory, Methods and Applications, Nov 2009.

[8] Belhumeour P.N., Hespanha J.P. Kriegman, D.J. Eigen faces vs Fisher faces: recognition using class specific linera projection. IEEE Transaction Pattern Analysis and Machine Intelligence, 19. pp.711-720. 1997.

[9] Wang X, Tang, X. A unified framework for subspace face recognition. IEEE Transactions on Pattern Analysis and machine Intelligence, 26. pp. 1222-1228, 2004.

[10] Guo Y., Hastie T., Tibshirani R. Regularized linear discriminant analysis and its application in microarrays. Biostatics, 8. pp.86-100, 2007.

[11] Chen L.F., Liao H.Y.M., Ko M.T., Lin J.C., Yu J.C. A new IDA-based face recognition system which can solve the small sample size problem. pattern Recognition, 33. pp.1713-1726, 2000.

[12] Park H., Jeon M., Rosen J.B. Lower Dimensional representation of text data based on centroids and least squares. BIT, 43. pp.1-22, 2003.

[13] Ye J. Characterization of a family of algorithms for generalized discriminant analysis on undersample problems. journal of Machine leraning Research, 6. pp.483-502, 2005.

[14] Deerwester S.C., Dumais S.T., Landauer T.K., Furnas G.W., Harshman A. Indexing by latent semantic analysis. Journal of the American society of Information Science, 41. pp.391-407. 1990.

[15] Heisterkamp D.R. Building a latent semantic index of an image database from patterns of relevance feedback. In ICPR (4), pp.134-137. 2002.

[16] Sahauria E., Zakhor A. Content Analysis of video using principal components. In ICIP, 3. pp. 541-545, 1998.

[17] Smaragdis P., Ray B., Shashanka M. A probabilistic latent variable model for acoustic Procesing at NIPS 2006, 2006.

[18] Chen X., Qi Y., Bai B., Lin Q., Carbonell J.G. Sparse Latent Semantic Analysis, SIAM, International Conference on Data Mining (SDM), 2011.

[19] Hyvannen A., Oja E. Independent Component Analysis: algorithms and Applications. Neural Networks, 13, pp.411-430, 2000.

[20] Hyvarinen A. Survey on Independent Component Analysis. Neural Computing Surveys 2, pp. 94-128, 1999.

[21] Comon P. Survey on Independent Component Analysis: a new concept?, Signal Processing 36. pp.287-314, 1994.

[22] Jutten C., Herault J. Blind Separation of Sources, Part I: an adaptive algorithm ased on neuromimetic architecture, Signal processing, 24. pp. 1-10, 1991.

[23] Weingessel A., Natter M., Hornik, K. Using Independent Component Analysis for feature extraction and Multivariate data projection. Working Paper 16, Adaptive Information Systems and Modelling in economics and Management Science, August 1998.

[24] Karlhunen J. Neural approaches to independent component analysis and source separation. In 4th European Symposium on Neural Networks, pp. 249-266., Bruges, Belgium, 1996.

[25] Blum A.L., Langely P. Selection of relevant features and examples in machine learning. Artificial Intelligence, Vol. 69 pp-.245-271, 1977.

[26] John G.H., Kohavi R., Pfleger K. Irrelevant feature and the subset selection problem. Proc of 11th International conference on machine learning, pp.121-129, 1994.

[27] Bne-Bassant. Pattern recognition and reduction of dimensionality, Handbook of statistics II, Krisnaiah and Kanal eds, pp.773-791, 1982.

[28] Mitra P. Murthy C.A. and Pal, S.K. Unsupervised Feature selection using feature similarity, IEEE transaction on Pattern Analysis and machine intelligence. Vol. 24, pp.301-312, 2002.

[29] Dash M., Liu H. Feature selection for classification. Intelligent data analysis: an international journal. Vol. 11, N°3, pp.131-156, 1997.

[30] Puronnen S., Tsymbal A., Skrypnik, I. Advanced local feature selection in medical diagnostics. Proc. 13th IEEE Symposum computer-based medical diagnostics, pp.25-30, 2000.

[31] Sofge D.A., Elliot D.L. Improved Neural Modelling of real world Systems using genetic algorithm based Variable Selection, proc. Conference on Neural Networks and Brain, Oct 1998.

[32] Kwak N., Choi C.H. Input feature selection for classification problems. IEEE trans. on neural networks, Vol. 13, pp.143-159, 2002.

[33] Lin J.Y., Ke H.R., Chien B.C., Yang W.P. Classifier design with feature extraction using layered genetic programming. Expert System with Applications, 34. pp.1384-1393.

[34] Cateni S., Colla V., Vannucci M. Variable Selection through Genetic Algorithms for classification purpose, IASTED International Conference on Artificial Intelligence and Applications, 2010, Innsbruck Austria, 15-17 February 2010.

[35] Wang S., Zhu J. Variable selection for model-based high dimensional clustering and its application on microarray data. Biometrics, 64. pp.440-448, June 2008.

[36] May R., Dandy G., Maier H. Review of input variable selection methods for artificial neural networks. Artificial Neural Network. Methodological Advances and Biomedical Applications. ISBN 978-953-307-243-2.

[37] Zhu Z., Ong Y.S., Dash M. Markov blanketembedded genetic algorithm for gene selection. Pattern Recognition, 40, pp.3236-3248, 2007.

[38] Khushaba R.N, Al-Ani A., Al-Jumaily A. Differential Evolution based Feature Subset Selection. 19th International Conference on Pattern Recognition, ICPR 2008. December 8-11, 2008. Tampa, Florida USA.

[39] Xiao Z., Dellandrea E., Dou W. Chen L. ESFS: A new embedded feature selection method based on SFS. Rapports de research, September 2008.

[40] Wu S., Flach P.A. Feature selection with labelled and unlabelled data. Proceeding of ECML7PKDD'02 Worshop on Integration and Collaboration Aspects of Data Mining, Decision Support and Meta-Learning, pp. 156-167, 2002.

[41] Yang, Y., Pedersen, J. O. A comparative study on feature selection in text categorization, Proc. of ICML'97, pages 412-420, 1997.

[42] Roobaert D., Karakoulas G, Nitesh V., Chawla V. Information Gain, Correlation and Support Vector Machines, StudFuzz 207, Springer- Verlag Berlin, pp. 463–470 (2006).

[43] Ladha L., Deepa T. Feature Selection methods and algorithms, International Journal on Computer Science and Engineering (IJCSE), Vol 3, N 5, May 2011.

[44] Yu L., Liu H. Feature Selection for high-dimensional data: a fast correlation-based filter solution. Proc. of the 20th International Conference on Machine Learning ICML-2003, Washington DC, 2003.

[45] Kohavi R., John G. Wrappers for feature selection. Artificial Intelligence, 97. pp. 273-324, December 1997.

[46] Guyon I., Elisseeff A. An introduction to variable and feature selection. The journal of Machine Learning Research, 3. pp.1157-1182, 2003.

[47] Cateni S., Colla V., Vannucci M. A Genetic Algorithm-based approach for selecting input variables and setting relevant network parameters of a SOM-based classifier. International Journal of Simulation Systems, Science & Technology. UKSim 4th European Modelling Symposium on Mathematical modelling and computer simulation, Vol.12, N°2, Aprile 2011.

[48] Huang C.L., Wang C.J. A GA-based feature selection and parameters optimization for support vector machines. Expert Systems with Applications 31. pp. 231-240, 2006.

[49] Vapnik V.N. The nature of statistical learning theory. New York, Springer, 1995.

[50] Cateni S. Colla V., Vannucci M. General purpose Input Variables Extraction: A Genetic Algorithm based Procedure GIVE A GAP, Proc of the 9th International Conference on Intelligence Systems design and Applications ISDA'09, November 30- December 2, 2009, Pisa, Italy.

[51] Patterson D. Artificial Neural Networks. Prentice Hall, New York Singapore 1996.

[52] Zhang Q., Benveniste A. Wavelet Networks. IEEE Transactions on Neural Network, Vol. 3, N°6, pp. 889-898, November 1992.

[53] Quinlan J.R. C4.5 Programs for Machine Learning. Morgan Kauffmann Publisher 1993.

[54] Kearns M.J., Mansur Y. A fast bottom up decision tree pruning algorithm with near-optimal generalization. In Proc. of the 15th International Conference on Machine Learning, 1998.

[55] Colla V., Vannucci M., Fera S., Valentini, R. Ca-treatment of Al killed steels: inclusion modification and application of Artificial Neural Networks for the prediction of clogging. Proc. 5th European Oxygen Steelmaking Conference EOSC'06, June 26-28, Aachen 2006, Germany, pp. 387-394.

[56] Asunction A., Newman D.J. UCI machine learning repository Irvine. CA: University of California, School of Information and Computer Science, 1997. [http://archive.ics.uci.edu/ml7datasets.htm]

[57] Kwak N., Choi C. Input Feature Selection for Classification Problems. IEEE Transaction on Neural Networks, Vol. 13 N°1, January 2002.

[58] Navil Lal T., Chapelle O., Weston J., Elisseeff A. Embedded Methods. Feature Extraction, Foundations and Applications, Springer-Verlag, Berlin/Heidelberg Germany, 2006, pp. 137-165.

[59] Weston J., Mukherjee S. Chapelle O., Pontil M., Poggio T., Vapnik V. Feature Selection for SVMs. In S.A. Solla, T.K.Leen and K-R Muller editors. Advances in Neural Information Processing Systems, Volume 12, pp. 526-532, Cambridge,MA, USA, 2000, MIT Press.

[60] Bo L., Wang L., Jiao L. Multi-layer Perceptrons with embedded feature selection with application in Cancer Classification. Chinese Journal of Electronics, 15. 2006. pp. 832-835.

[61] Tibshirani R. Regression shrinkage and selection via the LASSO. Journal of the Royal Statistical Society (B), vol. 58, pp.267-288, 1996.

[62] Donoho D., Elad M. Optimally sparse representations in general (nonorthogonal) dictionaries by l1 minimization. Proceedings of the National Academic of Science, Vol.100, pp. 2197-2202, 2003.

Chapter 6

Itaipu Hydroelectric Power Plant Structural Geotechnical Instrumentation Temporal Data Under the Application of Multivariate Analysis – Grouping and Ranking Techniques

Rosangela Villwock, Maria Teresinha Arns Steiner,
Andrea Sell Dyminski and Anselmo Chaves Neto

Additional information is available at the end of the chapter

1. Introduction

The monitoring of a dam structure can generate an enormous mass of data of which the analysis and interpretation are not always trivial. It is important to select the information that better "explain" the behavior of the dam, making possible the prediction and resolution of eventual problems that may occur.

The world largest hydroelectricity generator, Itaipu hydroelectric power plant, has more than 2.200 instruments that monitor its geotechnical and structural behavior, and these instruments have readings stored on a database for over 30 years. The high dimensionality and the large quantity of records stored on the databases are nontrivial problems that are kept so that one can pursue "knowledge" through these data.

The detailed analysis of the auscultation instrumental data requires a combination of knowledge of Engineering, Mathematics and Statistics, as well as the previous experience of the engineer or the technician responsible for the analysis of these data. That consumes a lot of time, and often makes it impossible to accomplish this task in an efficient way. This is the reason why the use of techniques and computational instrumentation to help the decisions maker is extremely important.

There are no records of the existence of methods that perform the classification of monitoring instruments in dams. In case of reading intensification this hierarchy could be useful to define which instrument to chose.

The aim of this paper is to identify the tools that are the most significant for the analysis of a dam behavior, which maximizes the effectiveness and efficiency of the analysis of the readings. It shows a methodology based on the field of Multivariate Analysis, applied to the Hierarchical Cluster Analysis in order to identify the groups of instruments similar to Ward's linkage method. The factor analysis of the strain gauge of each instrument group was also applied, performing the hierarchical cluster of monitoring instruments in dams, detecting the main instruments.

This chapter is organized as follows: Section 2 features the problem statement which addresses the importance of the safety on dams and the risks faced when dam rupture accident occurs. Section 3 describes the application area focusing on the safety of dams, on the conditions of load and on the conditions of the monitoring instrument. Section 4 approaches a "research course". Section 5 describes the used data and the Multivariate Statistical Analysis techniques. Section 6 shows the status. Section 7 shows the results. Section 8 approaches the future researches. Section 9 shows the results.

2. Problem statement

Once the potential risks and losses as a result of rupture accidents on a dam can reach large scales a safe project and adequate construction as well as a correct operation on dams are concerns of Brazilian and worldwide engineers. Additionally, an effectively done monitoring on large dams is essential for the safety of its structure. By aiming the safety of the dams, International Guidelines and many helpful discussions about this subject have been proposed and conducted, such as the one from the [1].

In Brazil, guidelines that aim the safety of the dams were published by the *Comitê Brasileiro de Grandes Barragens* (Brazilian Committee on Large Dams), see [2]. The *Comissão de Constituição e Justiça e Cidadania do Congresso Nacional)* (The Constitutional, Justice and Citizenship Committee of the National Congress) approved, on 06/23/2009, the proposal that requires the Executive Power to establish a National Policy on Dams Safety. Its aim was to endow the Public Power with a permanent instrument for the inspection of over 300 thousand dams in the country. The text that has been questioned is the surrogate for the Law Project 1181/03 [3]. The original proposal, the Law Project 1181/03, (*Projeto de Lei – PL 1181/03),* written by Leonardo Monteiro, defines safety guidelines for the construction of dams and landfills of industrial liquid wastes.

The concerns about the Brazilian Constitutional Public Powers is due to the recent rupture of the Dam of Câmara, (in the State of Pará - PA), in 2004; the rupture of the diversion structure of the Dam of Campos Novos, (in the State of Santa Catarina - SC), in 2006; the rupture of the Dam of Algodões I, (in the State of Piauí - PI), in 2009; and other accidents of smaller magnitude.

According to [4], the catastrophes have been opportune signs for the examination of the criteria of the existing projects and for the selection of more efficient methods and monitoring safety of dams.

In [5] show a table which contains the estimative for the most common causes of ruptures on dams. Among them, the following are highlighted: problems of the foundation; inappropriate spillway; structural problem; different declinations; extreme low-pressure; rupture of landfills; defective materials; incorrect operation; actions of war, and earthquakes. All these problems can be diagnosed with the monitoring of the dam instrumentation, with exception of the last two ones, which percentage of frequencies sum just 4%.

According to [6], the global experience shows that the expenses in order to guarantee the safety of a dam are little when compared to the costs of its rupture. The author quotes the importance of the use of a database of instrumentation for supporting the preliminary analysis of the readings in order to detect problems.

3. Application area

3.1. Safety of dams

The principles established on NBR 8681 – *Ações e Segurança das Estruturas* (Actions and safety of structures) [7] conceptualizes the safety of the concrete constructions of a dam. For concrete gravity-dam projects, some verification corresponding to the stability analysis are necessary in order to evaluate the safety of the movements of: sliding, overturning, floating, tension at base and on structure, deformations, consolidation and vibrations.

The stability of dams must be primary analyzed during the phase of the project. The geometry of the structures and the property of the materials involved must be well considered, as well as the load condition. Some of the basic load conditions are shown on Figure 1.

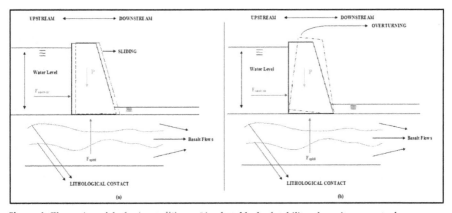

Figure 1. Illustration of the basic conditions of load and lack of stability of gravity concrete dams.

Through Physics, it is possible to explain that the difference of the water level (downstream-upstream) generates a hydraulic gradient between the dam downstream and upstream making the water of the reservoir to try passing through upstream in order to archive a hydraulic equilibrium. To do so, the water percolates through the foundation mass of the dam. During this process, the infiltrated water generates vertical forces acting upward over the dam, these forces are called uplift pressure in dam. The resultant of these forces is represented by F_{uplift}. Furthermore, the water from the reservoir generates horizontal forces that act downstream-upstream over the dam. These forces are called hydrostatic pressures against the dam wall. The resultants of these forces are represented by $F_{reservoir}$. These two resultant forces are called destabilizing forces. As for the force P (dam weight) it is a stabilizing structure force. The combination of F_{uplift} and $F_{reservoir}$ can cause the overturning and the slipping of the dam, not just because of the efforts and moment when it is directly applied, but also for the relief of the weight of the structure itself (in case of uplift pressure).

The above described effects of loads on dams can be observed on figure 1, where the slipping (a) and the overturning (b) are emphasized.

The loading conditions and the properties of materials can change over the lifecycle of a dam, and instrumentation can identify some of these changes.

Figure 2 shows the differences in the behavior of the dam in relation to summer and winter climate conditions, as well as its consequences. In summer, an expansion of the concrete occurs, and that causes the block to tumble downstream. This overturning causes the block to compress the foundation. In winter, the concrete is compressed causing the block to tumble upstream, returning to initial position. As a consequence the pressure that occurs in summer over the foundation to be relieved. In this way, it is possible to identify a cyclical behavior of the structure, intrinsically conditioned by the environmental conditions which involve the construction.

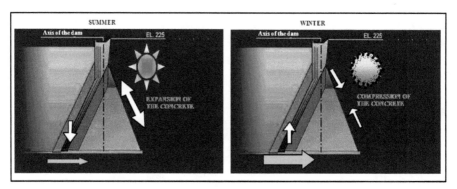

Figure 2. Behavior of the dam in relation to summer and winter climate conditions (Adapted from [8]).

According to [9], the instrumentation must be used as supplement to visual inspection when executing the evaluation of the performance and safety of dams. The careful inspection of the instrumentation data can reveal a critical condition.

In [10] shows correlations between the types of instruments that are usually used for the auscultation on concrete dams, and the primary types of deterioration of concrete dams. According to the author, the multiple extensometer for example, is related to the monitoring of deteriorations caused by sliding, different declinations, land subsidence of the upstream base, and the Alkali-Aggregate Reactivity.

The measurement of the declinations is one of the most important observations for monitoring a dam behavior during the period of construction, of dams filling and operation. The measurement of the declination can be performed through a multiple point rod extensometer installed on boreholes [10]. Figure 3 shows the multiple point rod extensometer and an example of a typical profile of a multiple point rod extensometer at *Itaipu*.

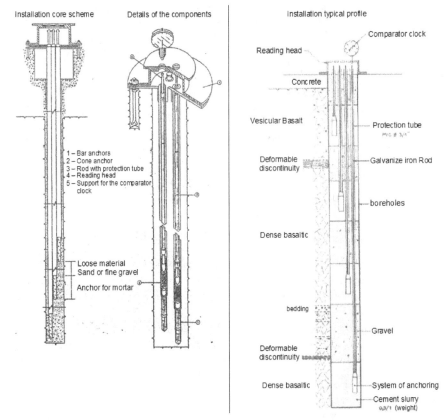

Figure 3. Multiple point rod extensometer and a example of a typical profile of a multiple point rod extensometer at *Itaipu* (Adapted from [11]).

The measurements of displacements and deformation can be performed in several parts of the foundation with the usage of various rods. Among these displacement and deformations are the contact of concrete and rock, joints and faults and other sub-horizontal discontinuities in the foundation. This approach was used at the Itaipu Dam, where different points of foundation mass were instrumented, specially the geological discontinuities. Figure 4 shows a typical geological profile of the foundation mass of the Itaipu Dam part, which has no tunnel in its right-side, where primary geological discontinuities can be found (contacts, joints, and gaps) of that specific site. In blocks where there is a transversal gallery access to the shaft, the installation of downstream-upstream extensometers can help in the measurement of the angular displacement of the dam with the foundation [10].

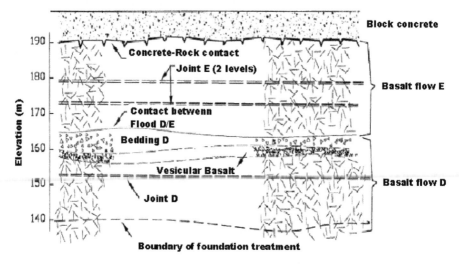

Figure 4. Schematic geological profile of the foundation of Itaipu (ITAIPU BINACIONAL, 1995, *apud* [8]).

The measurement of the horizontal displacement of the ridge is a relevant parameter which is affected by deflections of the concrete structure, by the rotation of the base of the structure (due to the deformability of the foundation), and by thermal and environmental influences. These displacements are affected by the characteristics of the concrete or by the proprieties of the foundation rock mass, resulting in important information for the auscultation of the behavior of the dam and of its foundation. The horizontal displacements of the ridge can be measured by a direct pendulum, usually installed at the end of the construction process. The measurements are done on the stages of reservoir spillway and of dam operation [10].

The stability of the structure in terms of sliding, overturning or floating is directly affected by the level of the piezometric pressures in the concrete-rock interface and in the sub horizontal discontinuities of low resistance that exists in the foundation. The measurements of low pressures on the concrete dam foundation are important for the monitoring of its safety conditions. The drainage is one of the most efficient ways to ensure adequate safety coefficients. The measurements of low pressure are performed by the piezometer [10].

4. Research course

4.1. Itaipu Binacional

The Itaipu Binacional, the largest energy producer of the world, had its construction started in 1973 at a river stretch of Rio Paraná known as Itaipu, which in Tupi language means "the singing boulder", located in the heart of Latin America, on the border of Brazil and Paraguay [12]. The construction of the dam ended in 1982 and the last generator unit was completed in 2008.

Nowadays, the Itaipu Dam has 20 generator units of 700 MW (megawatts) each, generating a total potential of 14.000 MW. Itaipu Binacional (Bi-national Itaipu) reached its record in producing energy in 2000, generating over 93,4 billions kilowatts-hour (KWh). It is responsible for supplying 95% of the energy consumed in Paraguay and 24% of all the Brazilian consumption.

The Itaipu Dam has 7.919m of extension and a maximum high of 196m; these dimensions made of the Itaipu construction a reference in concrete, and dam safety studies. Itaipu dam is made of two stretches of earth dam, one stretch of rock-fill dams and concrete stretches, and these forms the higher structures of it. Figure 5 illustrates the whole structure of the Itaipu dam, and table 1 shows the main characteristics of the stretches pointed on figure 5.

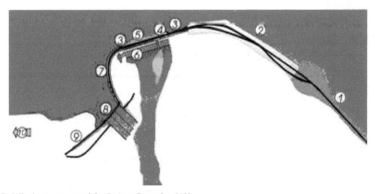

Figure 5. Whole structure of the Itaipu Complex [12].

It is possible to find in all the Itaipu extension an amount of 2.218 instruments (1.362 in the concrete, and 865 in the foundations and earthen embankments) and from this amount 270 of them are automated, to monitor the performance of the concrete structures and foundations. Furthermore, there are 5.239 drains (949 in the concrete and 4.290 in the foundations). The readings of these instruments occur in different frequencies, they can be, for example, daily, weekly, fortnightly, and monthly, depending on the type of instrument. These readings have been stored for over 30 years.

Even though, every stretch of the dam is instrumented and monitored, one of the stretches, called *Barragem principal* (main dam) (Denominated stretch F and identified as number "5" on Figure 5), should be highlighted in a deeper study. The turbines for generating energy can be found in stretch F. In addition, this stretch is the most high water column and the most instrumented one. This stretch is made of many blocks, and each of them has instruments in the concrete structures and in the foundation that provides data about its physical behavior. This study was developed based on the data collected in this stretch of the dam.

Stretch		Structure	Lenth (m)	Maximun high (m)
1	Auxiliary Dam (Saddle Dam)	Earth	2294	30
2	Auxiliary Dam (Saddle Dam)	Rock-filling	1984	70
3 and 7	Lateral Dams	Couterfort	1438	81
4	Deviation Structure	Concrete mass	170	162
5	Main Dam (TStretch F)	Reliefed Gravity	612	196
9	Auxiliary Dam	Terra	872	25
Other strwtches		Características		
6	Powerhouse	20 Generator units		
8	Spillway	350 m length		

Table 1. Characteristics of the stretches of Itaipu.

In the stretch F it is possible to find extensometers, piezometers, triothogonal meter, water level gauge and foundation instrumentation (seepage flow meter). Among these instruments, the multiple point rod extensometers, that are installed in boreholes, were selected for the analysis. This type of instrument is considered one of the most important because they are responsible for measuring the vertical displacement. That is one of the most important observations while monitoring the behavior of the dam structure. There are 30 extensometers located in stretch F.

The procedure for the methodology used for the analysis of the problem of *Itaipu* is the following:

In the first phase, the data were selected and it was decided that the methodology would be applied only to the extensometers located in stretch F.

In the second phase, the data given by *Itaipu* were converted into spreadsheets, from which the necessary data used for developing this study were extracted.

In the third phase, the data were standardized in order to receive the subsequent application of the clustering methods.

In the fourth phase, the Factor Analysis and the Clustering Analysis were applied at the same time. The Factor Analysis was also applied within each cluster formed through Clustering Analysis.

5. Method used

The methodology used for the analysis was applied to the data of 30 extensometers located in different blocks of stretch F of the dam, which having one or two point rods, totalizes 72 displacement measures. These measurements are identified as follow: equip4_1, meaning rod 1 of the extensometer 4, and so on.

The data used in this study are monthly stored and they correspond to the period of January/1995 to December/2004, totalizing 120 readings. This period was chosen as a suggestion of the engineer team of Itaipu because it is subsequent the construction of the dam and prior to the system of automatic acquisition of data. During the period of system implementation, some instruments ended up having no manual readings, in addition, a total of 11 automated instruments (totalizing 24 rods) went through modifications that might have influenced the subsequent readings; there was an exchange on the instrument head for a 70 cm longer one. In this way, the referred 120 readings were immune to these irregularities.

During the period of pre-processing the data, it was identified that most of the instruments readings are monthly, but some of them showed more than one reading per month, so for this cases, the monthly average was considered. Moreover, some instruments had missing readings, in these cases; interpolations were performed through temporal series, meaning that, an adequate model was established from the Box & Jenkins methodology, using the Statgraphics [13]. In this way, it was possible to assure that all the 120 instruments had 120 readings (10 years). See [14] for more information about the interpolation techniques with temporal series.

In this way, the Matrix of entrance of structural geotechnical instrumentation data (Matrix Q) is of order $a \times b$, where a is the number of patterns and b is the number of attributes. For the structural geotechnical instrumentation data of Itaipu, $a = 72$ (number of patterns) and $b = 120$ (number of attributes).

During the period of the Multivariate Analysis was applied and the patterns were grouped through the Ward's hierarchical clustering method. The grouping was performed in order to find out similar groups of instruments, and the aim of doing it was to establish the technical justifications for its formation. In addition, the Factor Analysis was applied to the referred data. The Factor Analysis was used to rank the rods of the extensometers through a balanced average of factor scores. Next, the Factor Analysis was applied within each group formed by the clustering analysis. Once having groups that have the instrumentations with a similar behavior, a raking of these instruments was performed within each group, in order to indicate the most relevant instruments, which would be chosen, for example, in cases of intensifying the reading.

5.1. Statistical multivariate analysis

5.1.1. Factor analysis

Factor Analysis is a multivariate statistical method, which objective is to explain the correlations between one large set of variables in terms of a set of unobserved low random variables called factors. Hence, suppose the random vector $\underline{X}$ resulted from p random variables; $\underline{X}' = [x_1\ x_2\ x_3\ ...\ x_p]$, and in order to study the covariance structure of this vector, in other words, if $\underline{X}$ is observed n times, it happens that its parameters $E(\underline{X}) = \mu$ e $V(\underline{X}) = \Sigma$ can be estimated and the relation between the evaluated variables represented by matrix of covariance Σ or of correlation p. The factor analysis makes a grouping of variables to explain the influence of latent variables (unobserved) or factors. Within a same group, the variables are highly correlated with each other, and from one group to another, the correlations are low. Each group represents a factor, which is responsible for the observed correlation.

The covariance matrix of the vector $\underline{X}$ can be placed in an exact form: $V(\underline{X}) = \Sigma = LL' + \Psi$, where matrix LL' has on the main diagonal the called communality defined for each variable considering m factors by: $h_i^2 = l_{i1}^2 + l_{i2}^2 + ... + l_{ip}^2$. However, considering the m main factors, it is given that $h_i^2 = l_{i1}^2 + l_{i2}^2 + ... + l_{im}^2$, $i = 1, 2, ..., p$ variables. In this way, the communality h_i^2 is the part of the variance of the random variable x_i that comes from m factors. And, the part of the variance of the random variable x_i due to the factors $p - m$ that are not important are called specific variance. Hence, $V(x_i) = h_i^2 + \Psi_i$, $i = 1, 2, ..., p$.

There are many criteria to define m number of factors. The most used one is the Kaiser criterion [15], which suggests that the number of extracted factors must be equal to the number of eigenvalues higher than one, of Σ or ρ.

If $\underline{X}$ is a random vector, with p components, and the parameters $E(\underline{X}) = \mu$ e $V(\underline{X}) = \Sigma$, in factor model ortogonal, $\underline{X}$ is linearly dependent upon several random unobserved variables, F_1, F_2, ... , F_m called common factors and p sources of joining variables: $\varepsilon_1, \varepsilon_2, ... , \varepsilon_p$, called errors or specific factors.

The model of Factor Analysis is represented below, where μ_i is the average of the i-th variable, ε_i is the i-th error, or specific factor, F_j is the j-th common factor and l_{ij} is the weight of the j-th F_j factor on i-th X_i variable. Equation 1 shows the model represented in matrix terms.

$$\begin{cases} X_1 - \mu_1 = l_{11}\ F_1 + l_{12}\ F_2 + ... + l_{1m}\ F_m + \varepsilon_1 & i = 1,2,...,p \\ X_2 - \mu_2 = l_{21}\ F_1 + l_{22}\ F_2 + ... + l_{2m}\ F_m + \varepsilon_2 & j = 1,2,...,m \\ ... \\ X_p - \mu_p = l_{p1}\ F_1 + l_{p2}\ F_2 + ... + l_{pm}\ F_m + \varepsilon_p & m \le p. \end{cases}$$

$$X = \mu + LL' + \Psi \tag{1}$$

In order to estimate the loading l_{ij} and the specific variables ψ_i, the method of principal components can be used, which is briefly described below [15].

If the pair of eigenvalues and eigenvectors are $(\lambda_i, \underline{e}_i)$ of the matrix of sample covariance S, with $\lambda_1 \geq \lambda_2 \geq \ldots \geq \lambda_p \geq 0$ and $m < p$ is the number of common factors the matrix of the estimated loadings is given by $L = CD^{1/2}$, where C is the matrix of the eigenvectors and D is a diagonal matrix of which the diagonal elements are the eigenvalues.

In the application of this method, the observations are primarily centralized or standardized, in other words, the matrix of correlation R (estimator of p) is used in order to avoid problems of scale. The specific variances estimated $\widehat{\Psi}_i$ are given by the diagonal elements of the matrix $\widehat{\Psi}_i = S - LL'$.

In multiple actions, it is necessary to estimate the value of the scores of each factor (unobserved) for an individual $\underline{X}$ observation. These factor values are called factor scores. The estimated factor scores to the original variables are $\underline{F} = (L'L)^{-1} L'(\underline{X} - \bar{X})$ and for the standardized variables are $\underline{F} = (L'L)'L\underline{z}_i$, that is, if the principal components are used in order to estimate the loadings.

According to [15], with the rotation of factors, a structure is obtained for the low or moderated loadings on the other factors. This leads to a more simplified structure to be interpreted. Kaiser suggested an analytical measure known as *Varimax* criteria [15] in order to make the rotation.

The rotation coefficient scaled by the square root of the communalities is defined by $\tilde{l}_{ij} = \frac{l_{ij}}{h_{ij}}$. The *Varimax* selects the orthogonal transformation T that turns V (given by equation 2) the largest possible, in other words, the procedure starts from $\sum LT'L'$ and gives the loadings $\underline{l}^*$ which comes from LT. Hence, the criterion is to maximize V.

$$V = \frac{1}{p} \sum_{i=1}^{p} \left[\sum_{i=1}^{p} L_{ij}^{*4} - \frac{\sum_{i=1}^{p}\left(L_{ij}^{*2}\right)}{p} \right] \tag{2}$$

In Factor Analysis, communality h_i^2 is the portion of the variance of the variable that is attributed to the factors and represents the percentage of variation of the variable which is not random but from the factors. Thus, the criterion used to classify the patterns is sort the variables (instruments) according to their factor scores. The factor scores were evaluated by a factor that distinguishes the behavior of the instrument, using it as a practical and simple quality control of the measurement of the instrument.

To perform the ranking of the variables (instruments), a final factor score was used, which is given by equation (3), where m is the number of factors extracted, λ_i are the eigenvalues and f_i are the factor scores.

$$final\_factor\_score = \frac{\sum_{i=1}^{m} \lambda_i f_i}{\sum_{i=1}^{m} \lambda_i} \tag{3}$$

The Factor Analysis was done with the aid of the computational *Statgraphics* [13].

5.1.2. Cluster analysis

The clustering is a manner of grouping in a way that those patterns inside the same group are very similar to each other, and different from patterns of the other groups. According to [16], cluster analysis is an analytical technique used to develop meaningful subgroups of objects. Its objective is to classify the objects in a small number of groups that are mutually exclusive. According, to [17], it is important to favor a small number of groups in cluster analysis.

The clustering algorithms can be divided into categories in many ways, according to its characteristics. The two main classes of clustering are: the hierarchical methods and the nonhierarchical methods.

The hierarchical methods include techniques that connection of the items assuming obtain various levels of clustering. The hierarchical methods can be subdivided into divisive or agglomerative ones. The agglomerative hierarchical method considers at the beginning each pattern as a group and interactively, clusters a pair of groups that are the most similar with a new group until there is only one group containing all patterns. In the other hand, the divisive hierarchical method, starts with a single group and performs a process of successive subdivisions [18].

The most popular hierarchical clustering methods are: Single Linkage, Complete Linkage, Average Linkage and Ward's Method. The most common method of representing a hierarchical cluster is using a dendrogram that represents the clustering of the patterns and the levels of similarity in which the groups are formed. The dendrograms can be divided in different levels, showing different groups [19].

In the dendrogram (figure 6), two groups can be seen by admitting a cut on the level represented by the figure. The first one composed by patterns P1, P2 and P5 and the second one composed by patterns P3 and P4.

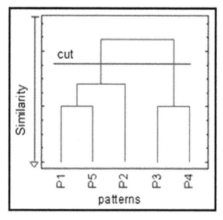

Figure 6. Example of dendrogram.

Methods that are not hierarchical or partitioning seek for a way of partitioning without the need of hierarchical associations. Optimizing some criteria, a partition of the elements on k group is selected [18].

The most known method among the nonhierarchical methods is the k-means cluster method [15]. Normally, the k clusters that are found are of better quality than the k clusters produced by the hierarchical methods. The methods of partitioning are advantageous in applications that involve larger series of data.

The methods of the Multivariate Statistics field were used because these are already common methods. The Multivariate Statistic Analysis is an old method that has been made feasibly recently with the advance of present, fast and economic computation.

The clustering of the patterns is based on the measure of similarity and dissimilarity. The similarity measure evaluates the similarities of the objects, in other words, the highest the measures value are the most similar are the objects. The most known mean of similarity is the correlation coefficient. The means of dissimilarity evaluates whether the objects are dissimilar, this is to say, that the highest the measure value are the less similar the objects are. The most known measure of dissimilarity is the Euclidean distance.

According to [15], Ward's method performs the join of two clusters based on the "loss of information". It is considered to be the criteria of "loss of information" the sum of the error square (SQE). For each cluster I, the measure of the cluster (or centroide) of the cluster and the sum of the cluster error square (SQE_i) which is the sum of the error square of each pattern of the cluster in relation to the measure. For cluster k there is SQE_1, SQE_2, ..., SQE_k, where SQE is defined by equation 4.

$$SQE = SQE_1 + SQE_2 + ... + SQE_k \qquad (4)$$

For each pair of cluster m and n, first, the measure (or centroide) of the formed cluster is calculated (cluster mn). Then, the sum of error for the square of cluster mn is calculated $(SQEmn)$, according to equation 5.

$$SQE = SQE_1 + SQE_2 + ... + SQE_k - SQE_m - SQE_n + SQE_{mn} \qquad (5)$$

The clusters m and n that show the lower increase on the sum of error square (SQE) (lower loss of information) will be gathered. According to [16], this method tends to obtain clusters of same size due to the deacrese of its internal variation.

Cluster Analysis was applied with the aid of the computational software *Statgraphics* [13]. The measure of dissimilarity used was the Euclidean distance. The data were standardized.

6. Status

This research was performed during the first author's (Rosangela Villwock) doctorate process, from 2005 to 2009, in the Post-graduation Program on Numerical Methods in Engineering, of the Federal University of Paraná, guided by the second author of this text

(Maria Teresinha Arns Steiner). This study was part of a project guide by the third author (Andrea Sell Dyminski), called *"Analise de Incertezas e Estimação de Valores de Controle para o Sistema de Monitoração Geotécnico-estrutural na Barragem de Itaipu"* (Estimation of Control Values for the System of Geotechnic-structural Monitoring in the Itaipu Dam). All the research process counted with the collaboration of the fourth author (Anselmo Chaves Neto) and it was also supervised by him.

As mentioned before, the aim of this paper is to identify the instruments that are the most significant to the analysis of the behavior of dams. There are no records of the existence of methods that perform the ranking of the instruments of monitoring dams. In order to achieve this aim, it is necessary to select, cluster and rank geotechnical-structural instruments of an electric power plant looking forward to maximizing the effectiveness and efficiency of the readings analysis, in our case the Itaipu Hydroelectric Power Plant. In case of needing to intensify the reading this hierarchy could be useful to define which instruments to choose.

The choice of instrumentation is performed with no previous knowledge about the location, features, or characteristics of the instruments. In this way, it is possible to think of applying the methodology when making decisions about the automation of the additional instruments. Approaches that are similar to this can be used in many other cases because there are hundreds of large Civil Engineering construction works that rely on systems of instrumentation in Brazil which the data must have an appropriate treatment.

7. Results

In the cluster Analysis, the patterns are the rods of the extensometers, and its readings along the months which are compared in order to determine the clusters. The dendrogram on figure 7 shows the formation of the clusters for these data.

Considering the first cut, there are two clusters left. The first cluster, here denominated "cluster 1", is formed by the rods of the extensometers that are considered extremely important to the monitoring of the dam. They are rods of extensometers installed in the axis of the block upstream the dam and inclined 60° towards upstream.

Notice that there is a formation of two additional clusters in the second cut. The first one denominates "cluster 2" which most of its rods of the extensometer installed in the balsatic rocks B, C and D (A and B are called the deepest rocks; C and D are called the superficial rocks), and on the lithological contacts B/C and C/D. The second cluster, denominated "cluster 3" has most of the rods of the extensometers installed in the joints (between the rock layers) A and B and on the lithological contact A/B.

This was the quantity of clusters which are been considered (3 clusters), since it was possible to obtain technical justification for its formation. In a larger subdivision, such justification was not observed.

Notice that at this point it was possible to cluster the instruments according to the relevant geological characteristics of the foundation mass, even though they weren't explicitly showed to the technician. However, on cluster 2, three rods of extensometers installed in joint B were observed, and in cluster 3, three rods of extensometers installed in the basaltic rocks B and C and in the lithological contact B/C were observed.

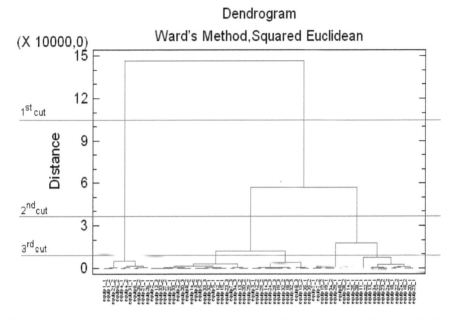

Figure 7. Dendrogram showing the formation of the clusters in different types of cuts (Ward's method).

Figure 8 shows the graphic of all the rods of the extensometer during the period of study. The lines were colored according to the cluster of which the rods belong to (black, blue and yellow for clusters 1, 2 and 3, respectively). It is possible to note the distinction between the clusters. This distinction of clusters is not easily recognized when there is no previous knowledge about these three clusters. The task would not be possible if a larger cluster of data hat to be analyzed, hence, the importance of this type of analysis.

Cluster 1, which is composed by rods of extensometers installed on the upstream of the dam, clearly shows the effects of summer and winter. The clusters 2 and 3 are separated due to the absolute measures. This separation can be justified by the fact that they are indifferent conditions, which is more superficial in cluster 2, and deeper in cluster 3. Once the readings of the most superficial rods and the readings of the deepest rods are summed up, these measures are larger.

Table 2 shows the most important rod for each of eight factors, for instances, the rod dominating each factor. Notice that in table 2 the factor 2 is dominated by the rod equip1_1, equip1_2, equip4_1, equip4_2, equip6_1, equip6_2, equip8_1, equip8_3, equip21_1, equip21_2, equip25_3, equip26_2 e equip31_1. This factor has 10 of the 11 rods that are part of cluster 1, it means that there is an external phenomenon influencing them. As mentioned before, these rods reflect the effects of the summer and winter. In the same way, each factor is dominated by a set of rods and there is an external phenomenon that explains each set of rods or factor, even though it is not easy to interpret them.

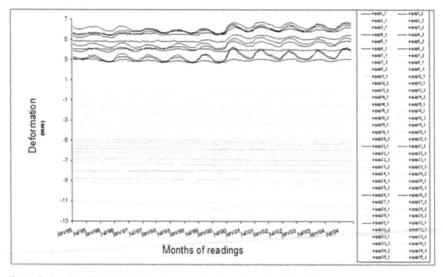

Figure 8. Graphic of all rods of the extensometers from the period of study.

	equip7_1	equip7_2	equip7_3	equip11_1	equip12_1	equip12_2	equip13_1
factor1	equip13_2	equip14_1	equip14_2	equip14_3	equip19_2	equip20_2	equip20_3
	equip22_1	equip22_2	equip22_3	equip23_1	equip23_2	equip23_3	equip24_1
	equip24_2	equip24_3	equip25_1	equip25_2	equip27_2	equip28_1	equip28_2
	equip29_1	equip29_2	equip32_3	equip33_1	equip33_2	equip33_3	equip34_1
	equip34_2	equip34_3	equip35_1	equip35_2			
factor2	equip1_1	equip1_2	equip4_1	equip4_2	equip6_1	equip6_2	equip8_1
	equip8_3	equip21_1	equip21_2	equip25_3	equip26_2	equip31_1	
factor3	equip2_1	equip2_2	equip3_1	equip3_2	equip5_1	equip5_2	
factor4	equip13_3	equip18_1	equip18_2	equip18_3	equip19_1	equip19_3	
factor5	equip15_1	equip15_2					
factor6	equip8_2	equip20_1	equip32_2				
factor7	equip26_1						
factor8	equip32_1						

Table 2. Rods of extensometers that are important to each factor, according to its weights in the Factor Analysis.

A community is the portion of the variation of the extensometer rods which is explained by its factors. A low community within a rod indicates that the same is not greatly affected by the factor because a community is the sum of contributions of each rod in each square factor. Thereon, in this case the influence mainly comes from a random factor. Notice that none of the extensometer rods showed lower community than 0.71, it means that none of the random variations are over 29%. A community that is equal to 0.71 indicates that the 71% of the rods extensometer variations is ascribed to the factors and that only 29% of those variations is random, it means that these correlated rods are working properly. A low community would indicate a need of investigating the rods.

Table 3 shows 25 rods of extensometers with the highest communalities. In case of reading intensification, these rods are the recommended ones. The highlighted rods are part of the system of automatic data acquisition of Itaipu. 24 of the 74 rods that were analyzed were automated by the engineers' team of Itaipu. The method of ranking that was proposed (without the previous clustering of the rods) indentified 14 of the 24 automated rods.

Communality	0,988861	0,981763	0,976523	0,975655	0,972231	0,971971
Rod	equip29_1	equip21_2	equip23_1	equip22_1	equip3_1	equip1_1
Communality	0,971798	0,970804	0,970397	0,968213	0,968083	0,967029
Rod	equip22_3	equip11_1	equip1_2	equip23_2	equip4_1	equip21_1
Communality	0,966602	0,965999	0,965522	0,964925	0,963139	0,960121
Rod	equip4_2	equip29_2	equip34_3	equip6_1	equip6_2	equip22_2
Communality	0,957609	0,953036	0,950395	0,949394	0,949108	0,948646
Rod	equip14_3	equip25_1	equip33_2	equip24_2	equip24_1	equip5_1
Communality	0,943644					
Rod	equip28_1					

Table 3. Shows the 25 rods of extensometers with the highest communalities.

After forming three clusters, the ranking of the rods was performed within each cluster with the help of the Factor Analysis. The hierachization within each group can also be used to identify rods used on readings intensification. The advantage of application of ranking within each group is that a separation of the rods with similar behavior is firstly obtained then the indicated rods will well represent the variability of the cluster. Note that the rods of the automated extensometers are, mostly, among the first in the ranking of each cluster.

As mentioned above, a low communality of a rod indicates that this rod is not strongly influenced by the factors and, in this case, the influence comes from random factors. In the application of Factor analysis within each cluster, there are rods of extensometers with communities between 0,6 and 0,7, in other words, random variation between 30% and 40%. It is indicated that the investigation on the rods is performed in this case.

Furthermore, in order to identify the 24 rods that are the most relevant, we opted, in first place, to identify the 8 best ranked rods from each cluster. In this case, there would be 15 out of the 24 automated rods. This number of rods coinciding with the automated ones in Itaipu would increase with the aid of a specialist for a better interpretation of the results. This specialist would detect that cluster 1, for example, is formed by rods that are extremely important for the monitoring of dams, and that all rods from this cluster should be automated.

This type of analysis was not found in literatures, for this reason the contribution of this study is relevant. It is recommended that this Analysis (process of hierarquization) is repeated periodically (according to the needs indicated by the specialists in this field – in this case, by the engineers' team of Itaipu) what could be done, for example, every two years. This can show the appearance of new rods that are indicated by the performing of readings intensification (that should be investigated), the same could occur with rods that would no longer be indicated.

When there are rods within the clusters with low communalities, it is recommended that they are investigated. Low communality indicates a high percentage of randomness in the data and that can be an indicator of problems with the rods.

These identifications of similar rods can also be used in projecting the control values. In this case, the values of control for each rod can be associated to the readings of the rods that belong to a same cluster.

The final factorial score performs the hierachization of the attributes. In this case the patterns are vectors of which the components (attributes) are the readings of the rods of the extensometers in a certain month. Therefore, the final factorial score performs the hierachization of the months showing whether there is any month that is rather relevant and that deserves greater attention.

Table 4 shows the first 15 months with a higher final factorial score and the last 15 months with lower final factorial scores, considering the 72 rods of extensometers. The values of the 15 first months with a higher final factorial score reveal that all the months are important; there is no month that is rather relevant. Only the month of December does not appear in the first 15 months. Notice that 1995 was the most relevant year and in analyzing the ambient temperature during the period of study it was possible to verify that this occurred due to the high temperature variation. The values of the last 15 months with least final factorial scores revealed that the months of April, May, and June are the most important one, identifying the effects of summer.

As mentioned, cluster 1 shows the effect winter/summer in its readings. For this reason the final factorial score was calculated in order to perform a ranking of the months for cluster 1, to show whether there is any month or some months with greater relevance.

The first 15 months with a higher final factorial score and the last 15 months with least final factorial scores were observed considering only the 11 rods of the extensometer of cluster 1. The values of the 15 first months with higher final factorial scores reveal that the months of September, October, and November are the most relevant ones, identifying the effects of winter. The values of the last 15 months with least final factorial score reveal that the months of March, April, May and June are the most important ones, identifying the effects of summer.

The identification of the months with more significant readings for an external effect (in this case, the effect of summer and of winter on the readings of the rods of the extensometers), can be useful, for example, in the projection of the values of control. Admitting that there are differences in the readings of the rods for the months related above, only the readings performed in these months would be used to define specific values of control for these months.

15 first		15 last	
Final factorial score	Month	Final factorial score	Month
1,755	January/98	-0,761	April/02
1,217	August/95	-0,816	July/03
1,153	January/95	-0,821	Febrary/03
1,091	Febrary/95	-0,821	June/00
0,992	June/95	-0,856	June/02
0,914	March/95	-0,877	May/03
0,902	April/95	-0,904	Febrary/00
0,877	November/96	-0,924	May/00
0,794	May/95	-0,934	May/02
0,781	July/95	-0,965	April/00
0,776	April/97	-0,971	April/04
0,749	October/95	-1,050	April/03
0,741	November/95	-1,061	June/03
0,710	September/95	-1,135	May/00
0,709	Febrary/96	-1,152	March/03

Table 4. Shows final factorial scores of the months in which the readings of the 72 rods of the extensometers were performed.

8. Further research

The application of this methodology is suggested for other instruments and other periods, and the implementation of it in order to define values of control and for anomaly detection. Once the process of ranking is repeated in several periods (every 2 years, for example.) it can show the appearance of new rods which are indicated for performing readings intensification or the appearance of rods that could no longer be indicated (these should be investigated).

9. Conclusions

This manuscript shows a methodology that uses some techniques of the field of Multivariate Analysis, which aim is to select, cluster and rank geotechnical-structural instruments of a Hydroelectric power plant, in our case, the Itaipu hydroelectric power plant, in order to maximize the efficiency and effectiveness of the analysis of the readings.

The methodology showed was applied to the instruments called extensometers, locates in different points of block F of the dam, a total of 30 extensometers that with one, two or three point rods totalized 72 measures of monthly displacement. This measures were stored over a period of 10 years, totalizing 120 readings (January/1995 to December/2004). It is important to remember that 24 measures out of the 72 were automated by the company. The ranking of the instruments would be a way to choose the instruments without any previous knowledge about its location, features, or other characteristics. In this way, it is possible to think in applying this methodology in further decision-making when it relates to the automation of additional new instruments.

The methodology used to analyze the problem of the research was composed by the following form: Ward's method was applied in order to cluster 72 rods of extensometers; at the same time, the Factor Analysis was applied in order to rank the rods; latter, the Factor Analysis was applied within each cluster formed by Clustering Analysis.

In the Factor Analysis applied to the 72 rods, there was not need of investigation for any of the rods, once the communality was high for each of them. Observing the 25 rods of extensometers with the highest communality, 14 rods were identified among the ones that were automated by the team of engineers of Itaipu (the automated rods are the ones considered the most important), in other words, the proposed hierachization method (without previous clustering of the rods) identified 14 of the 24 automated rods.

The Clustering Analysis shows that it is possible to find technical justification for the formation of three clusters. The instruments were clustered according the relevant geological characteristics of the foundation mass, although they were not explicitly shown to the technicians.

By observing the clusters 1, 2, and 3, the factor analysis was applied within each cluster in order to perform the ranking of the rods of the extensometers. It was possible to notice that the rods of the automated extensometers are, most of the time, among the first ones of the ranking of each cluster.

In order to identify the 24 rods that are the most relevant, we decided to identify the 8 best ranked rods from each cluster. In this case, there would be 15 of the 24 automated rods. This number of rods coinciding with the automated ones in Itaipu would increase with the aid of a specialist for a better interpretation of the results. For instance, this specialist would detect that cluster 1is formed by rods that are extremely important for the monitoring of dams and that all rods from this cluster should be automated.

Approaches that are similar to this can be used in many other cases, since there are thousands of large construction works of Civil Engineering that use the system of instrumentation, of which the data can and must receive an appropriate treatment.

The approach of an important problem of engineer, the analysis of the instrumentation data of large construction works, clustering techniques and other techniques were applied, in the context of the Multivariate Statistical Analysis, aiming the identification of the instruments that are the most significant ones to the analysis of the behavior of dams.

Author details

Rosangela Villwock *
Mathematics division, Western Paraná State University, Cascavel, Brasil

Maria Teresinha Arns Steiner, Andrea Sell Dyminski and Anselmo Chaves Neto
PPGMNE, Federal University of Paraná, Curitiba, Brasil

Acknowledgement

The authors would like to thank Itaipu's Civil Engineering team for instrumentation data and technical contributions.

10. References

[1] Icold - International Commission on Large Dams. http://www.icold-cigb.org, 2008.

[2] CBGB - Comitê Brasileiro de Grandes Barragens. Diretrizes para a inspeção e avaliação de segurança de barragens em operação. Rio de Janeiro, 1983. 26 p.

[3] Brasil. Projeto de Lei Nº 1.181/2003. Estabelece diretrizes para verificação da segurança de barragens de cursos de água para quaisquer fins e para aterros de contenção de resíduos líquidos industriais. Disponível em http://www.emtermos.com.br/ADMS/PL_1181.pdf. Acessoem 19/06/2009.

[4] Kalustyan, E. S. Assessment and role of risk in dam building. Hydrotechnical Construction, v. 33, n. 12, 1999.

[5] Yenigun, K.; Erkek, C. Reliability in dams and the effects of spillway dimensions on risk levels. Water Resources Management, v. 21, p. 747-760, 2007.

[6] MenescaL, R. de A. Gestão da Segurança de Barragens no Brasil - Proposta de um Sistema Integrado, Descentralizado, Transparente e Participativo. 769 f. Tese (Doutorado em Engenharia Civil) - Departamento de Engenharia Hidráulica e Ambiental, Universidade Federal do Ceará, Fortaleza, 2009.

[7] ABNT – Associação Brasileira De Normas Técnicas. Ações e Segurança nas Estruturas (NBR 8681), 2003.

[8] Osako, C. I. A Manutenção dos Drenos nas Fundações de Barragens - O Caso da Usina Hidrelétrica de Itaipu. 126 f. Dissertação (Mestrado em Construção Civil). – Setor de Ciências Exatas, Universidade Federal do Paraná, Curitiba, 2002.

[9] FEMA – Federal Emergency Management Agency, Federal Guidelines For Dam Safety, U. S. Department Of Homeland Security, USA, 2004.

[10] Silveira, J. F. A. Instrumenatação e Comportamento de Fundações de Barragens de Concreto. São Paulo: Oficina de Textos, 2003.

[11] Matos, S. F. Avaliação de Instrumentos para Auscultação de Barragem de Concreto. Estudo de caso: Deformímetros e Tensômetros para Concreto na Barragem de Itaipu.

---

* Corresponding Author

106 f. Dissertação (Mestrado em Construção Civil). – Setor de Ciências Exatas, Universidade Federal do Paraná, Curitiba, 2002.

[12] ITAIPU – Itaipu Binacional. Disponível em http://www.itaipu.gov.br/. Acessoem 28/08/2008.

[13] Statgraphics Plus 5.1 – Statgraphics Plus 5.1, Statistical Graphics Corp., Rockville, 2001.

[14] Box, G.E.P.; Jenkins, G.M. Time Series Analysis, forecasting and control. Ed. Holden Day, 1976.

[15] Johnson, R.A.; Wichern, D.W. Applied Multivariate Statistical Analysis. Sixth Edition. New Jersey: Pearson Prentice Hall, 2007.

[16] Hair Jr, J.F.; Anderson, R.E.; Tatham, R.L.; Black, W.C. Análise Multivariada de Dados. Tradução de: Santanna, A. S.; Chaves Neto, A. Porto Alegre: Bookman, 2005.

[17] Freitas, A. A. Data Mining and Knowledge Discovery with Evolutionary Algorithms. New York: Springer, 2002.

[18] Diniz, C. A. R.; Louzada Neto, F. Data mining: uma introdução. São Paulo: ABE, 2000.

[19] Jain A. K., Murty M. N., Flynn P. J. Data clustering: a review. ACM Computing Surveys. v. 31, n. 3, 1999.

Multivariate Analysis in the Sciences: Chemometrics Approach

Chapter 7

Chemometrics: Theory and Application

Hilton Túlio Lima dos Santos, André Maurício de Oliveira,
Patrícia Gontijo de Melo, Wagner Freitas and Ana Paula Rodrigues de Freitas

Additional information is available at the end of the chapter

1. Introduction

This chapter aims to present a chemometrics as important area in chemistry to be able to help work with many among of data obtained in analysis. The term *chemometrics* was introduced in initial 70th years by Svant Wold (Swede) and Bruce Kowalski (USA). According International Chemometrics Society, founded in 1974, the accept definition to chemometrics is (i) the chemical discipline that uses mathematical and statistical methods to design or select optimal measurement procedures and experiments (ii) to provide maximum chemical information by analyzing chemical data [1]. When the study involving many variable became the study in a multivariate analysis, so it is necessary to building a typical matrix and is normal to do a pre-processing. Pre-processing is a procedure to adjust the different factors with different units in values than allow give for each factor the same change to contribute to the model. After, next step is usually the Pattern Recognition method, to find any similarity in your data. In This method is common using the unsupervised group where there are the HCA and PCA analysis and the supervised group where there is the KNN. The HCA analysis (Hierarchical Cluster Analysis) is used to examine the distance among the samples in two dimensional plot (dendogram) and cluster samples with similarity. (Figure 1). Now PCA analysis (Principal Component analysis) is used to try decrease the size data set, without lost information about samples (Figure 2) and KNN used to classify samples using cluster previously know [2].

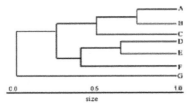

Figure 1. Example of dendogram

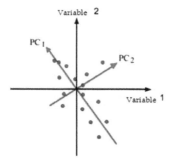

Figure 2. Clustering by PCA

Thus, the chemometrics show to be wide may be used in several area of knowledge.

2. Pattern recognition

In analytical chemistry when we have the data set, it is important find similarities and differences between samples based on measurements. For this is necessary to use methods according with information about the samples. And can be: Unsupervised (HCA and PCA) and Supervised methods (KNN)

2.1. Unsupervised methods

In this group there are two methods: Hierarchical Cluster Analysis (HCA) and Principal Components Analysis (PCA), and the goal is to evaluate if there is any clustering in data set without using the class about samples.

2.1.1. Hierarchical Cluster Analysis (HCA)

The Hierarchical Cluster Analysis is a technique to evaluate the distance between de samples and group in a plot calling dendogram. Theses distance can be calculated utilizing different methods as Euclidean or Mahalanobis or Manhattan distance, for example. For the Euclidean distance is using the equation 1, for Mahalanobis distance is using the equation 2 and for Manhattan distance is using equation 3:

$$\text{Distance} = \sqrt{(X_1 - Y_1)^2 + (X_2 + Y_2)^2 + \cdots + (X_n + Y_n)^2} \qquad (1)$$

Where:
X_n and Y_n are the coordinates of sample X and Y in the nth dimension of row space.

$$\text{Distance} = \sqrt{(X_i - Y_j)^T C^{-1}(X_i + Y_j)} \qquad (2)$$

Where:
X_i and Y_j are column vectors for objects i and j, respective and C is the covariance matrix.

$$\text{Distance} = \sum_{i=1}^{p} |X_i - Y_i| \tag{3}$$

Where:

X_i and Y_i are vectors.

When performed the estimate for distance, so is possible plot the dendogram. A general dendogram is showing below (Figure 3). In this dendogram is possible to see the samples (letters) and the distances (numbers). Samples belonging to clusters A, has a distance of 0,2 from one another. Same time the sample B has a distance 0,5 from cluster A. The value of distance can change according with the distance used to calculate.

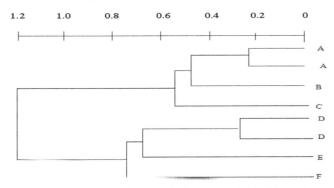

Figure 3. The general dendogram where above are the distances and right side are the samples

2.1.2. Principal Components Analysis (PCA)

The Principal Components Analysis (PCA) has the goal available the distances between the points using few axes in the row plot. In a matrix, each row is the point in the graphic below (Figure 2). So the aim is study the relationship between these samples to find the similarity and differences. In this general example are using two principal components (PC1 and PC2). The first PC (PC1) describes the major points in the graph and the maximum amount of variance, while the PC2 explain the remaining points. It is important to know that the sum of percentage described by PC's must be close 100%. Another propriety of PC's is about de position. The PC's are always perpendiculars one with another.

The PCA technical can be used to define which variables are more important in a process. For this analysis is necessary use the factors (column in the matrix) and objects (row in the matrix). When the aim is to determine which variable are more important for the process is used *loading* and when want studying the relationship between objects is used *scores*

2.2. Supervised methods

The Supervised methods are using when want to construct a model using the class membership for future samples. In this group, KNN is a technical widely used when the goal is this.

2.2.1. K- Nearrest Neighbor (K-NN)

The KNN technical allows use the samples or clusters to identify another samples or clusters. For this is necessary to calculate the distances between them, using a Euclidean or Mahalanobis or Manhattan distance, for example. The minimum distance is calculated and the object is assigned to the corresponding class. A classification is dependent on the number of objects in each class.

3. Chemometrics in medicinal chemistry

3.1. The QSAR principle: Hansch analysis

The development of new drugs is a continuous challenge, before uncountable diseases the lack an adequate pharmaceutical approach. The modern medicinal chemists concern specially with methods based upon rational and quantitative procedures, aiming to focus on potentially efficient candidates. In that context, the use of chemometric methods is very important, in quantitative structure-activity relationship (QSAR) studies, and it presupposes that the biological activity (BA), measured through a biological response (BR), keeps a relationship with chemical structure (CS):

$$BR = f(CS) \tag{4}$$

The first attempt to quantitatively relate chemical structure to chemical behavior in a series of structuraly kindred compounds remounts to 1940's, with Hammett [3] who, studying the meta- and para-substituted benzoic acids at 25°C, stablished linear relationships between the R = X substituted benzoic acid ionization constant (KX) and the ionization constant of the non-substituted benzoic acid (R = H):

$$(m-/p-R)C_6H_4COOH \rightarrow (m-/p-R)C_6H_4COO^- + H^+$$

$$\tag{5}$$

$$\sigma = \log\left(\frac{K_X}{K_H}\right) = \log(K_X) - \log(K_H)$$

The σ constant is group-specific, and represents the electronic effect (inductive and resonance type) pursuit by R group. In 1964, Corwin Hansch [4] combined the use of the electronic constants to the lipophylic parameter (π), which represents the contribution of each R group to the overall lipophylicity:

$$\pi = \log\left(\frac{P_X}{P_H}\right) = \log(P_X) - \log(P_H) \tag{6}$$

where P_X is the X-substituted compound octanol-water partition coefficient, and P_H, the partition coefficient for a non-substituted compound. Thus, a QSAR equation evolves some kind of RB, for example, the negative logarithm of the minimal inhibitory concentration (MIC) for am antimicrobial compounds series (-log(MIC)), and the electronic (σ) and lipophylic effect (π) of the R groups, the makes distinction among the several series representatives, can be expressed as

$$-\log(MIC) = \log\left(\frac{1}{MIC}\right) = a \cdot \sigma + b \cdot \pi + c \tag{7}$$

where a, b and c are the multiple regression coefficients.

The Hansch's hypothesis that RB may be related to specific physico-chemical to each substituent present in the basic skeleton in a congener series of similar BA led to the proposition of numerous descriptors, of different kinds, useful to the identification of the principal effects that show up in drug action.

3.2. Physico-chemical descriptors

There are several physico-chemical descriptors, useful in QSAR studies that can be divided in categories: constitutional, topological, stereochemical and electronic ones, beside the so called indicator variables.

3.2.1. Constitutional descriptors

This kind of descriptor is related to the presence of structural characteristics that can affect the BA, such as: amount of unsaturated bonds, amount of hydrogen-bond donors, average ring size, etc.

3.2.2. Topological descriptors

These are descriptors that represent shape and connectivity, such as: ramifications, spacing groups, unsaturations, etc. The Kier [5] and Wiener [6] descriptors are typical.

3.2.3. Steric (or stereochemical) descriptors

Steric descriptors exist to describe effects related to the size of chemical groups and hindrance behavior. Taft steric descriptor, Es, [7] is a common example.

3.2.4. Eletronic descriptors

These variables are related to molecular electronic densities, and are used to be calculated by quantum methods. One can mention as examples: dipole moments, atomic partial charges, highest occupied molecular orbital energy (HOMO) and lowest unoccupied molecular orbital energy (LUMO).

3.2.5. Indicator variable and Taylor analysis

Indicator variables represent a useful way to convert a qualitative information into quantitative once, just as the occurrence of some kind of structural feature – setting 1 when this feature is present, and 0 otherwise. The Taylor QSAR [8] approach employs indicator variables.

3.3. Chemometric methods applied to drug design

Chemometric statistical methods find in QSAR a large application field, considering that the multivariate problems are inherent to it.

3.3.1. Discriminatory and classificatory methods

Those methods aim the grouping and classification of compounds and variables in classes or categories that share resemblances, and are very interesting in pattern recognition situations and in dimensionality reduction of complex systems.

3.3.2. Principal Component Analysis (PCA)

Principal component (PCs) methods aim to combine correlated variables, projecting them in a new coordinate system, so that fewer variables are obtains, without any intercorrelation. The former coordinates are projects in a new axis system, in which the system variability is maximum along PC1, decreasing along the other axises (PC2, PC3...), all of the orthogonal each other, what allows one to deal just with the first components (usually PC1, PC2 and PC3). Thus, from a multi-variable universe, commonly multicolinear, one can obtain a simpler system with almost the same amount of information. Naming X the data matrix, with I×J dimension (I molecules and J descritors), a PCA generates two matrices, T e L, so that

$$X = TL^T \tag{8}$$

The matrix T is of scores, and represents the position of the compounds in a a novel coordinate system in which the components are its axises, and L is the loading matrix. Plotting the PCs instead of the original descriptors, one obtains groups governed by the similarities among the data.

3.3.3. Hierarchical Cluster Analysis (HCA)

This analysis is also useful to the classification of compounds, permitting visually distinguish the patterns and cluster. The plot resembling a tree, called dendogram, presents similar compounds at the same branches. Those branches are plotted based upon a similarity matrix, **S**, and each component of it is given by the similarity index between two samples k and l, Skl:

$$S_{kl} = 1.0 - \frac{d_{kl}}{d_{max}} \tag{9}$$

In this expression, d_{kl} is the Euclidian distance between k and l, and d_{max}, the maximum distance. Ferreira [9] describes a PCA/HCA analysis for a 25-compound series of 1,4-

naphtoquinones with antitumour activity. Using electronic descriptors, it was possible to distinguish active from inactive compounds (Figure 4). The loadings values indicate that the presence of high-density groups in side chain and terminal positions favours activity. The same profile arise from the dendogram analysis.

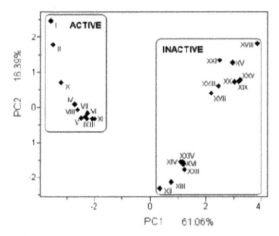

Figure 4. PC1 versus PC2 scores plot.

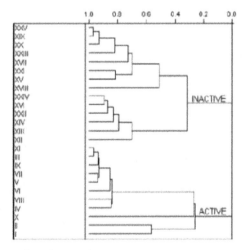

Figure 5. Dendogram for a naphtoquinone series

3.4. Multivariate regression

To construct a QSAR equation (Eq. 1), it is necessary to adopt some kind of multivariate fitting method in order to correlate the descriptors with the BR. The main methods are:

multilinear regression (MLR), principal component regression (PCR) and partial-least squares (PLS).

3.4.1. Multilinear regression (MLR)

The objective of this method is obtaining a relationship among a number of descriptors limited to 1/5 of the number of compounds and the BR, as an equation of the form:

$$BR = \alpha_1\left(\pm\varepsilon_1\right)\cdot D_1 + \alpha_2\left(\pm\varepsilon_1\right)\cdot D_2 + \alpha_3\left(\pm\varepsilon_1\right)\cdot D_3 + \cdots + \varepsilon \tag{10}$$

in which i are the regression coefficients, D_i are the descriptors, ε_i, the coefficients confidence interval and ε, the independent term. The model statistical validation is very important, and it requires the consistency in the D_i descriptors unit, as well as in values magnitude (necessarily). Statistical parameter like the fitting coefficient (r), the sample standard deviation (s), the cross-validation coefficient (q^2) and the Fischer test (F) are used in this task. The MLR is quite sensitive to multicollinearity: variables intercorrelated (tipically, com $r^2 > 0.6$) must not be used together. This is a common problem in multi-descriptor system that may be dealed with other regression methods.

3.4.2. Principal component regression (PCR)

In order to avoid multicollinearity, it is possible to make the regression, not with the descriptors themselves, but with their principal components (PCs) generated in a PCA treatment. The main advantage of this approach is the assurance that every variable are independent and no n-correlated, despite it is necessary to analyze the loading matrix (**L**). In this kind of regression, the variables are defined to maximize the descriptor matrix variance, without force a correlation with the BR

3.4.3. Partial least square (PLS)

Similarly to PCR, the PCs are employed, but in this case, the BR matrix has maximum variability, so that each loading matrix component (**L**) is a good predictor for each BR matrix component. This is the most used regression method, and it is adequate for dealing with 3D-QSAR problems, in which a set of compounds preciously aligned is put within a grid of interaction points with a molecular probe. Each point energy is a variable in the QSAR equation, which are by their turn corrlated with the BR to achieve a tridimensional profile of the critical sites that favours or disfavours the interaction with a hypothetical biological receptor.

4. Design of experiments

The exploration for new sources of energy such as biodiesel is of great importance today as well as their production processes. The factorial design is an important tool to reduce the search time, waste of reagents and hence operating costs [10]. A factorial design is performed with the interest to determine the experimental variables and interactions between variables that have significant influence on the different responses of interest [11]. After selecting the significant variables, we must evaluate the experimental methodology and the influence of a particular variable on the yield of the reaction, a statistical experimental design, full factorial type, in which the independent variables are: the nature and concentration of catalyst temperature and the molar ratio between alcohol and oil and the dependent variable is the yield of esters produced. The variables that were not selected must be fixed throughout the experiment [12]. In a subsequent step must be chosen which planning used for estimating the effect (the effect) of the different variables results in a reduced number of conducting experiments. In the screening study the interactions between the variables (main interactions) and second order, usually obtained by full or fractional factorial designs. In the experiments are evaluated best experimental conditions, as well as their simultaneous effects that influence the yield of the reaction are therefore extremely important for understanding the behavior of the system [13]. The values of "p" and greater than or equal to 0.05 indicate that the factors: variable (1), variable (2), variable (3), variable (4) and the interactions of the variables are statistically significant at 95% reliable, since they are greater than 0.05. These parameters were evaluated at a low level (-1) and high (+1) are significant to the process of positive or negative manner. The Figure. 6 shows the profile of the Pareto chart [7]

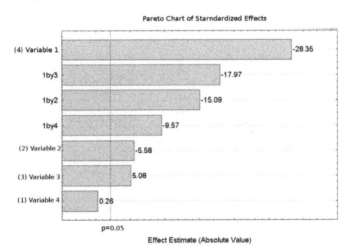

Figure 6. Pareto chart of the resulting fractional factorial design to evaluate the effects of each variable and their interactions in the reaction yield.

The analysis parameters obtained by means of multivariate optimization consists in choosing the conditions for preliminary assessment of experimental variables (fractional factorial design) followed by a response surface methodology (central composite design) made from the screening of the variables that may affect the synthesis of biodiesel. Generated model and the set of significant effects can evaluate through the study of response surface methodology, as shown in Figure 7 and 8, and their interference in the response, ie the yield of the reaction, in which the dark area demonstrates the conditions that process has higher yield.

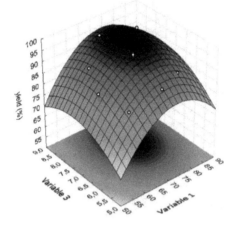

Figure 7. (a) Response surface generated by the central composite design for optimization of variables 1 and 3

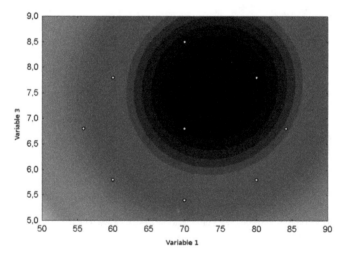

Figure 8. Zoom applied to the surface region of response.

Thus, the statistical analysis shown to be an important tool to evaluate, select and propose new technological routes, either through raw materials and / or process evaluation of the parameters that most influence the transesterification reaction to obtain for biofuels.

5. Conclusion of chapter

This chapter had as aim to show the versatility tools chemometrics in several areas. Was showed application chemometrics theory in drug design, natural products chemistry but it is not limited in theses area. Well, we hope to have expanded the range of chemometrics

Author details

Hilton Túlio Lima dos Santos and Wagner Freitas
University of São Paulo (USP), Brazil

André Maurício de Oliveira
Federal Center of Technology – Minas Gerais (CEFET - MG), Brazil

Patrícia Gontijo de Melo
Federal University of Uberlândia (UFU), Brazil

Ana Paula Rodrigues de Freitas
State University of São Paulo (UNESP), Brazil

6. References

[1] Otto M. Chemometrics- Statistic and Computer Application in Analytical Chemistry. Ed. Wiley-VCH. 1999
[2] Beebe K., Pell R., Seasholtz M., Chemometrics – A Practical Guide. Ed.Wiley Interscience Publication. 1998.
[3] Hammett, Louis P. (1937). J. Am. Chem. Soc. 59: 96.
[4] Hansch, C. (1969) A Quantitative Approach to Biochemical Structure-Activity Relationships. Acct. Chem. Res. 2: 232-239.
[5] Hall, Lowell H.; Kier, Lemont B. (1976). Molecular connectivity in chemistry and drug research. Boston: Academic Press.
[6] Wiener, H. (1947). "Structural determination of paraffin boiling points". J. Am. Chem. Soc. 1 (69): 17–20.
[7] R. W. Taft, Linear free energy relationships from rates of esterification and hydrolysis of aliphatic and ortho-substituted benzoate esters. J. Am. Chem. Soc. 1952, 74, 2729-2732.
[8] Hansch, C.; Sammes, P. G.; Taylor, J. B.; Comprehensive medicinal chemistry: the rational design, mechanistic study & therapeutic application of chemical compounds, Pergamon Press: Oxford, 1990, vol. 4.
[9] Ferreira, M.M.C. J. Braz. Chem. Soc., Vol. 13, No. 6, 742-753, 2002
[10] Charoenchaitrakool, M., & Thienmethangkoon, J. (2011). Statistical optimization for biodiesel production from waste frying oil through two-step catalyzed process. Fuel Processing Technology, 92(1), 112-118.
[11] Berrios, M., Gutiérrez, M. C., Martín, M. A., & Martín, A. (2009). Application of the factorial design of experiments to biodiesel production from lard. Fuel Processing Technology, 90(12), 1447-1451.

[12] Melo, P. G. (2012). Production and characterization of obtained from Macaúba (Acrocomia aculeata). Master degree thesis. Univesity of Federal of Uberlandia – Brazil.

[13] Atadashi, I. M., Aroua, M. K., & Aziz, A. A. (2010). High quality biodiesel and its diesel engine application: A review. Renewable and Sustainable Energy Reviews, 14(7), 1999-2008.

[14] Mingoti, S. A., (2007). Data analysis through methods of multivariete statistical approach applied. Federal University of Minas Gerais

Multivariate Analysis in Vibrational Spectroscopy of Highly Energetic Materials and Chemical Warfare Agents Simulants

John R. Castro-Suarez, William Ortiz-Rivera, Nataly Galan-Freyle, Amanda Figueroa-Navedo, Leonardo C. Pacheco-Londoño and Samuel P. Hernández-Rivera

Additional information is available at the end of the chapter

1. Introduction

The detection of harmful materials in bulk and trace levels present in different matrices: gases/vapors, liquids, and solids is an important consideration for the development of sensors and standoff detection systems for use in National Defense and Security applications. Hazardous chemicals such as highly energetic materials (HEM), homemade explosives (HME), chemical and biological agents are classified as imminent threats, providing terrorists with ways to cause damage to civilians or troops. Chemical warfare agents (CWA) are usually classified as skin-damaging, nerve agents and toxins [1]. Examples of exposures have occurred since World War I with the development of chlorine, phosgene, cyanide and sulfur mustard which were also used in the Iran-Iraq war. In recent times, terrorist attempts involving chemical warfare agents have occurred all over the World as in the case of Sarin (Japan, 1994) and Ricin (London and Paris, 2003) [2]. Threat perception of chemical warfare agents has increased since September 11, 2001 [3,4]. Exposure to low levels of these chemical agents can cause respiratory problems, eye irritation, choking and blisters. LD50 (mg/kg) values for Nerve agents include Tabun (0.08), Sarin (0.01), Soman (0.025) and VX (0.007) [5].

Most studies that have been published about detection of these compounds are based on spectroscopic and chromatographic (GC and HPLC) methodologies [6-11]. Vibrational spectroscopy has demonstrated to be valuable for the detection of HEM, HME, CWA and Simulants (CWAS) and Toxic Industrial Compounds (TIC). In particular, infrared spectroscopy (IRS) and Raman spectroscopy (RS) in various modalities have played unique roles in threat compounds detection [6,12-19]. IRS and RS can be employed for detection of

Explosives and Chemical Warfare Agents, as well as other chemical and biological threats in airports, in military environments, in government buildings and other public safety places. Raman Spectroscopy employs a non-invasive approach that provides high resolution and specificity. Some applications of IRS and RS includes lab based characterization studies as well as forensic field studies of organic and inorganic substances through their vibration signatures.

Optical Fiber Probes (OFP) have been employed in biomedical applications, in communications, in coupling instrumentation to sensing probes and other important modern applications. Moreover, their uses have been extended to excitation and detection of Raman and infrared signals [16, 20]. Fiber optics applications to Raman Spectroscopy can take advantage of a favorable excitation radiation distribution within the sample; allowing the use of higher laser power levels which, in turn, can yield an elevated signal-to-noise ratio (SNR) for a given experiment without increasing the risk of photo-damaging analytes [21, 22]. In 2011 Ramírez-Cedeño et al. utilized Optical Fiber Coupled Raman Spectroscopy (OFC-RS) to detect hazardous liquids concealed in commercial products [6]. They proved that an optical fiber coupled Raman probe was able to discriminate hazardous liquids inside consumer products from common drinks. Elliason et al. (2007) have also reported drug and liquid explosives detection in concealed in colored plastic containers [23].

Recently infrared spectroscopy has shown progress in the use of more powerful IR sources, such as Quantum Cascade Lasers (QCL) by incorporating these devices in IR reflectance, IR transmission and even in IR microscopy applications [24]. QCL-based setups are being developed for in the field applications such as breath analysis, environmental research, airborne measurements, security applications, laser-based isotope ratio measurements, and many others. In particular, for security applications, optical methods are advantageous because of their capability for remote and standoff detection [14, 25, 26]. Due to improvements in QCL development, mid infrared lasers operating at room temperature with high output powers in the CW regime are commercially available and make it possible to set up a ruggedized system that allows sensing of explosives and others materials outside the laboratory and the ability to enter real world scenarios. With laser based standoff spectroscopy, the detection distance can be a few meters to tens of meters. Because of the inverse square dependence of light intensity, larger distances require high power, collimated light sources such as lasers. For homeland security applications such as detection of suicide bombers or improvised explosive devices, a distance of 50-100 m is generally sufficient.

In this chapter we illustrate the usefulness of incorporating powerful statistical routines to all traditional chemistry disciplines: Chemometrics is the application of statistical tools to plan, execute and analyze experiments in chemistry. To illustrate the power of Chemometrics techniques to analyze experiments in chemistry we have chosen three case studies, all involving identification, quantification, discrimination and classification of chemical threats in different matrices from vibrational spectroscopy multivariate data.

In the first case study a remote Raman detection study was performed for quantification of HEM such as pentaerythritol tetranitrate (PETN) present in different mixtures. The remote measurements were carried out at 10 m by employing a frequency-doubled 532 nm Nd:YAG pulsed laser as excitation line, the quantification study was performed by using partial least squares regression analysis (PLS), Interval-PLS (iPLS) and Synergy-PLS (siPLS) as chemometrics tools to achieve the best correlation between the remote Raman signal and the concentration (%) of PETN explosive in a mixture with pharmaceutical compound.

In the second case study discussed, Optical Fiber Coupled Raman Spectroscopy (OFP-RS) was employed at 488 nm excitation wavelength for detection of a Chemical Warfare Agent Simulant (CWAS): triethyl phosphate (TEP) inside different commercial bottles: green-plastic, green-glass, clear-plastic, clear-glass, amber-glass and white plastic. Aqueous solutions were also used to discriminate on various bottle materials in commercial beverage products.

In a third case study a Fourier Transform infrared interferometer with MCT detector was used for recording vibrational infrared signals from nitroaromatic and peroxide explosives in the gas phase. Furthermore, a dispersive IR HEM detection system using a quantum cascade laser was used to record MIR spectral signals of 2,4,6-trinitrotoluene, pentaerythritol tetranitrate and cyclotrimethylenetrinitramine on travel baggage surfaces. Several models were generated with and without preprocessing throughout MIR spectrum.

2. Description of methodologies

Explosives compounds employed in the studies illustrated were pentaerythritol tetranitrate (PETN) cyclotrimethylenetrinitramine (RDX), triacetone triperoxide (TATP), 2,4-dinitrotoluene (2,4-DNT), 2,4,6-trinitrotoluene (TNT) were synthesized in the laboratory according to methods described by Urbanski [27] and pharmaceutical active compound: acetaminophen (APAP) was purchased from Aldrich-Sigma Chemical Co. (Milwaukee, WI). Powder mixtures were prepared employing the both compounds (PETN and APAP) mentioned above and the compositions of PETN in the mixtures was varied from 1 to 34% w/w. Components of the mixtures were carefully weighed and mixed using an agate mortar ensuring homogeneity throughout the sample with a total weight of 200 mg.

Figure 1. Commercial bottles (glass and plastic) used to TEP detection using Optical Fiber Coupled Raman spectroscopy.

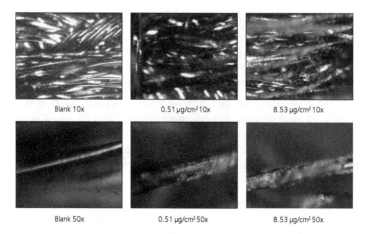

Figure 2. Microscopic Views of PETN on travel baggage substrates; zoom used was 10x and 50x.

A chemical warfare agent simulant: (CWAS) triethyl phosphate 99% (TEP) from Acros Organics (New Jersey, USA) was used to demonstrate the detection and quantification capabilities of this kind of compound by Optical Fibers Coupled Raman spectroscopy. Several formulations were made with the stimulant in their commercial containers: Snapple® Kiwi-Strawberry (Snapple Group USA), Pepsi (PepsiCo Inc., USA), Mountain Dew® (PepsiCo Inc., USA), Heineken® (Mendez & Company, PR), Mott's apple juice® (Mott's LLP., Rye Brook, NY), Leche Suiza® Low Fat Grade A (Suiza Dairy Corp., Puerto Rico) and Malta India® (PR Brewing Co., Mayaguez, PR). The containers can be seen in Figure 1.

For gas phase measurements of 2,4-DNT and TATP using infrared spectroscopy vapors were collected in a gas cell (10 cm long and 3.5 cm diameter) by slowly heating the sample to generate vapors. Finally, traces of PETN, TNT and RDX were placed on travel baggage surface with size of 1 in^2. Figure 2 shows a view of how PETN was deposited on travel baggage substrates at different surface concentration. Figure 3 shows a summary the experiments carried out using vibrational spectroscopy techniques such as infrared and Raman. This figure shows the modalities used, the target tested and the chemometrics models utilized.

For detection of PETN mixed with APAP, Raman spectra of mixtures were acquired by employing a Remote Raman system. This system has been described in detail previously [16]. The prototype was modified using a Headwall Photonics Raman Explorer™ spectrograph with optical layout for 532 nm (Headwall Photonics, Inc.) instead of the Andor spectrometer. The remote Raman system consisted of a MEADE ETX-125 Maksutov-Cassegrain telescope (125 mm clear aperture, 1900 mm focal length f /15). The reflecting collector was coupled to the Raman spectrometer with non-imaging, 200 μm diameter optical fiber (model SR-OPT-8024, Andor Technology, Belfast, Northern Ireland). A frequency-doubled 532 nm Nd:YAG pulsed laser system (Quanta Ray INDI Series, Newport-Spectra Physics, Mountain View, CA) was used as the excitation source. The maximum energy/pulse of the laser at 532 nm was 25 mJ, and it operated at a repetition rate of 10 Hz. The pulse width was approximately 5-8 ns, and the beam divergence was less than 0.5 mrad. A gateable, intensified CCD detector (iStar™ ICCD camera, Model DH-720i-25F-03, Andor Technology, Belfast, Northern Ireland) was used as the photon detector. Andor Technology Solis™ software for spectroscopic, imaging and time-resolved studies was used for spectral data acquisition and processing from the intensified and gated CCD detector. Using this software, the data could be acquired in both imaging and spectroscopic modes. In this experiments, each mixture was placed into a stainless steel sample holder of 0.6 cm in diameter where 30 ft·lb of pressure was applied to generate a tablet. Remote Raman spectra of mixtures were measured at a target at telescope standoff distance of 10 m, in the Raman Shift region 450-3000 cm^{-1} using an pulsed laser operating at 532 nm excitation line with a constant energy of 25mJ/pulse (at head) and 100 pulses were applied to achieve spectra with good Signal to Noise. A total of 10 spectra were collected for each mixture acquiring around 56 spectra in the specific Raman shift range.

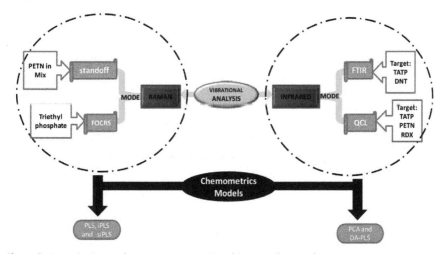

Figure 3. General scheme of experiments using IR and Raman vibrational spectroscopy.

In the detection of TEP chemical warfare simulant in commercial bottles, Raman experiments were performed with a custom built setup (Figure 4) using the strong blue excitation line from an argon ion laser INNOVA 310/8 from Coherent, Inc. at 488.0 nm. The first strand of optical fiber (non-imaging, 600 μm diameter, model AL 1217, Ocean Optics, Inc.) as well as the second (200 μm diameter, model SR-OPT 8024, Andor Technologies Inc.) were used to couple the Raman probe to which a set of laser line filter (to clean satellite lines) and Semrock RazorEdge™ edge filter was used to filter the Rayleigh scattered light. An Andor Technologies spectrograph: Shamrock SR-303i (aperture: f/4; focal length: 303 mm; wavelength resolution: 0.1 nm or 4.2 cm^{-1} at the excitation wavelength) equipped with a 1200 grooves/mm grating was used to analyze the Stokes scattered light. A high performance, back thin illuminated CCD camera (Andor Technologies model # DU970N-

UVB) with quantum efficiencies of 90% (200 cm^{-1}) to 95% (3600 cm^{-1}) served as light detector (Figure 4) and calibration was performed using cyclohexane. Detection was performed with a light source in order to be carried out in the high-background environment conditions. In this experiment, six different bottle materials: clear-glass, green-glass, brown-glass, clear-plastic, white-plastic and green-plastic were used to measure the amount of simulant (triethyl phosphate) within the container. Mixtures ranged from 0% to 100% (v/v) of simulant and water, simulant and commercial beverage product were analyzed.

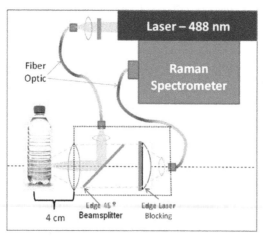

Figure 4. Experiment setup for detection of chemical warfare simulant in commercial bottles.

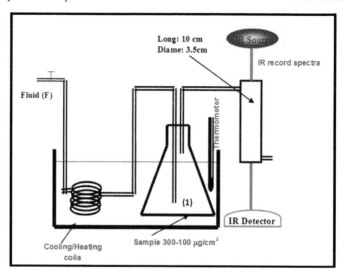

Figure 5. Schematic diagram of experimental setup used in the IR detection. Traces of explosives in gas phase were dragged by air flow and transported to a gas cell for detection.

The IR equipment used for the experiments was a model IFS 66v/S interferometer (Bruker Optics, Billerica, MA). For the experiments described, the system was equipped with a DTGS detector and a potassium bromide (KBr) beamsplitter. A spectroscopic measurement averaged 20 scans at a resolution of 4 cm^{-1} using OPUS Version 4.2 software in the range of 7500 – 400 cm^{-1}. Target chemicals were TATP, 2,4-DNT and 2,4,6-TNT. Second, an EM-27 Open Path FT-IR interferometer (Bruker Optics, Billerica, MA) was used to obtain the IR spectral information of gas phase TATP samples with a (TE) cooled MCT detector. Third: Quantum Cascade Laser (QCL) based dispersive IR spectrometer LaserTune™ (Block Engineering, Marlborough, MA) was used to obtain the IR spectral information of TATP samples. An Agilent 6890 gas chromatograph (GC) coupled to an Agilent 5893 mass selective detector (MSD) with a capillary column: HP-5 MS 5% phenyl methyl siloxane, Length: 30.0 m, 250.0 μm in diameter and 0.25 μm of film thickness was used for detecting the presence of explosive TATP, 2,4-DNT and 2,4,6-TNT in the gas phase.

Figure 5 shows a schematic diagram of the experimental setup used in the investigation. Samples of 100-300 $\mu g/cm^2$ of explosives were placed on the bottom of a 500 mL Erlenmeyer flask at the position labeled (1) in Figure 5. A flow of dry air (1-16 mL/s) at temperatures of 0-38°C was used to transfer the solid explosives to the gas phase. The measurements as function of temperature were done in two forms, scanning the range of temperature and fixed temperature point measurements. Traces of explosives in gas phase were dragged from the surface by the air flow and transported to an IR gas cell for detection. Spectra were recorded using the instrument first at 4 cm^{-1} of resolution and 25 scans were used for the experiments. A total of 1089 spectra of air with 2,4-DNT, 1194 spectra of air with TATP and 2200 spectra of air were recorded to generate the models. On the OP EM-27 active mode experiments were carried out at lab temperature (25°C) at 30 scans and 4 cm^{-1} resolution. The spectral range used was from 700 to 1600 cm^{-1}. Experiments using QCL LaserTune™ active mode experiments were carried out at lab temperature of 20 °C at 1 spectrum and 4 cm^{-1} resolution. The spectral range used was from 830 to 1430 cm^{-1}. The presence of TATP in air was determined by GC-MS, and the concentration of 2,4-DNT in air for different flow conditions and temperatures were calculated by calibration curves from GC-μECD. Finally, explosive traces (PETN, TNT and RDX) were deposited on travel baggage of 1 in^2 size of and analyzed with the QCL spectrometer.

3. Chemometrics to vibrational spectral analysis

The automation and computerization of laboratories have been carried out with various important consequences. One of them is the rapid acquisition of large amounts of data. However, it is well know that acquiring such large amount of data is far from to providing appropriate answers quicker. Obtaining vibrational spectroscopy multivariate data is not synonymous with possessing vibrational information. The later must be interpreted and placed in context to convert it into useful information for the user. Chemometrics is the field of chemistry that provides the user with the required tools to enable that capability.

A great deal of chemometrics tools have been developed and tested. The most used of these tools to identify, quantify and classify data sets are those that make use of principal components analysis (PCA), partial least squares (PLS), discriminant analysis (DA), and their combined usage: PLS-DA and hierarchical cluster analysis (HCA). PCA transforms a set of variables into fewer variables (called factors, rank, dimensions or principal components) which contain most of the information (variance) of the initial data set [28-31].

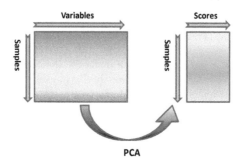

Figure 6. Simplified scheme for a PCA analysis.

The PCA algorithm seeks to save the information from a large number of variables in a small number of uncorrelated components, with minimal loss of information. The main reasons for performing a PCA are: reduction of the number of variables to fewer dimensions that contain as much information as possible and have uncorrelated dimensions (used to avoid multi-collinearity in multiple regressions, among other things). An important method for qualitative analysis of spectral data is principal component analysis. PCA is a method for the investigation of the variation within a multivariable data set. The first step in PCA is to subtract the average value or spectrum from the entire data set, this is called mean centering. The largest source of variation in the data set is called principal component PC1. The 2nd largest source of variation in the data, which is independent of PC1, is called PC2. Principal components form a set of orthogonal vectors. For each one of the data points, the projection of the data point onto the P1 or P2 vector is called a score value. Plots of sample score values for different principal components, typically P1 versus P2 are called score plots. Score plots provide important information about how different samples are related. Principal component plots, also called loading plots, provide information about how different variables are related to each other. In practical cases, PCA uses a single X matrix which is represented by the infrared spectra. PCA is a purely qualitative analysis (does not give a quantitative value that establishes how different are a spectral dataset) to visualize if there is variability between a set of IR spectra. PCA can thus also be used to detect the presence of outliers. Figure 6 shows a simplified PCA scheme [28-29].

Partial least squares (PLS) regression is a quantitative spectral decomposition technique that is closely related to PCA regression. The importance of PLS is that it is used to design and build robust calibration models for multivariate quantitative analysis. PLS actually uses the concentration information during the decomposition process. This causes spectra containing higher constituent concentrations to be weighted more heavily than those with lower concentrations. The main idea of PLS is to get as much concentration information as possible into the first few loading vectors (number of component, factors, ranks or principal components). PLS regression consists of two fundamental steps. First, to transform the X predictive matrix (spectra) of order n × p (n = number of samples and p = number of variables: cm^{-1} or nm), in an matrix of components or latent variables uncorrelated, T = (T1, ..., Tp) of order n × p, called PLS components, using the Y response vector (concentrations) of order n × 1; this contrasts with the principal component analysis in which the components are obtained using only the X predictive matrix . Second, to calculate the estimated regression model using the Y response original vector as predictive, PLS components. The dimensionality reduction can be applied directly on the components as they are orthogonal. The number of PC required for the regression analysis must be much smaller than the number of predictors. There is a number of ways of expressing these, a convenient one being (Eq.1 and 2) [29]:

$$X = T.P + E \tag{1}$$

$$c = T.q + f \tag{2}$$

Figure 7 illustrates a simplified scheme for PLS: X represents the experimental measurements (e.g. spectra) and c (or Y) the concentrations. The first equation above appears similar to that of PCA, but the scores matrix also models the concentrations, and the vector q has some analogy to a loadings vector. The matrix T is common to both equations. E is an error matrix for the X block and f an error vector for the c block. The scores are orthogonal, but the loadings (P) are not orthogonal, unlike in PCA, and usually they are not normalized.

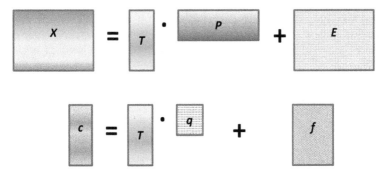

Figure 7. Simplified scheme for a PLS transformation.

Chemometrics techniques have improved the last years in order to save time and computational resources in different models to be used without compromising the quality of results. In 2000 Norgaard and co-workers [32,33], developed different algorithms useful in Chemometrics field called interval partial least squares (iPLS) and this tool was presented for use on NIR spectral data. Recently, this new graphically oriented local modeling procedure has been implemented in many areas of research such as petrochemicals, pharmaceutical and beverage industry [34-36].

The principle of the iPLS is to optimize the predictive capability of PLS regression models and to support in interpretation. This algorithm which develops local PLS models on equidistant subintervals of the full-spectrum region. Its major objective is to provide an overall perspective of the significant information in different spectral subdivisions, thereby focusing on important spectral regions and removing interferences from other regions. The sensitivity of the PLS algorithm to noisy variables is highlighted by the informative iPLS plots [32]. For synergy interval PLS (siPLS), the basic principle of this algorithm is the same as iPLS first, it is to split the data set into a number of intervals (variable-wise), next, to develop PLS regression models for all possible combinations of two, three or four intervals. Thereafter, RMSECV is calculated for every combination of intervals. The combination of intervals with the lowest root mean square error of cross-validation (RMSECV) is selected.

Finally, cluster analysis is the name given to a set of techniques that seeks to determine the structural characteristics of multivariate data sets by dividing the data into groups, clusters, or hierarchies. For cluster analysis, each sample is treated as a point in an n-dimensional measurement space. The coordinate axes of this space are defined by the measurements used to characterize the samples. Cluster analysis assesses the similarity between samples by measuring the distances between the points in the measurement space. Samples that are similar will lie close to one another, whereas dissimilar samples are distant from each other [28].

In this chapter, remote Raman detection experiments were performed to quantify HEM such as PETN present in mixtures with non-HEM. The remote measurements were carried out at 10 m employing a frequency-doubled 532 nm Nd:YAG pulsed laser as excitation source. The quantification study was performed by using PLS, iPLS and siPLS as chemometrics tools to achieve the best correlation between the remote Raman signal and the concentration (%) of PETN explosive in a mixture with pharmaceutical compound. Discrimination of chemical warfare agent simulant (CWAS) TEP concealed within commercial beverage bottles using Optical Fiber Coupled Raman Spectroscopy with the use of different chemometrics techniques such as PLS, PLS-DA. Finally infrared spectroscopic information analysis using Chemometrics was designed and implemented in the detection of HEM: 2,4-DNT, TATP, PETN and RDX, present at trace level on surfaces and in air were analyzed by Chemometrics Enhanced Vibrational Spectroscopy.

4. Multivariate Detection and Quantification from Vibrational Spectra

4.1. Remote raman experiments

Different preprocessing methods such as vector normalization (VN), mean centering (MC), auto scaling (AS), multiple scattering correction (MSC), standard normal variate (SNV) and first and second derivatives have been developed to improve a good multivariate quantification. The 56 remote Raman spectra taken from PETN detection in mixes with APAP were randomly split into two groups: a first group with the 70% of the data for calibration and cross validation (training set) and a second group for external validation (test set) formed by the remaining 30% of the data. The quantitative model was performed by using chemometrics tools, such as PLS, iPLS and siPLS. The PLS program used was from PLS-ToolBox™ (Eigenvector Research Inc.) for use with MatLab™. The iPLS and siPLS algorithms used in this work were carried out by employing iToolbox™, (downloaded from http://www. models.kvl.dk). The performance of the final PLS, iPLS and siPLS models were evaluated according to the root mean square error of cross-validation (RMSECV), a leave-one-sample-out cross-validation method and the predictive ability of the models were assessed by the root mean square error of prediction (RMSEP) and the correlation coefficient (R). In general for all the PLS models RMSECV were calculated as follows:

$$RMSECV = \sqrt{\frac{\sum_{i=1}^{ncal}(c_p-c_i)^2}{n_{cal}}} \qquad (3)$$

Where c_i and c_p are the experimental and predicted concentration, respectively, of the ith calibration sample when situated in a left out segment, n_{cal} is the number of calibration samples in the training set. The number of PLS components included in the model is selected according to the lowest RMSECV. This procedure is repeated for each of the preprocessed spectra. For the test set, the root mean square error of prediction (RMSEP) is calculated as follows:

$$RMSEP = \sqrt{\frac{\sum_{i=1}^{ntest}(c_i-c_p)^2}{n_{test}}} \qquad (4)$$

The best model with the overall lowest RMSECV will be selected as final model. Correlation coefficients between the predicted and the true concentration are calculated for both the calibration and the test set, which are calculated as follows from Equation 5, where $\bar{C}_i$ is the mean of the experimental measurement results for all samples in the train and test sets.

$$R = \sqrt{1 - \frac{\sum_{i=1}^{n}(c_p-c_i)^2}{\sum_{i=1}^{n}(c_i-\bar{c}_i)^2}} \qquad (5)$$

The implementation of new methodologies for enhanced detection of hazardous compounds such as explosives is always attractive for many countries principally for defense and security applications. Terrorist employ different ways to pose threats and make illegal acts against military and civilian people. According to this situation our study is focused on detection of explosives present in mixture prepared intentionally with a pharmaceutical product by employing remote Raman detection and chemometrics tools. Remote Raman spectra of PETN, APAP in mixtures of them are illustrated in Figure 8. The results show that mean centering (MC) pre-processing method was the most successful method for correcting background and was selected for construction of further models because they presented small improvement in RMSEC.

The full spectrum was split in 20 independent intervals and the RMSECV values for PLS models constructed with different intervals is shown in Figure 9. Models with no intervals were better than PLS models with all variables (dotted in line) and the intervals 6 (1185.2-1328.9 cm⁻¹), 9 (1619.8 -1755.4 cm⁻¹), and 19 (2878 -2988.4 cm⁻¹), presened the lowest RMSECV values where more variability exists. These values are shown in Table 1. The number of latent variables required for the models obtained using different intervals is the numbers shown inside the rectangles.

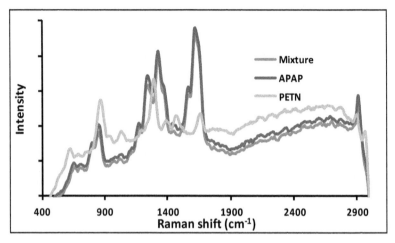

Figure 8. Remote Raman spectra of PETN, APAP and mixture of them, collected at 10 m of target to collector distance employing 532 nm laser with 100 pulses of 25 mJ/pulse.

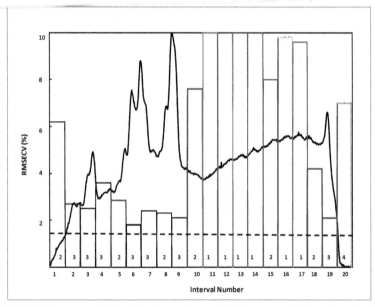

Figure 9. RMSECV values for PLS models obtained for the 20 different intervals (bars) used in iPLS models. The horizontal dotted line represents the RMSECV value for the PLS model with all variables. Numbers inside the rectangles are the optimal number of latent variables.

Models	LV[a]	Intervals	NV[b]	RMSEC V (%)	RMSEP (%)	R$_{CV}$	R$_P$
PLS	6	All	730	1.8	2.2	0.978	0.979
iPLS	3	6	37	2.0	2.8	0.986	0.976
	3	9	37	2.5	3.1	0.976	0.969
	3	19	36	2.7	2.4	0.972	0.988
siPLS	7	3,9,19	110	1.4	1.8	0.993	0.992

a Latent variable b Total number of variables.

Table 1. Full-cross-validated PLS, iPLS, and siPLS models for prediction of PETN in the range 1.0–34.0% Remote Raman spectra. All models are based on MC data.

In synergy interval-PLS (siPLS) model calibration, the number of intervals was also optimized according RMSECV values. Table 1 shows the results of siPLS model calibration when the spectra were split into different number of intervals. The optimum siPLS model was obtained with the combination of 3 intervals (3, 9 and 19) and 7 PLS components. The lowest RMSECV was 1.4, compared with RMSECV values obtained for PLS model with all variables and iPLS models. According to the statistical results illustrated in Table 1, it is important to establish that iPLS or siPLS models with 4 or more intervals (data not shown) including intervals 10-18 were explored. These intervals correspond to noisy areas which were not eliminated in order that the models could choose the spectral region of larger variability. The capability of prediction of siPLS models was better when compared to the other models As shown in the correlation plots in Figure 10, there is a good relationship between the True and Predicted concentration (%) for PETN, with R$_{CV}$ values of 0.993. This can also be appreciated by the good prediction of the test set of samples with values of RMSEP of 1.8% for the corresponding explosives. The final model separated the vibrational spectra into 20 intervals, 7 latent variables were used and the intervals number 3, 9 and 19 were combined The selected intervals included regions of 724.2 - 876.7cm^{-1},1619.8-1755.4 cm^{-1} and 2878 -2988.4 cm^{-1}, The first Raman shift region correspond to NO$_2$ scissoring mode and O-N stretching band; the second region is relevant for NO$_2$ asymmetric stretching mode and C=O stretching band; the third region represents the C-H stretching mode [37-39].

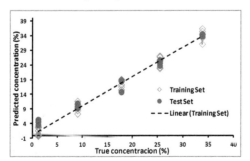

Figure 10. Predicted vs. True PETN concentration for siPLS model using 3, 9, and 19, intervals and 7 latent variables.

4.2. Optical fiber probe raman spectroscopy experiments

In the optical fibers coupled Raman spectrum of TEP, shown in Figure 11, the CWAS has characteristics peaks at 733 cm^{-1} (PO$_3$ symmetric stretching mode), 813 cm^{-1} (PO$_3$ asymmetric stretch), 1032 and 1098 cm^{-1} (C–O stretch), 1162 cm^{-1} (CH$_3$ rocking) and 1279 cm^{-1} (P–O symmetric stretch) [6]. Mixtures of TEP with commercial liquids were measured in their corresponding commercials bottles. TEP concentration varied from 0 to 100 (%v/v). In Figure 12, TEP Raman spectra are shown for different bottle materials. At all concentrations, the TEP characteristic peaks could be distinguished within the different types of materials of the container with the exception of brown glass and white plastic. These two bottle materials had lower transmittance in the 200 to 1400 cm^{-1} region and TEP characteristic peaks in the 2700 to 3200 cm^{-1}region. UV-VIS spectra (data not shown) show the increased absorbance in bottle materials such as white plastic and amber glass (Malta™). This confirms nature of the low intensity Raman peaks in the region (200-1400 cm^{-1}) shown in Figure 12. When light scatters turbid materials, such as amber glass or white plastic, the material is absorbing or blocking the light when compared to clear glass and clear plastic. Thickness of the bottle material and coloration also play a role in absorbance and transmission. The high intensity peak at 2300 cm^{-1} corresponds to the background light (mercury vapor from fluorescent lamps). This peak is shown with higher intensity in Raman spectra of brown glass and white plastic in comparison to the rest of spectra due to the increase in integration time for these two bottle materials. All bottle materials were subject to background light in order to simulate real-time conditions found in military, airport and other environments where a light source is involved. This analysis is based on increased absorbance shown in the UV-VIS Spectra for different bottle materials (data not shown).

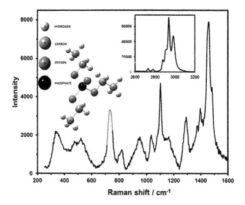

Figure 11. Raman vibrational spectrum of TEP excited at 488 nm.

Calibration models were performed with PLS regression model to distinguish between the samples that contain TEP in aqueous solutions compared to the solutions with TEP and the commercial product. In Figure 13, eight PLS regression models are chosen in order to show the marked difference between the best and the worst regression model, each of these with and without pre-processing steps. Since integration times were normalized for each bottle, Limits of Detection were similar with the exception of amber/brown glass (Malta™). The aqueous solutions show a better R^2 values than the mixtures with the commercial product. For clear glass (Snapple™), the R^2 value is 0.9925 for aqueous solutions compared to 0.9747 for the mixtures with the commercial product. The R^2 values for Malta™ in aqueous solutions showed a significant increase with optimization (0.4193 without preprocessing and 0.9508 with optimization). However, optimization with Malta™ shows a lower R^2 value 0.7646 compared to 0.8047 without preprocessing.

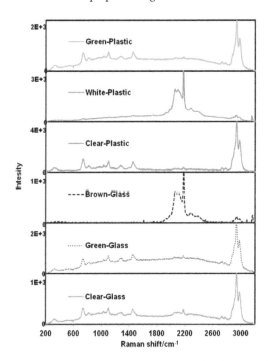

Figure 12. Raman spectra of Triethyl Phosphate in various types of bottle materials

It is clear that the R^2 values increase in PLS regression models for aqueous solutions since water does not present strong signatures in Raman Spectroscopy. Every other PLS regression model (green plastic, green glass, clear plastic, clear glass, and white plastic) in aqueous and beverage solution presented nearly similar limits of detection. Each of these limits improved with their respective preprocessing step (vector normalization, standard normal variate and mean centering). With the help of integration time for each bottle material, normalization was achieved with the limits of detection and root-mean-squared error cross-validation (RMSECV). These values were found as acceptable in an average between the best models of approximately 2.5%. The Limits of Detection for PLS methods were estimated using the equation 6 [40]:

$$LOD = \Delta\,(\alpha,\beta,\upsilon) \times RMSEC(\sqrt{1+h_0}) \qquad (6)$$

Root mean squared error of calibration (RMSEC) was obtained from the square fit errors $[(c_{predicted} - c_{true})2/\upsilon]^{1/2}$ where the sum extends to all samples of the calibration set. The degrees of freedom were then calculated as $\upsilon = n - F - 1$ where F is the number of latent variables and n is the number of samples in the set. The distance of the predicted sample from zero concentration to the calibration set's mean is the leverage h_0. Ultimately, $\Delta\,(\alpha,\beta,\upsilon)$ corresponds to a statistical parameter that notices the α and β probabilities of falsely stating presence/absence of the chemical warfare agent stimulant. Since $\upsilon \geq 25$, we used $\alpha = 3.4$ for the LOD. LOQ values as per Eq. 7 were studied at a concentration with a Relative Standard Deviation (RSD) of 15% as stated by Felipe-Sotelo *et al.* [40]:

$$LOQ = 100x(RMSECx(1 + h_0)^{0.5}RSD(\%) \qquad (7)$$

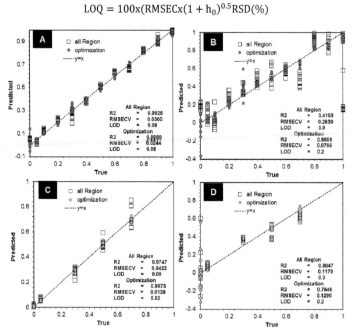

Figure 13. A) PLS models of TEP in aqueous solution in Snapple™ container (clear glass materials) with (vector normalization) and without preprocessing. B) PLS models of TEP in aqueous solution inside Malta™ container (amber glass materials) with (mean centering, standard normal variate) and without preprocessing. C) PLS models of TEP mixtures with the commercial product Snapple™ (clear glass materials) with (vector normalization) and without preprocessing. D) PLS models of TEP mixtures with the commercial product Malta™ (amber glass materials) with (mean centering) and without preprocessing.

Comparing limits of detection (Figure 13) the same integration times were used for aqueous and commercial beverage bottle solutions. A and B (Figure 5) show Snapple™ and Malta™ in aqueous solutions with TEP. Figures 13C and 13D in the same figure show mixtures of

TEP with commercial products and with less data (5, 30, 70 and 0 %v/v) due to limited time. Snapple has lower limits of detection which is favorable for detection of chemical warfare stimulants in commercial bottles made out of various materials. When comparing limits of detection for aqueous solutions versus solutions with commercial beverage product inside commercial bottles, limits of detection are considerably lower. R^2 prediction values were higher in aqueous solutions since water does not present significant Raman signal. Limits of detection were found as low as 1 percent for white plastic. Optimization also improves or lowers the limits of detection as shown in Figure 13.

Table 2 shows Limits of Detection and Quantification (LOD and LOQ respectively) for various commercial beverage bottle solutions with TEP for the best models. Preprocessing options include Vector Normalization (V.N.), No preprocessing (N/A), Mean Centering (M.C.), Constant Offset Normalization (C.O.N.), First Derivative (F.D.) and Multiplicative Scatter Correction (M.S.C). Higher limits of detection and quantification for amber glass and clear plastic were presented due to their dark coloration in bottle material (amber) and commercial beverage product (Pepsi and Malta). An unexpected low value for limits of detection and quantification for white plastic was observed. This may be due to the low amount of trials (5 instead of 10 for 5, 30, 50 and 70 (%v/v of TEP) as was done with other bottle materials due to the high integration times for this material. Even though TEP, a surfactant agent, did not present a homogeneous solution with milk, integration times were normalized in order to obtain a better model of a clear linear regression with an R^2 value of 0.9987 and excellent limits of detection of 0.01(1%).

COMMERCIAL BEVERAGE MIXTURES					
Green Glass	White Plastic	Amber Glass	Clear Glass	Clear Plastic	Green Plastic
LOD (%) 3	1	26	4	22	3
LOQ (%) 8	3	77	11	66	9
Preprocess V.N.	V.N.	N/A	M.C. + V.N.	C.O.N.	M.S.C. + M.C.
AQUEOUS MIXTURES					
LOD (%) 11	7	16	8	8	4
LOQ (%) 33	21	48	22	25	12
Preprocess V.N.	F.D. + V.N.	F.D. + V.N.	V.N.	V.N.	N/A

Table 2. Limits of Detection and Quantification for the PLS models of TEP in commercial beverage bottles and aqueous mixtures along with their respective preprocessing methods.

4.3. Gas phase infrered spectroscopy experiments

Multivariate calibration methods such as Partial Least Squares (PLS) models can be formulated as a regression equation [41, 42]. The equation in metrical form is $Y = XB$, where

B is computed as $B = W(PTW)^{-1} QT$ and **W** is the matrix of weights of **X**, **Q** is the loadings matrix of **Y**, and **P** is the **X** loadings matrix. In this study, the **Y** matrix represents the dependent variables but this is changed from continuous to discrete variation, and contains information about different classes of objects [43-45], it is a simple two states function: 1 represents the condition for the presence of explosive in the sample and 0 stands for the absence of explosive in the sample analyzed. By these means it will be possible to decide if an explosive substance is present or not in a sample. The values originating from the analysis: wavenumber range or parts of spectra are the independent variables (**X** matrix). In this study the loading vectors or number of component (**B** matrix) were used for independent variables in the DA.

TATP and 2,4-DNT in air were detected using FTIR spectroscopy. At trace levels, the vibrational signatures are not easily perceptible. Vibrational signatures of explosive can be confused with vibrations arising from the background air components. Thus the first task was to determine the possible interference of the two spectra. Figures 14a and 14b show the spectra of flowing gas that contains TATP and 2,4-DNT traces. The characteristic infrared signals of TAPT at 1200 cm^{-1} and at 1550 cm^{-1} for 2,4-DNT can be observed in Figure 14 which confirms the presence of these compounds in air. Linear Combination Analysis in the form of Partial Least Squares (PLS) was calculated for all FTIR spectra (7500-600 cm^{-1}). Two and four vectors were required to find the perturbation produced by TATP and 2,4-DNT respectively, on the normal flowing air IR spectrum. The discriminating function used was a two position switch type function: On – Off (Yes/No). The nomenclature in the DA was for classification of samples in terms of "Disc-1=TATP present" or "Disc-0 = TATP not present" in air, for TATP; and "Disc-1 = 2,4-DNT present" or "Disc-0 = 2,4-DNT not present" in air, for 2,4-DNT. The results were presented in the form of histogram, where the y-axis is the frequency and x-axis is the discrimination function. Also the prediction of new sample was present in this form, (Figures 15 and 16) in these graphs, the improvement of models, when vectors are added successively is observed.

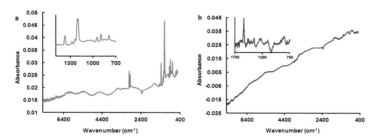

Figure 14. FTIR vibrational spectra of gas explosive in air: a. TATP and b. 2,4-DNT traces.

The best discriminant function was selected based on statistical significance (p) and the percentage of cases correctly classified (PCCC) [46]. The validation was done by internal jackknifing validation and external validation. Internal validation: in this method, each spectrum was successively removed from the data set, and then it was discriminated from a new model built from the remaining spectra. This procedure was done for each one of the spectra in the data set, and the predicted discriminations were then compared with the experimental observations. The generated percentage of cases correctly classified is called the cross-percentage of cases correctly classified (PCCCC). External validation: before making the model, 100 spectra of air, 100 spectra air with TATP and 50 spectra air with 2,4-DNT were taken from the data set randomly. These spectra were analyzed by the validation model.

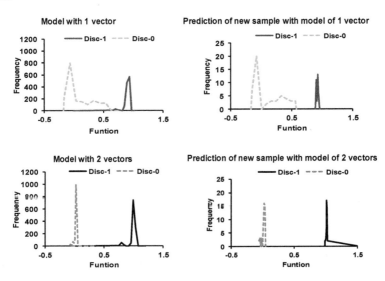

Figure 15. Histogram for discrimination models of TATP and external validation.

For the PCA analysis of TATP in air spectra were recorded using the EM-27 and the LaserScope™ instruments. A total of 60 spectra were recorded from clean air and 120 spectra from air with TATP present using EM-27 and 35 spectra were recorded from clean air and 30 spectra from TATP present in air using LaserScope™. All PCA analysis including any preprocessing in the spectral data were run using PLS-Toolbox software. PCA runs were made with the raw data and using different preprocessing treatments. The preprocessing treatments used were: auto scale, smoothing, SNV-standard normal variation, Mean center, auto scale + 1st derivate, auto scale + 2nd derivate, mean center + 1st derivate, mean center + 2nd derivative, MSC-multiplicative scattering correction. The algorithm used to carryout smoothing and derivatives was that ofSavitzky-Golay (every 11, 17, 21 and 31 points). During the PCA runs it was not necessary to eliminate spectral data.

The infrared data from clean air and air with TATP were run together in the PCA model for each instrument used. Figure 17 shows the Scores plots for the PCA obtained. Figure 17a shows the first two principal components from spectral data using the EM-27 FTIR spectrometer with a Globar source Figure 17b shows the first two principal component analyses from spectral data of TATP detection from LaserScope™ spectrometer using

Quantum Cascade Laser Source. The best results achieved for both PCA models (illustrated in Figures 17a and 17b) were using raw data. Both results allowed classifying gas phase TATP explosive from clean air. In Figure 17 can be noticed that PC1 tends to relate the differences between the IR dataset two.

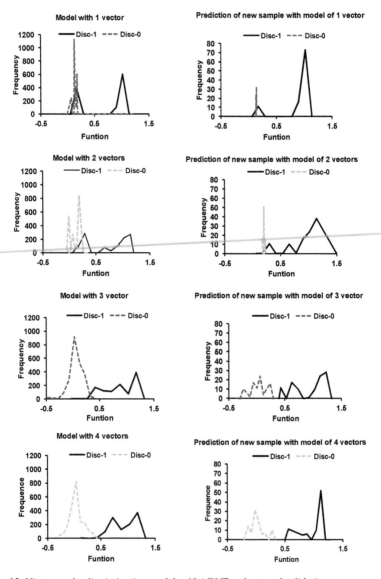

Figure 16. Histogram for discrimination models of 2,4-DNT and external validation.

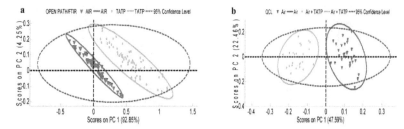

Figure 17. Score plots for the PCA, presented as (a) PC2 vs. PC1 for TATP detection from EM-27 FTIR spectrometer using Globar source and (b) PC2 vs. PC1 for TATP detection from LaserScope™ spectrometer using QCL source.

Other hand, the loadings plot were analyzed too to support the results from PCA with the finality of knowing which spectral signals cause differences between the dataset. Figure 18 shows the PC1 loading from Figure 17b, in this it can be seen than the spectral features are equal to infrared vibrational signal of reference TATP. Some signal recording can be tentatively assigned according to B. Brauer and J. Oxley as [47,48]: 891.8 cm^{-1} to O–C–O and Me–C–Me sym str, and Me–C–O asym str; 946 cm^{-1} to C-O str; 1197.6 cm^{-1} to O–C–O and Me–C–Me asym str, Me–C–O sym str; 1205 cm^{-1} to O–C–O and Me–C–Me sym str and finally 1234 cm^{-1} to C-C str,

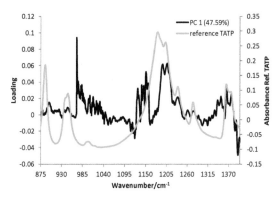

Figure 18. Figure 18. Loading plot for PC1 from PCA for TATP detection from LaserScope™ spectrometer using QCL source.

4.4. Quantum cascade laser based ir reflectance experiments

OPUS 6.0 Software (Bruker Optics, Billerica, MA, USA) was used to analyze the data obtained. Four spectra were obtained for each sample. The spectra were carried out using as backgrounds: substrate without explosive. PLS was applied to the data using different preprocessing treatments: raw data, auto scale. Mean center, auto scale + 1st derivative, auto scale + 2nd derivative, mean center + 1st derivative, mean center + 2nd derivative. The spectral range was 1000-1600 cm⁻¹. PLS shown below was that best results obtained. Figure 19 shows PLS plots of RDX deposited on TB. The best result was achieved using the spectral region of 1000-160 cm⁻¹ and using mean centering as preprocessing. A total of 10 latent variables or factors were necessary to obtain a R^2 and RMSECV equal to 0.9915 and 2.32 µg/cm2, respectively.

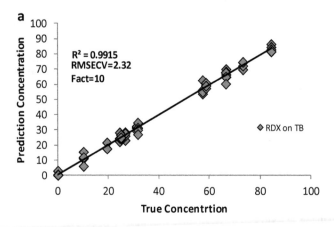

Figure 19. PLS of RDX on travel baggage (TB) as substrate.

Figure 20 shows PLS of PETN deposited on TB. The best resulted was achieved using the spectral region of 1000-1600 cm⁻¹ and using mean centering as preprocessing treatment. A total of 10 latent variables or factors were necessary to obtain a R^2 and RMSECV equal to 0.9994 and 1.82 µg/cm2, respectively.

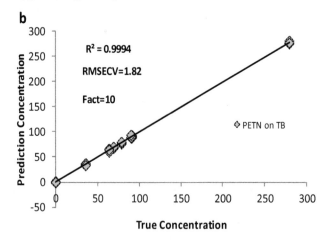

Figure 20. PLS of PETN on Travel Baggage as substrate.

5. Conclusion

Raman and infrared vibrational techniques were used for the detection of highly energetic materials and chemical warfare agents simulants in different matrices such as pharmaceutical mix, commercials bottles and travel baggage. The analysis of the spectral data allows emphasizing certain results. Satisfactory results were found for the quantification of explosives with good values of R^2cv, RMSECV. Reliable predictions obtained by remote sensing based on Raman spectroscopy at remote distance of 10 m employing 532 nm laser as excitation source. Remote Raman system using the appropriate chemometrics tools such as PLS, iPLS and siPLS promises to be a reliable technique for finding the existence of highly energetic material such as PETN deliberately hidden in matrices with similar chemical structures.

Partial Least Squares (PLS) calibration models reported limits of detection very low for white plastic in commercial beverage bottle solutions which was the best model. Due to the bottle material and commercial beverage product coloration, Malta was the worst model with reported limits of detection more elevated. Limits of Detection and Quantification for commercial bottles were compared in aqueous and mixtures. It is observed that limits of Detection were significantly lower for mixtures of TEP with the commercial product. Integration times were the same for both aqueous and commercial beverage bottle solutions (each normalized with respect to bottle material, color and thickness). Water does not transmit significant Raman signal, which would make limits of detection lower for aqueous solutions. However, commercial beverage bottles mixtures showed lower limits of detection than aqueous solution since the beverage solutions inside each bottle showed significant Raman signal and, therefore, increasing CWAS presence in the spectra.

PLS-DA model and discriminant analysis was done to detect TATP and 2,4-DNT traces in fluid air. The region of 600 to 7500 cm^{-1} was highly significant in the discrimination with p < 0.00001 and 100 % discrimination for two vectors for TATP and four vectors for 2,4-DNT. These results show the ability of the Chemometrics methods to discriminate between vapor phase explosive (2,4-DNT) and air.

Results obtained from principal component analysis to determine the presence of peroxides explosives such as TATP when they are in gas phase mixed with air shown be useful for distinction between TATP vapors and air. The principal component analysis from infrared spectral data used little PC for predict the variability of the spectral data, being the first two PC more important. PC1 loadings confirm the results from the PCA because it contained features from TATP spectrum. Other hand, the PLS model were shown chemometrics tool for quantify explosive such as RDX and PETN on substrate of the real world such as travel baggage.

In general, vibrational spectroscopy systems designed based on this work should be useful for National Defense and Security applications, for screening hazardous liquids in government installations, seaports and in public installations to improve defense against terrorist attacks.

Author details

John R. Castro-Suarez, William Ortiz-Rivera, Nataly Galan-Freyle,
Amanda Figueroa-Navedo, Leonardo C. Pacheco-Londoño
and Samuel P. Hernández-Rivera
ALERT DHS Center of Excellence, Department of Chemistry
University of Puerto Rico-Mayagüez, Mayagüez, PR

Acknowledgement

Support from the U.S. Department of Homeland Security under Award Number 2008-ST-061-ED0001 is also acknowledged. However, the views and conclusions contained in this document are those of the authors and should not be considered a representation of the official policies, either expressed or implied, of the U.S. Department of Homeland Security.

This contribution was supported by the U.S. Department of Defense, Proposal Number: 58949-PH-REP, Agreement Number: W911NF-11-1-0152. The authors also acknowledge contributions from Dr. Richard T. Hammond from Army Research Office, DOD.

6. References

[1]   Augerson W.S. A Review of the Scientific Literature as it Pertains to Gulf War Illnesses vol. 5. Rand; 2000.

[2]   Vale A., Bradberry S., Rice, P. & Marrs, T.C., Chemical Warfare and Terrorism. The Medicine 2003;31(9) 26-29.

[3]   Goozner B., Lutwick L.I. & Bourke E. Chemical Terrosism: a primer for 2002. J. Assoc. Acad. Minor. Phys. 2002;13(1) 14-18.

[4]   Rosenbloom M., Leikin J.B., Vogel S.N., Chaudry Z.A. Biological and Chemical agents: A brief synopsis. Am. J. Ther. 2002;9(1) 5-14.

[5]   Gendering C., Roggan Y., Collet C. Pharmaceutical applications of vibrational chemical imaging and chemometrics: A review. Journal of Pharmaceutical and Biomedical Analysis 2008;48(3) 533-553.

[6]   Ramırez M.L, Gaensbauer N., Felix H., Ortiz-Rivera W.; Pacheco-Londoño L.C., Hernandez-Rivera S.P. Fiber Optic Coupled Raman Based Detection of Hazardous Liquids Concealed in Commercial Products. International Journal of Spectroscopy 2012;1(1) 1-7.

[7]   Caron T., Guillemot M., Montméat P., Veignal F., Perraut F., Prené P., Serein-Spirau F. Ultra-trace detection of explosives in air: Development of a portable fluorescent detector. Talanta 2010;81(1-2) 543-548.

[8] Hilmi A., Luong J. Micromachined Electrophoresis Chips with Electrochemical Detectors for Analysis of Explosive Compounds in Soil and Groundwater. Environ. Sci. Technol. 2000;34(14) 3046-3050.

[9] Yinon J. Trace analysis of explosives in water by gas chromatography—mass spectrometry with a temperature-programmed injector. J. Chromatogr. A. 1996;742(1-2) 205-209.

[10] Szakal C., Brewer T.M. Analysis and mechanisms of cyclotrimethylenetrinitramine ion formation in desorption electrospray ionization. Anal. Chem. 2009;81(13) 5257-5266.

[11] Miller C.J., Yoder T.S. Explosive Contamination from Substrate Surfaces: Differences and Similarities in Contamination Techniques Using RDX and C-4. Sens. Imaging: An International Journal 2010;11(2) 77-87.

[12] Pacheco-Londoño L.C., Ortiz-Rivera W., Primera-Pedrozo O.M, Hernández-Rivera S.P. Vibrational spectroscopy standoff detection of explosives. Anal. Bioanal. Chem. 2009;395 (2) 323-335.

[13] Banas K., Banas A., Moser H.O., Bahou M., Li W., Yang P., Cholewa M., Lim, S.K. Multivariate Analysis Techniques in the Forensics Investigation of the Postblast Residues by Means of Fourier Transform-Infrared Spectroscopy. Anal. Chem. 2010;82(7) 3038–3044.

[14] Van Neste C.W., Senesac L.R., Thundat T. Standoff spectroscopy of surface adsorbed chemicals. Anal. Chem. 2009;81(5) 1952–1956.

[15] Hildenbrand J., Herbst J., Wollenstein J., Lambrecht A., Razeghi M., Sudharsanan R., Brown G.J. Explosive detection using infrared laser spectroscopy. Proc. SPIE 7222(1), 72220B; 2009.

[16] Ortiz-Rivera W., Pacheco-Londoño L.C., Hernandez-Rivera S.P. Remote Continuous Wave and Pulsed Laser Raman Detection of Chemical Warfare Agents Simulants and Toxic Industrial Compounds. Sensing and Imaging: An International Journal 2010;11(3) 131-145.

[17] Ortiz W., Pacheco L.C., Castro J.R., Felix H., Hernandez-Rivera, S.P. Vibrational spectroscopy standoff detection of threat chemicals. Proc. SPIE Int. Soc. Opt. Eng. 8031: 803129; 2011.

[18] Castro J.R., Pacheco L.C., Vélez M., Diem M., Tague T.J., Hernandez S.P. Open-Path FTIR Detection of Explosives on Metallic Surfaces. in Fourier Transforms: New Analytical Approaches and FTIR Strategies. G. S. Nikolić, ed. InTech Open, Croatia, 978-953-307-232-6; 2011.

[19] Castro J.R., Pacheco L.C., Vélez M., Diem M., Tague T.J., Hernandez S.P. Passive Mode FT-IR Standoff Detection of Nitroaromatic High Explosives on Aluminum Substrates. (MS No.11-06229R2). Submitted and accepted in Applied Spectroscopy; 2012.

[20] Primera O.M., Soto Y.M., Pacheco L.C., Hernández S.P. Detection of High Explosives Using Reflection Absorption Infrared Spectroscopy with Fiber Coupled Grazing Angle Probe/FTIR. Sens. Imaging: An International Journal 2009;10(1-2)1-13.

[21] Blades M.W., Schulze H.G., Konorov S.O., Addison C.J., Jirasek A.I., Turner, R.F.B. New Tools for Life Science Research Based on Fiber-Optic-Linked Raman and Resonance Raman Spectroscopy. ACS Symposium Series; Vol. 963 1-13; 2007.

[22] Boere I.A., Bakker Schut T.C., van den Booger J., de Bruin R.W.F., Puppels G.J. Use of fibre optic probes for detection of Barrett's epithelium in the rat oesophagus by Raman Spectroscopy. Vibrational Spectroscopy 2003;32(1) 47-55.

[23] Eliasson C., Macleod N., Matousek P. Noninvasive Detection of Concealed Liquid Explosives Using Raman Spectroscopy. Analytical Chemistry 2007;79(21): 8185-8189.

[24] Curl R.F., Capasso F., Gmachl C, Kosterev A.A., McManus, B., Lewicki R., Pusharsky M., Wysocki G., Tittel, F.K. Quantum cascade lasers in chemical physics. Chem. Phys. Lett. 2010;487(1–3) 1-18.

[25] Hildenbrand J., Herbst J., Wollenstein J., Lambrecht A., Razeghi M., Sudharsanan R.; Brown G.J. Explosive detection using infrared laser spectroscopy. Proc. SPIE 7222(1), 72220B; 2009.

[26] Hinkov B, Fuchs F., Kaster J. M., Yang Q., Bronner W., Aidam R., Kohler K., Carrano J.C., Collins C.J. Broad band tunable quantum cascade lasers for stand-off detection of explosives. Proc. SPIE 7484(1), 748406; 2009.

[27] Urbanski T. Chemistry and technology of explosives. New York: Macmillan Company; 1964.

[28] Beebe K.R., Pell R.J., Seasholtz M.B. Chemometrics: A Pactrical Guide. New York: John Wiley & Sons; 1998.

[29] Brereton R. G. Applied Chemometrics for Scientists. The Atrium, Southern Gate: John Wiley & Sons Ltd. Chichester; 2007.

[30] Massart D.L., Vandeginste B.G.M., Buydens L.M.C. Data Handling in Science and Technology Handbook of Chemometrics and Qualimetrics Part B. The Netherlands: Elsevier Science B.V.; 1997.

[31] Massart D.L, Vandeginste B.G.M., Buydens L.M.C., Handling in Science and Technology Handbook of Chemometrics and Qualimetrics Part A. The Netherlands: Elsevier Science, B.V.; 1997.

[32] Nørgaard L., Saudland A., Wagner J., Nielsen J.P., Munck L., Engelsen S.B. Interval Partial Least Squares Regression (iPLS): A Comparative Chemometrics Study with an Example from Near-Infrared Spectroscopy, Applied Spectroscopy 2000;54(3) 413-419.

[33] Leardi R., Nørgaard L. Sequential application of backward interval PLS and Genetic Algorithms for the selection of relevant spectral regions. Journal of Chemometrics 2004;18(11) 486-497.

[34] Delfino I., Camerlingo C., Portaccio M., Della Ventura B., Mita L., Mita D.G., Lepore M. Visible micro-Raman spectroscopy for determining glucose content in beverage industry. Food Chemistry 2011;127(2) 735–742.

[35] Nørgaard L., Hahn M., Knudsen LB., Farhat I.A., Engelsen S.B. Multivariate near-infrared and Raman spectroscopic quantifications of the crystallinity of lactose in whey permeate powder. International Dairy Journal 2005;15(12) 1261-1270.

[36] Chena Q., Zhao J., Liu M., Jianrong C., Jianhua L. Determination of total polyphenols content in green tea using FT-NIR spectroscopy and different PLS algorithms. Journal of Pharmaceutical and Biomedical Analysis 2008;46 (3) 568-573.

[37] Gruzdkov Y.A., Gupta Y.M.J. Vibrational Properties and Structure of Pentaerythritol Tetranitrate. Phys. Chem. A. 2001;105(25) 6197-6202

[38] Lewis I.R., Daniel N.W., Griffiths P.R. Interpretation of Raman Spectra of Nitro Containing Explosive Materials. Part I: Group Frequency and Structural Class Membership. Applied Spectroscopy 1997;51 1854-1867.

[39] Pestaner J.P., Mullick F.G., Centeno J. A. Characterization of acetaminophen: molecular microanalysis with Raman microprobe spectroscopy. J. Forensic. Sci. 1996;41 1060-1063.

[40] Felipe M., Cal M.J., Ferre J., Boque R., Andrade J.M., Carlosena A. Linear PLS regression to cope with interferences of major concomitants in the determination of antimony by ETAAS. J. Anal. At. Spectrom. 2006;21(1) 61-68.

[41] Miller J.N., Miller J.C. Statistics and Chemometrics for Analytical Chemistry. Fourth edition, Pearson Prentice Hall; 2000.

[42] McLachlan G.J. Discriminant Analysis and Statistical Pattern Recognition. Hoboken, New Jersey: John Wiley & Sons Inc. Chichester; 1992.

[43] Liu C.L., Sako H., Fujisawa H. Discriminative Learning Quadratic Discriminant Function for Handwriting Recognition. IEEE Transactions on Neural Networks 2004;15(2), 430-444.

[44] Alsberg B.K., Kell D.B., Goodacre R. Variable Selection in Discriminant Partial Least-Squares Analysis. Anal. Chem. 1998;70(19) 4126-4133.

[45] Brereton R.G. Chemometrics. Data Analysis for Laboratory and Chemical Plant. The Atrium, Southern Gate: John Wiley & Sons Ltd. Chichester; 2003.

[46] Olivero J., Vivas R., Pacheco L., Johnson B., Kannan K. Discriminant analysis for activation of the aryl hydrocarbon receptor by polychlorinated naphthalenes. Journal of Molecular Structure: Theochem. 2004;678(13) 157–161.

[47] Brauera B., Dubnikova F., Zeiri Y., Kosloff R., Gerbera R.B. Vibrational spectroscopy of triacetone triperoxide (TATP): Anharmonic fundamentals, overtones and combination bands. Spectrochimica Acta Part A. 2008;71 1438–1445.

[48] Oxley J., Smith J., Brady J., Dubnikova F., Kosloff R., Zeiri L., Zeiri Y. Raman and Infrared Fingerprint Spectroscopy of Peroxide-Based Explosives. Applied Spectroscopy 2008;62(8) 906-915.

Classification and Ordination Methods as a Tool for Analyzing of Plant Communities

Mohammad Ali Zare Chahouki

Additional information is available at the end of the chapter

1. Introduction

Community ecologists aim at understanding the occurrence and abundance of taxa (usully species) in space and time and the goal of all studies in plant ecology, is finding spatial and temporal interactions add to the complexity of vegetation systems. Hence for this purpose, it is necessary to imply best statistical methods (Causton, 1988)

In this study, some important classification and ordination methods such as cluster analysis (CA), Two way Indicator Species Analysis (TWINSPAN), Polar Ordination (PO), Nonmetric Multidimensional Scaling (NMS), Principal component analysis (PCA), Detrended Correspondence Analysis (DCA), Canonical correspondence analysis (CCA), Redundancy analysis (RDA) will be explained briefly.

Ordination (or inertia) methods, like principal component and correspondence analysis,and clustering and classification methods are currently used in many ecological studies (Anderson, 1971; Gauch et aL, I982a; Orloci, 1978; Whittaker et al, 1967; Legendre & Legendre, 1998).

The choice of the mathematical method of analysis is mainly determined by availability rather than an accurate knowledge of the properties and limitations of the possible different methods (Legendre & Legendre, 1998).

This study aims to explain these methods as tool for analyzing of plant Communities. The use of multivariate analysis has been extended much more widely over the past 20 years. Much more is included on techniques such as Canonical Correspondence Analysis (CCA) and Non-metric Multidimensional Scaling (NMS), Principal component analysis (PCA) and another technique to include plant communication and plant-environment relationships (Kent, 2006). It is a main objective in data analysis to distinguish random from deterministic components. Therefore spatial and temporal interactions add to the complexity of vegetation systems (Wildi, 2010).

Some basic knowledge of Classification and Ordination methods that influence vegetation ecology might be needed to understand the examples presented in this study.

Studying the vegetation distribution pattern is a basic aspect of the design and management (Zhang et al., 2006). Quantitative separation was studied by previous scholars to investigate the contribution of environmental factors to the whole or different layers of plant community distribution pattern. (Zhang et al., 2004). Actually, natural plant communities are distributed continuously, and they are composed of plant communities at different succession stages which response to environmental factors differently.

2. Data

Commonly, data interpreted using Classification and ordination, are collected in a species by sample data matrix, similar to the matrixes presented below.

Species abundances as main data matrix will also use the standardized set of no redundant environmental variables for use with clustering and indicator species analysis. Will be not need a second matrix, although Cluster analysis will produce one for use during this exercise. For explaining the issue, using data from Study area that is located in the North-East of the Semnan province in center of Iran (35º 53′ N, 54º 24′ E to 35º50′ N, 53º43′ E) (Fig 1).

270	plots					
9	Species					
	Q	Q	Q	Q	Q	Q
	Ar.si	Se.ro	Eu.ce	St.ba	Zy.er	...
1	10	0.5	0.5	0.5	0.5	...
2	1.75	3.75	0.5	0.5	0.5	...
3	1	0.5	3.75	1	0.5	...
4	3.75	0.5	3.75	0.5	0.5	...
5	6.25	0.5	0.5	1.75	0.5	...
6	1	0.5	3.75	1	0.5	...
7	10	0.5	1	1	0.5	...
8	3.75	0.5	1	0.5	0.5	...
9	3.75	0.5	1	0.5	0.5	...
10	6.25	0.5	1.75	0.5	0.5	...
11	6.25	1.75	3.75	0.5	0.5	...
12	3.75	0.5	0.5	0.5	1	...
13	10	0.5	15	1	0.5	...
14	3.75	0.5	1.75	0.5	0.5	...

Table 1. Data matrix using in Classification (using ordinal scale of Van-der-Marrel)

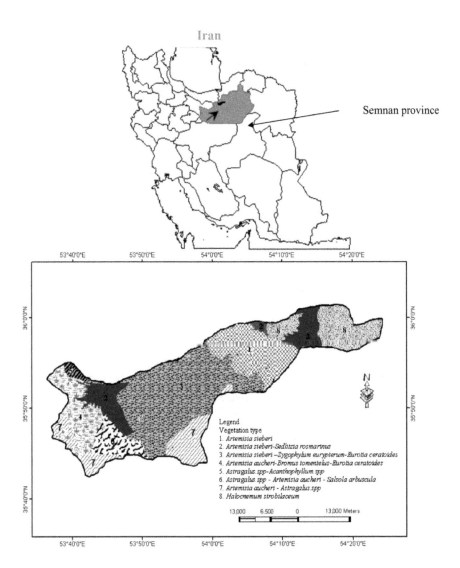

Figure 1. Location of study area and the distribution of the vegetation types.

The below is a relatively simple data set. However, it is easy to imagine that a true data set may encounter dozens of species over 270 of samples. Complex sample by species matrices represent dozens to 270 of dimensions which are impossible to visualize or interpret. Even graphed, species response curves of large community data sets can be nearly impossible to interpret.

A quantitative survey of the vegetation is carried out during 2009-2010. In each of the studied types, soil and vegetative attributes were described within quadrates located along three 150m transverse transects. Quadrate size was determined for each vegetation type using the minimal area method. Considering variation of vegetation and environmental factors, forty five quadrates with a distance of 50m from each other were established in each vegetation type. Sampling method was randomized systematic. Floristic list, density and canopy cover percentage were determined in each quadrate. Vegetation cover data were recorded using ordinal scale of Van-der-Marrel (1979).

In fact, the cover data transformed using an eight-point scale ((0–1=0.5, 1–2.5=1.75, 2.5–5=3.75, 5–7.5=6.25, 7.5–12.5=10, 12.5–17.5=15, 17.5–22.5=20, 22.5–27.5=25, >27.5=30)

Sample data may include measures of density, biomass, frequency, importance values, presence/absence, or any number of abundance measures.

Ordination can help us find structure in these complicated data sets. By using various mathematical calculations, ordination techniques will identify similarity between species and samples. Results are then projected onto two dimensions in such a way that species and samples most similar to one another will be close together, and species and samples most dissimilar from one another will appear farther apart (as shown at this study).

6	type				
22	factor				
	Q	Q	Q	Q	Q
	gr1	gr2	clay1	clay2	...
A.sieberi-E.ceratoides	28.2016	45.6333	22.1667	21	...
H.strobilaceum	8.04E+00	2.83667	26.8	29.3333	...
A.sieberi-Z.eurypterum	35.5167	50.0333	17.5	16	...
Z.eurypterum-A.sieberi	27.5933	36.44	16.6667	23.6667	...
A.au-As.ssp-B.tomentelus	28.48	47.6433	26.4533	33.1667	...
S.rosmarinus	28.15	37.475	22.8333	20.6667	...

Table 2. Data matrix using in Ordination

Data analysis was performed on the species, averaging all plots per site. All numerical analyses were done with the PC-ORD, V. 4 package (McCune and Mefford, 1999).

3. Methods of classification analysis

Classification method is an act of putting things in groups. Most commonly in community ecology, the "things" are samples or communities. Classification can be completely subjective, or it can be objective and computer-assisted (even if arbitrary). Hierarchical classification means that the groups are nested within other groups. There are two general kinds of hierarchical classification: divisive and agglomerative. A Divisive method starts with the entire set of samples, and progressively divides it into smaller and smaller groups. An agglomerative method starts with small groups of few samples, and progressively groups them into larger and larger clusters, until the entire data set is sampled (Pielou, 1984).

Cluster analysis, on the other hand, seeks to divide the n quadrates into groups of high internal similarity with respect to species or characters used. In the classical approach of Williams & Lambert (1959), the so-called Association-Analysis, communities are defined by the presence or absence of single species. This is highly dependent on the vagaries of sampling; many workers have felt the method may result in botanical over simplification, so that nowadays polythetic methods are more usually applied.

From the above discution, it can be seen that ordination and cluster analysis are not competing approaches and provided the ecologist is cautious in making inferences, both can reasonably be applied in the examination of multivariate samples (Pritchard & Anderson, 1971).

In classification of species the basic idea is that a characteristic species combination (or at least a group of differentiated species) should gather samples containing these species into clusters of similar samples (Tavili & Jafari, 2009).

In fact, Classification assumes from the outset that the species assemblages fall into discontinuous group, whereas ordination starts from the idea that such assemblages very gradually

3.1. Cluster analysis

Clustering, sometimes simply a synonym of classification, but more usually referring to agglomerative classification.

Clustering is a straightforward method to show association data, however, the confidence of the nodes are highly dependent on data quality, and levels of similarity for cluster nodes is dependent on the similarity index used. Krebs (1999) shows that mean linkage is superior to single and complete linkage methods for ecological purposes because the other two are extremes, either producing long or tight, compact clusters respectively. There are, however, no guidelines as to which mean-linkage method is the best (Swan, 1970).

The objective of Cluster Analysis is to graphically show the relationship between cluster analyses and your individual data points.

The resulting graph makes it easy to see similarities and differences between rows in the same group, rows in different groups, columns in the same group, and columns in different groups. Groups of rows and columns relate to each other, could be seen graphically. Two-way clustering refers to doing a cluster analysis on both the rows and columns of your matrix, followed by graphing the two dendrograms simultaneously, adjacent to a representation of your main matrix. Rows and columns of your main matrix are re-ordered to match the order of items in your dendrogram (Mucina, 1997).

Fig 1 showed dendrogram of Cluster analysis (study area: North East of Semnan rangelands, Iran). Grouping was performed using Euclidean distance and the Ward method. Species with less than 2 entries in the matrix were deleted from the analysis.

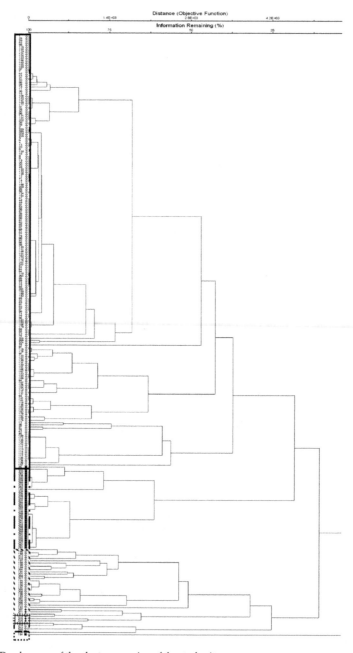

Figure 2. Dendrogram of the cluster grouping of the study sites

Cluster analysis can be performed using either presence–absence or quantitative data. Each pair of sites is evaluated on the degree of similarity, and then combined sequentially into clusters to form a dendrogram with the branching point representing the measure of similarity.

In fact, the aim is to form a hierarchical classification (i.e. groups, containing subgroups) which is usually displayed by a dendrogram (as shown in above). The groups are formed from the most similar objects are first joined to form the first cluster, which is then considered an object, and the joining continues until all the objects are joined in the final cluster, containing all the objects (fig 2).

The procedure has two basic steps: in the first step, the similarity matrix is calculated for all the pairs of the objects (the matrix is symmetric, and on the diagonal there are either zeroes – for dissimilarity – or the maximum possible similarity values). In the second step, the objects are clustered (joined, amalgamated) so that after each amalgamation, the newly formed group is considered to be an object, and the similarities of the remaining objects to the newly formed one are recalculated. The individual procedures (algorithms) differ in the way they recalculate the similarities (Leps & Smilauer, 2003).

Major types of hierarchical, agglomerative, polythetic clustering strategies followed:

1. Nearest Neighbor
2. Farthest Neighbor
3. Median
4 Group Average
5. Centroid: It (weighted) mean of a multivariate data set. Can be represented by a vector. For many ordination techniques, the centroid is a vector of zeros (that is, the scores are centered and standardized). In a direct gradient analysis, a categorical variable is often best represented by a centroid in the ordination diagram.
6. Ward's Method (Ward's is also know as Orloci's and Minimum Variance Method)
7. Flexible Beta
8. McQuitty's Method

This analysis of the vegetation - environment relations and the classification of the Semnan rangelands, is also relevant for the rangelands of arid and semi arid in Iran, and provides a base line for other studies intended to conserve and restore this ecosystem.

Although clustering is an agglomerative classification technique and TWINSPAN is divisive, both produced comparable results. In addition, TWINSPAN provided indicator species.

In addition, to identify species with particular diagnostic value and to confirm clustering results, the floristic data were classified with the two way indicator species analysis (TWINSPAN) (Hill, 1979).

3.2. TWINSPAN

The TWINSPAN method is one of the more popular classification programs used in plant community ecology (Hill 1979; Hill et al. 1975). The two approaches differ between two classification methods is that, TWINSPAN creates groups and also finds indicator species for those groups, while Cluster analysis requires a before-the-fact assignment of group membership as input. In this case, will be used hierarchical clustering to identify groups for vegetation classification. TWINSPAN produces no graphical output. The biggest volume of the result is the description of each division. For each division, TWINSPAN identifies the indicator pseudo species and their signs (positive or negative for one end of the ordination or the other) and lists the samples assigned to each subgroup. Two popular agglomerative polythetic techniques are Group Average and Flexible. McCune et al. (2002) recommend Ward's method in addition. Gauch (1982a) preferred to use divisive polythetic techniques such as TWINSPAN.

This method works with qualitative data only. In order not to lose the information about the species abundances, the concepts of pseudo-species and pseudo-species cut levels were introduced. Each species can be represented by several pseudo-species, depending on its quantity in the sample. A pseudo-species is present if the species quantity exceeds the corresponding cut level.

TWINSPAN is a program for classifying species and samples, producing an ordered two-way table of their occurrence. The process of classification is hierarchical; samples are successively divided into categories, and species are then divided into categories on the basis of the sample classification. TWINSPAN, like DECORANA, has been widely used by ecologists.

For example, TWINSPAN was performed for vegetation analysis in 270 plots using ordinal scale of Van-der-Marrel (1979). The end of results file is the two-way ordred table summarizing the classification (Fig3). The table has species (not pesudo species) as rows and samples as columns.The results of TWINSPAN classification are presented in Fig.4. According to the above-mentioned table, figure, and also eigenvalue of each division, vegetation of the study area was classified in to six main types. Each type differs from the other in terms of it's environmental needs.

These types are as follows:

1. *Artemisia sieberi-Eurotia ceratoides*
2. *Artemisia aucheri, Astragalus spp., Bormus tomentellus*
3. *Artemisia sieberi–Zygophylom eurypterum*
4. *Zygophylom eurypterum- Artemisia sieberi*
5. *Seidlitzia rosmarinus*
6. *Halocnemum strobilaceum*

4. Methods of ordination analysis

Ordination serves to summarize community data (such as species abundance data) by producing a low-dimensional ordination space in which similar species and samples are plotted close together, and dissimilar species and samples are placed far apart (Peet, 1980)

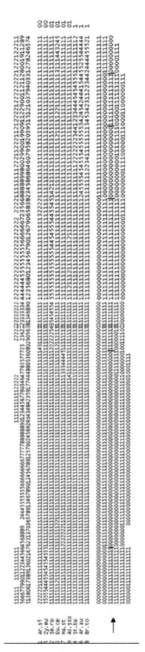

Figure 3. TWINSPAN of the vegetation cover in 270 quadrates and 9 species

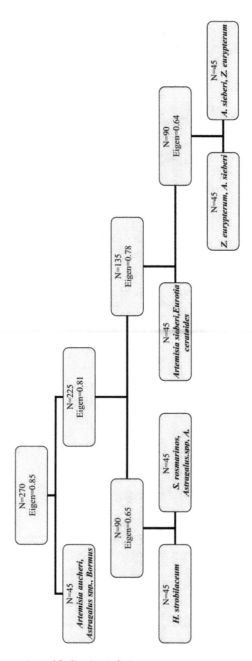

Figure 4. Schematic comparison of Ordination techniques

Ordination methods can be divided in two main groups, direct and indirect methods. Direct methods use species and environment data in a single, integrated analysis. Indirect methods use the species data only (Fig 5). Finally, ordination techniques are used to describe relationships between species composition patterns and the underlying environmental gradients which influence these patterns. Although community ecology is a fairly young science, the application of quantitative methods began fairly early (McIntosh,. 1985).

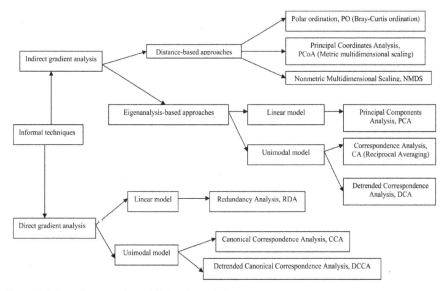

Figure 5. Schematic comparison of Ordination techniques

In 1930, began to use informal ordination techniques for vegetation. Such informal and largely subjective methods became widespread in the early 1950's (Whittaker 1967). In 1951, Curtis and McIntosh developed the 'continuum index', which later lead to conceptual links between species responses to gradients and multivariate methods. Shortly thereafter, Goodall (1954) introduced the term 'ordination' in an ecological context for Principal Components Analysis.

Each method was applied to data from a North east of Semnan (In Iran). If objective of study is examining the distribution patterns of six plant type in the rangelands, ordination could be used to determine which species are commonly found associated with one another, and how the species composition of the community changes with increase and decrease in each environment factor (Zare Chahouki et al, 2010). The objective of this method was to establish a monitoring system that may serve to identify and predict future vegetation changes and to assess impacts of conservation and management practices.

There are several different ordination techniques, all of which differ slightly, in the mathematical approach used to calculate species and sample similarity/dissimiarity. Rather than reinventing the wheel by discussing each of these techniques. Our example study illustrates the most frequent use of ordination methods in community ecology, we will offer only a brief description of the most commonly used methods here. Further details can be found in the following.

Polar Ordination (PO)

Bray and Curtis (1957) developed polar ordination, which became the first widely-used ordination technique in ecology.

Polar Ordination arranges samples with respect to poles (also termed end points or reference points) according to a distance matrix (Bray and Curtis 1957). These endpoints are two samples with the highest ecological distance between them, or two samples suspected of being at opposite ends of an important gradient. This method is especially useful for investigating ecological change (e.g., succession, recovery).

For example, Fig 6 shows ordination diagram for vegetation types and soil variables by Bray-Curtis analysis.

Endpoints for axis 1 was *Halocnemum strobilaceum*, *Artemisia aucheri-Astragalus spp-Bromus tomentellus*. Distances (ordination scores) are from *Halocnemum strobilaceum* Sum of squares of non-redundant distances in original matrix was .199621E+12. Axis 1 extracted 100.00% of the original distance matrix. Sum of squares of residual distances remaining is .672048E+05. Regression coefficient for this axis was -6.40 and Variance in distances from the first endpoint was 0.65.

Endpoints for axis 2: *Artemisia sieberi-Zygophylum eurypterum*, *Ar.au-As.spp-Br.to* distances (ordination scores) were from *Artemisia siberi-Zygophylum eurypterum*. Regression coefficient for this axis was -3.53. Variance in distances from the first endpoint was 0.0.

Axis 2 extracted 1.87% of the original distance matrix, Cumulative was 98.15%. Sum of squares of residual distances remaining was .948501E-01.

Polar ordination has strengths and weaknesses. The advantage of this method is that: (Beals 1984).

1. It is Simple, easy to understand geometric method, easily taught.
2. It is Ideal for evaluating problems with discrete endpoints. Polar Ordination ideal for testing specific hypotheses (e.g., reference condition or experimental design) by subjectively selecting the end points

The weaknesses of Polar Ordination method is that: (Beals 1984).

1. Axes are not orthogonal. With large data sets, it may be difficult to get a consistent ordination.
2. Not completely objective won't always get the same answer. However, this is a function of the decision regarding reference stands, and is really amounts to viewing the ordination from different angles, although the problem of nonorthogonal axes can cause considerable distortion to the ordination space.

Some of this problem can be overcome by using rules to define the reference stands.
3.   Distances are not metric (i.e., they are relative only)
4.   No explicit statement of underlying model.

In the earliest versions of PO, these endpoints were the two samples with the highest ecological distance between them, or two samples which are suspected of being at opposite ends of an important gradient (thus introducing a degree of subjectivity).

Beals (1984) extended Bray-Curtis ordination and discussed its variants, and is thus a useful reference. The polar ordination, simplest method is to choose the pair of samples, not including the previous endpoints, with the maximum distance of separation.

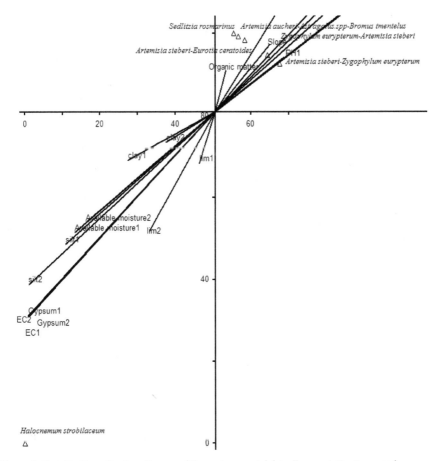

Figure 6. Bray-Curtis–ordination diagram of the environmental data. For vegetation types and variables abbreviations. (Δ) is the representative of the vegetation types.

These patterns are consistent with others in the literature (cited and reanalyzed in Palmer 1986).

Principal Components Analysis (PCA)

Principal Components Analysis (PCA) was one of the earliest ordination techniques applied to ecological data. PCA uses a rigid rotation to derive orthogonal axes, which maximize the variance in the data set. Both species and sample ordinations result from a single analysis. Computationally, Principal components analysis is the basic eigen analysis technique. It maximizes the variance explained by each successive axis.

The sum of the eigenvalues will equal the sum of the variance of all variables in the data set. PCA is relatively objective and provides a reasonable but crude indication of relationships.

PCA was invented in 1901 by Karl Pearson (Dunn,et al,1987) Now it is mostly used as a tool in exploratory data analysis and for making predictive models.

PCA is a method that reduces data dimensionality by performing a covariance analysis between factors (Feoli and Orl¢ci. 1992).

This method is a mathematical procedure that uses an orthogonal transformation to convert a set of observations of possibly correlated variables into a set of values of uncorrelated variables called principal components.

The number of principal components is less than or equal to the number of original variables. This transformation is defined in such a way that the first principal component has as high a variance as possible (that is, accounts for as much of the variability in the data as possible), and each succeeding component in turn has the highest variance possible under the constraint that it be orthogonal to (uncorrelated with) the preceding components (ter Braak and S ˇ milauer, 1998).

PCA method was used to determine the association between plant communities and environmental variables, i.e. in an indirect non-canonical way (ter Braak and Loomans, 1987).

For example to determine the most effective variables on the separation of vegetation types, PCA was performed for 22 factors in six vegetation types. The results of the PCA ordination are presented in Table 3 and Fig.5. Broken-stick eigenvalues for data set indicate that the first two principal components (PC1 and PC2) resolutely captured more variance than expected by chance. The first two principal components together accounted for 86% of the total variance in data set. Therefore, 61% and 25% variance were accounted for by the first and second principal components, respectively. This means that the first principal component is by far the most important for representing the variation of the six vegetation types.

Considering the characteristics of solidarity with the components, the first component includes silt and gravel in 20-80 depth, Available moisture in 0-20 depth, sand, gypsum and EC of both the depths. The second component consists of clay in 0-20 depth and lime in both depths.

AXIS	Eigenvalue	% of Variance	Cum.% of Var.	Broken-stick Eigenvalue
1	13.494	61.335	61.335	3.691
2	5.512	25.053	86.388	2.691
3	1.460	6.636	93.024	2.191
4	0.968	4.398	97.422	1.857
5	0.567	2.578	100.000	1.607
6	0.000	0.000	100.000	1.407
7	0.000	0.000	100.000	1.241
8	0.000	0.000	100.000	1.098
9	0.000	0.000	100.000	0.973
10	0.000	0.000	100.000	0.862

Factor	1	2	3	4	5	6
gr_1	-0.2636	0.0012	-0.0447	-0.0562	0.3161	0.1371
gr_2	-0.2589	0.0904	0.0166	-0.1657	0.2022	0.0355
$clay_1$	0.1792	0.3148	0.1002	-0.0093	0.1005	-0.1242
$clay_2$	0.1504	0.2595	-0.3168	-0.3208	-0.3702	-0.2055
$silt_1$	0.2476	0.0278	0.1910	0.3450	0.0191	0.1166
$silt_2$	0.2691	0.0624	-0.0028	0.0323	0.0133	-0.0807
$sand_1$	-0.2437	-0.1583	0.0828	-0.2235	-0.0573	-0.0706
$sand_2$	-0.2356	-0.1862	0.1819	0.0264	0.1395	0.0824
lim_1	0.0828	-0.3939	-0.0644	-0.0424	0.2794	0.0946
lim_2	0.1606	-0.3190	0.0101	-0.1881	0.3162	0.0212
$O.M_1$	-0.0253	0.3944	-0.0388	-0.0561	0.4768	0.0649
$O.M_2$	-0.0768	0.2109	0.2962	0.3680	0.0688	-0.0525
$A.W_1$	0.2440	0.1148	-0.2414	0.1038	0.2249	0.1069
$A.W_2$	0.2353	0.1306	-0.2399	0.0725	0.3501	0.1342
gyp_1	0.2662	-0.0688	0.0925	-0.0716	0.0125	-0.1236
gyp_2	0.2662	-0.0688	0.0925	-0.0716	0.0125	-0.1257
EC_1	0.2662	-0.0693	0.0957	-0.0628	0.0188	-0.1148
EC_2	0.2653	-0.0729	0.1017	-0.0773	0.0127	-0.1281
pH_1	-0.1360	-0.1130	-0.6739	0.0644	-0.1513	0.2438
pH_2	-0.2205	-0.1334	-0.2747	0.3324	0.2260	-0.8329
elevat	-0.1945	0.2594	0.0252	0.3383	-0.1141	0.0904
sl	-0.1345	0.2559	0.1863	-0.5878	0.1327	-0.1505

*Non-trivial principal component as based on broken-stick eigenvalues

Table 3. PCA applied to the correlation matrix of the environmental factors in the study area

In the study area, environmental conditions in *Halocnemum strobilaceum* type differ from the others. With attention to the position of this type in the four quarter of the diagram, it has a high correlation with the first axis. Therefore, this type has the most relation with variables of the first axis.

Because of the bigger distance of *H. strobilaceum* type from the second axis, this type has a weak relation with factors such as clay and lime. *Artemisia sieberi-Eurotia ceratoides* and *Seidlitzia rosmarinus* types have inverse relation with indicator environmental characteristics of the first and second axes except for clay, sand and gravel. *A. aucheri–Astragalus. spp.-Bromus tomentellus* type has more relation with indicator characteristics of the first and second axes.

Indicator environmental factors of the first and second axes in *A. sieberi–Zygophylom eurypterum* and *Z. eurypterum-A. sieberi* types are approximately similar. *A. sieberi–Z. eurypterum* type has a direct relationship with gravel and sand, and an inverse relationship with EC, silt, available moisture and gypsum. While *A. aucheri-As. spp.-B. tomentellus* type has a direct relationship with clay and inversely related to lime.

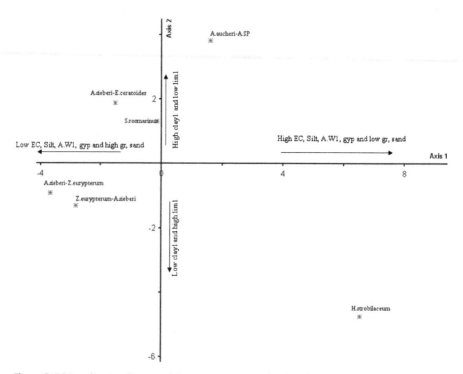

Figure 7. PCA–ordination diagram of the vegetation types related to the environmental factors in the study area. For vegetation types abbreviations, see Appendix A.

PCA operation can be thought of as revealing the internal structure of the data in a way which best explains the variance in the data. It is a way of identifying patterns in data, and expressing the data in such a way as to highlight their similarities and differences. Since patterns in data can be hard to find in data of high dimension, where the luxury of graphical representation is not available, PCA is a powerful tool for analyzing data

The one advantage of PCA is that once you have found patterns in the data, and you compress the data, ie by reducing the number of dimensions, without much loss of information and While PCA finds the mathematically optimal method (as in minimizing the squared error), it is sensitive to outliers in the data that produce large errors PCA tries to avoid. It therefore is common practice to remove outliers before computing PCA.

However, in some contexts, outliers can be difficult to identify. For example in data mining algorithms like correlation clustering, the assignment of points to clusters and outliers is not known beforehand.

A recently proposed generalization of PCA based on Weighted PCA increases robustness by assigning different weights to data objects based on their estimated relevancy.

Although it has severe faults with many community data sets, it is probably the best technique to use when a data set approximates multivariate normality. PCA is usually a poor method for community data, but it is the best method for many other kinds of multivariate (Bakus, 2007).

In general, once eigenvectors are found from the covariance matrix, the next step is to order them by eigenvalue, highest to lowest. This gives you the components in order of significance. Now, if you like, you can decide to ignore the components of lesser significance. You do lose some information, but if the eigenvalues are small, you don't lose much. If you leave out some components, the final data set will have less dimensions than the original.

To be precise, if you originally have dimensions in your data, and so you calculate eigenvectors and eigenvalues, and then you choose only the first eigenvectors, then the final data set has only dimensions. What needs to be done now is you need to form a feature vector, which is just a fancy name for a matrix of vectors. This is constructed by taking the eigenvectors that you want to keep from the list of eigenvectors, and forming a matrix with these eigenvectors in the columns.

Deriving the new data set is the final step in PCA, and is also the easiest. Once we have chosen the components (eigenvectors) that we wish to keep in our data and formed a feature vector, we simply take the transpose of the vector and multiply it on the left of the original data set, transposed.

In the case of keeping both eigenvectors for the transformation, we get the data and the plot found in Figure 5. This plot is basically the original data, rotated so that the eigenvectors are the axes. This is understandable since we have lost no information in this decomposition.

In figure 5 showed sample of PCA–ordination diagram of the vegetation types related to the environmental factors.

In contrast to Correspondence Analysis and related methods (see below), species are represented by arrows. This implies that the abundance of the species is continuously increasing in the direction of the arrow, and decreasing in the opposite direction.

Canonical correspondence analysis (CCA)

Canonical correspondence analysis (CCA) is a direct gradient analysis that displays the variation of vegetation in relation to the included environmental factors by using environmental data to order samples (Kent & Coker, 1992). This method combines multiple regression techniques together with various forms of correspondence analysis or reciprocal averaging (Ter Braak, 1986, 1987). The statistical significance of the relationship between the species and the whole set of environmental variables was evaluated using Monte Carlo permutation tests.

The CCA analysis method Ordination is a combination of conventional linear Environment variables with the highest value of dispersion Species shows. In other words, the best weight for CCA describes environment variables with the first axis shows. Species information structure using a reply CCA Nonlinear with the linear combination of variables will consider environmental characteristics of acceptable behavior characteristics of species with environment shows. CCA analysis combined with non-linear species and environmental factors shows the most important environmental variable in connection with the axes shows.

In ecology studies, the ordination of samples and species is constrained by their relationships to environmental variables.

The adventag of CCA Analysis is that: (Palmer, 1993)

1. Patterns result from the combination of several explanatory variables. And many extensions of multiple regressions (e.g. stepwise analysis and partial analysis) also apply to CCA.
2. It is possible to test hypotheses (though in CCA, hypothesis testing is based on randomization procedures rather than distributional assumptions).
3. Another advantage of CCA lies in the intuitive nature of its ordination diagram, or triplot. It is called a triplot because it simultaneously displays three pieces of information: samples as points, species as points, and environmental variables as arrows (or points).
    If data sets are few, CCA triplots can get very crowded then should be separate the parts of the triplot into biplots or scatterplots (e.g. plotting the arrows in a different panel of the same figure) or rescaling the arrows so that the species and sample scores are more spread out. And we can only plotting the most abundant species (but by all means, keep the rare species in the analysis).
4. When species responses are unimodal, and by measuring the important underlying environmental variables, CCA is most likely to be useful.

And one of limitations to CCA is that correlation does not imply causation, and a variable that appears to be strong may merely be related to an unmeasured but 'true' gradient. As with any technique, results should be interpreted in light of these limitations (McCune 1999).

It was used to examine the relationships between the measured variables and the distribution of plant communities (Ter Braak, 1986). CCA expresses species relationships as linear combinations of environmental variables and combines the features of CA with canonical correlation analysis (Green, 1989). This provides a graphical representation of the relationships between species and environmental factors.

Canonical Correlation Analysis is presented as the standard method to relate two sets of variables (Gittins, 1985). However, the latter method is useless if there are many species compared to sites, as in many ecological studies, because its ordination axes are very unstable in such cases.

The best weight for CCA describes environment variables with the first axis shows. Species information structure using a reply CCA Nonlinear with the linear combination of variables will consider environmental characteristics of acceptable behavior characteristics of species with environment shows. CCA analysis combined with non-linear species and environmental factors shows the most important environmental variable in connection with the axes shows.

In Canonical Correspondence Analysis, the sample scores are constrained to be linear combinations of explanatory variables. CCA focuses more on species composition, i.e. relative abundance.

When a combination of environmental variables is highly related to species composition, this method, will create an axis from these variables that makes the species response curves most distinct. The second and higher axes will also maximize the dispersion of species, subject to the constraints that these higher axes are linear combinations of the explanatory variables, and that they are orthogonal to all previous axis.

Monte Carlo permutation tests were subsequently used within canonical correspondence analysis (CCA) to determine the significance of relations between species composition and environmental variables (ter Braak, 1987)

The outcome of CCA is highly dependent on the scaling of the explanatory variables. Unfortunately, we cannot know a priori what the best transformation of the data will be, and it would be arrogant to assume that our measurement scale is the same scale used by plants and animals. Nevertheless, we must make intelligent guesses (Bakus, 2007).

It is probably obvious that the choice of variables in CCA is crucial for the output. Meaningless variables will produce meaningless results. However, a meaningful variable that is not necessarily related to the most important gradient may still yield meaningful results (Palmer 1988).

Explanatory variables need not be continuous in CCA. Indeed, dummy variables representing a categorical variable are very useful. A dummy variable takes the value 1 if the sample belongs to that category and 0 otherwise. Dummy variables are useful if you have discrete experimental treatments, year effects, different bedrock types, or in the case of the bryophyte example, host tree species (Bakus, 2007).

If many variables are included in an analysis, much of the inertia becomes 'explained'. Any linear transformation of variables (e.g. kilograms to grams, meters to inches, Fahrenheit to Centigrade) will not affect the outcome of CCA whatsoever.

There are as many constrained axes as there are explanatory variables. The total 'explained inertia' is the sum of the eigenvalues of the constrained axes. The remaining axes are unconstrained, and can be considered 'residual'. The total inertia in the species data is the sum of eigenvalues of the constrained and the unconstrained axes, and is equivalent to the sum of eigenvalues, or total inertia, of CA. Thus, explained inertia, compared to total inertia, can be used as a measure of how well species composition is explained by the variables. Unfortunately, a strict measure of 'goodness of fit' for CCA is elusive, because the arch effect itself has some inertia associated with it (Bakus, 2007).

The ordination diagrams of canonical correlation analysis and redundancy analysis display the same data tables; the difference lies in the precise weighing of the species (ter Braak, 1987, 1990; ter Braak & Looman, 1994). Recent, good ecological examples of canonical correlations analysis, with many more sites than species, are Van der Meer (1991) and Varis (1991).

For example, according to Tables 4 and5, first axis (Eigenvalue=0.869) accounted for 98.7% variation in environmental factors data. Correlation between the first axis and species–environmental variables was 0.99 and Monte Carlo permutation test for the first axis was highly significant ($P=0.01$). The second axis (Eigenvalue=0.182) explained 0.4% variation in data set. Correlation between the second axis and species–environmental variables was 0.92. In addition, the Monte Carlo test for the second axis was highly significant ($P=0.02$).

	Axis 1	Axis 2	Axis 3
Eigenvalue	0.869	0.003	0.003
Variance in species data			
% of variance explained	98.7	0.4	0.3
Cumulative % explained	98.7	99.1	99.4
Pearson Correlation, Spp-Envt*	0.998	0.920	0.959
Kendall (Rank) Corr., Spp-Envt	0.481	0.706	0.584

* Correlation between sample scores for an axis derived from the species data and the sample scores that are linear combinations of the environmental variables. Set to 0.000 if axis is not canonical.

Table 4. Canonical correspondence analysis for environmental data.

Axis	Spp-Envt Corr.	Mean	Minimum	Maximum	p
1	0.998	0.838	0.195	0.996	0.0100
2	0.920	0.607	0.072	0.935	0.0200
3	0.959	0.342	0.032	0.709	0.0100

p = proportion of randomized runs with species-environment correlation greater than or equal to the observed Species-environment correlation; i.e., p = (1 + no. permutations >= observed)/(1 + no. permutations)

Table 5. Mont Carlo test result –Speacies-Enviroment

Species responses to environmental conditions cannot be inferred in a causal way from multivariate analysis or any other statistical method; however, these techniques are useful to identify spatial distribution patterns and to assess which of the included environmental variables contribute most to species variability and which factors should be experimentally tested (D ı́ez et al, 2003).

The results of CCA ordination are presented in Fig.8. Each environmental factor is an indicator of the specific habitat. *Artemisia sieberi-Eurotia ceratoides*, *A. sieberi–Zygophylum eurypterum* and *Zygophylom eurypterum- A. sieberi types* have nonlinear relation with gravel, sand, silt, clay, lime, organic matter and available moisture. Relation power depends on the relative distance between indicator points of soil characteristics and vegetation types. *H. strobilaceum* type has non linear relation with gypsum and EC in both layers that is, EC and gypsum are indicator of habitat of this type. *A. sieberi–Z. eurypterum* and *Z. eurypterum- A. sieberi* types have non linear relation with them while *A.aucheri-As.sp.* and *S. rosmarinus* types are different from each other and they have less non linear relation with ecological factors.

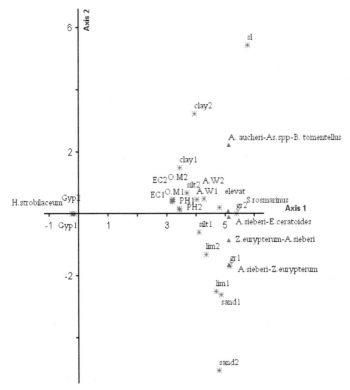

Figure 8. CCA–ordination diagram of the environmental data. For vegetation types and variables abbreviations, see Appendix A. (Δ) is the representative of the vegetation types. (*) is the representative of the environmental factors.

Reciprocal Averaging (RA) - Correspondence Analysis

RA is an ordination technique related conceptually to weighted averages. Because one algorithm for finding the solution involves the repeated averaging of sample scores and species scores (citations), Correspondence Analysis (CA) is also known as reciprocal averaging (Gittins, 1985).

RA places sampling units and species on the same gradients, and maximizes variation between species and sample scores using a correlation coefficient. It serves as a relatively objective analysis of community data.

CA is a graphical display ordination technique which simultaneously displays the rows (sites) and columns (species) of a data matrix in low dimensional space (Gittins, 1985). Row identifiers (species) plotted close together are similar in their relative profiles, and column identifiers plotted close together are correlated, enabling one to interpret not only which of the taxa are clustered, but also why they are clustered (Zhang et al,2005). Reciprocal analysis and canonical correlation analysis are linear methods. So, if well produced, their ordination diagrams are biplots or the superposition of biplots (a triplot). For illustration I use the Dune Meadow Data from Jongman et al. (1987). Reciprocal averaging is performed in PC-ORD by selecting options in program. Reciprocal averaging (RA) yields both normal and transpose ordinations automatically. Like DCA, RA ordinates both species and samples simultaneously. RA is the new technique that selects the linear combination of environmental variables that maximizes the description of the species scores. This gives the first RA axis. In RA, composite gradients are linear combinations of environmental variables, giving a much simpler analysis and the non-linearity enters the model through a unimodal model for a few composite gradients, taken care of in RA by weighted averaging. It provides a summary of the species-environment relations. This method is an ordination technique related conceptually to weighted averages. Results are generally superior to the results from PCA. However, RA axis ends are compressed relative to the middle, and the second axis is often a distortion of the first axis, resulting in an arched effect.

For example the analysis of variance showed in table.4 that there was a significant correlation among species and soil axis. The eigenvalues represent the variance in the sample scores. RA axis 1 has an eigenvalue of 0.86. RA axis 2 with an eigenvalue of 0.017 is less important. Table 6 shows the score classified site. Total variance (inertia) in the species data is 0.8887.

The results of RA ordination are presented in Fig 6. Six group sites were determined in relation to the environmental factors. Sites were determined in relation to the environmental factors.

The eigenvalue of the CA axis is equivalent to the correlation coefficient between species scores and sample scores (Gauch 1982b, Pielou 1984). It is not possible to arrange rows and/or columns in such a way that makes the correlation higher. The second and higher axes also maximize the correlation between species scores and sample scores, but they are constrained to be uncorrelated with (orthogonal to) the previous axes.

Since CA is a unimodal model, species are represented by a point rather than an arrow (Figure 7). This is (under some choices of scaling; see ter Braak and Šmilauer 1998) the weighted average of the samples in which that species occurs. With some simplifying assumptions (ter Braak and Looman 1987), the species score can be considered an estimate of the location of the peak of the species response curve (Figure 7).

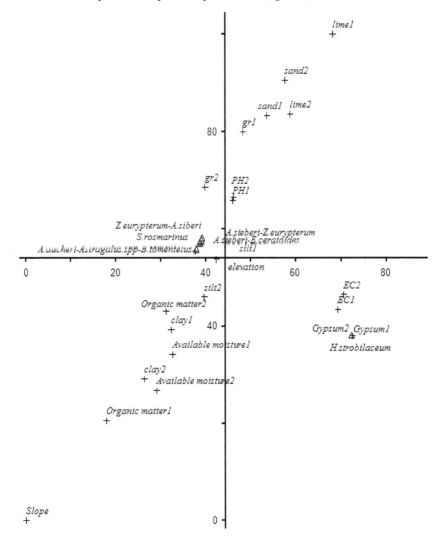

Figure 9. RA–ordination diagram of the environmental data. For vegetation types and variables abbreviations. (Δ) is the representative of the vegetation types. (+) is the representative of the environmental factors.

However, RA axis ends are compressed relative to the middle, and the second axis is often a distortion of the first axis, resulting in an arched effect.

N NAME	AX1	AX2	AX3	RANKED 1		RANKED 2	
				EIG=0.861		EIG=0.017	
1 Ar.si-Er.ce	2443	55	-97	1 Ar.si-Er.ce	2443	5 Ar.au-As.spp-B.to	206
2 Ha.sp	-25	0	0	3 Ar.si-Zy.eu	2441	2Ha.st	55
3 Ar.si-Zy.eu	2441	-73	-72	5Ar.au-As.spp-B.to	2435	1 Ar.si-Er.ce	0
4 Zy.eu-Ar.si	2421	-69	-25	4Zy.eu-A.si	2421	4Zy.eu-A.si	69
5 Ar.au-As.spp-B.to	2435	206	76	6Se.ro	2399	3 Ar.si-Zy.eu	73
6 Se.ro	2399	-161	131	2Ha.st	-25	6Se.ro	161

Table 6. Sample scores - which are weighted mean species scores

Row identifiers (species) plotted close together are similar in their relative profiles, and column identifiers plotted close together are correlated, enabling one to interpret not only which of the taxa are clustered, but also why they are clustered (Bakus,2007).

Reciprocal averaging (RA) yields both normal and transpose ordinations automatically. Like DCA, RA ordinates both species and samples simultaneously. Instead of maximizing 'variance explained', CA maximizes the correspondence between species scores and sample scores.

If species scores are standardized to zero mean and unit variance, the eigenvalues also represent the variance in the sample scores (but not, as is often misunderstood, the variance in species abundance).

The CA distortion is called the arch effect, which is not as serious as the horseshoe effect of PCA because the ends of the gradients are not incurved. Nevertheless, the distortion is prominent enough to seriously impair ecological interpretation (Bakus, 2007).

In other words, the spacing of samples along an axis may not affect true differences in species composition. The problems of gradient compression and the arch effect led to the development of Detrended Correspondence Analysis.

Detrended Correspondence Analysis (DCA)

Detrended correspondence analysis (DCA), an ordination technique used to describe patterns in complex data sets, and produced the following sequence of ordination axis scores (ter Braak,1986).

DCA is an eigenvector ordination technique based on Reciprocal Averaging, correcting for the arch effect produced from RA. Hill and Gauch (1980) report DCA results are superior to those of RA. Other ecologists criticize the detrending process of DCA. DCA is widely used for the analysis of community data along gradients. DCA ordinates samples and species simultaneously. It is not appropriate for the analysis of a matrix of similarity values between community data (Gauch, 1982b).

Detrended Correspondence Analysis (DCA) eliminates the arch effect by detrending (Hill and Gauch 1982). There are two basic approaches to detrending: by polynomials and by segments (ter Braak and Šmilauer 1998). Detrending by polynomials is the more elegant of the two: a regression is performed in which the second axis is a polynomial function of the first axis, after which the second axis is replaced by the residuals from this regression. Similar procedures are followed for the third and higher axes. Unfortunately, results of detrending by polynomials can be unsatisfactory and hence detrending by segments is preferred. To detrend the second axis by segments, the first axis is divided up into segments, and the samples within each segment are centered to have a zero mean for the second axis (see illustrations in Gauch 1982). The procedure is repeated for different 'starting points' of the segments. Although results in some cases are sensitive to the number of segments (Jackson and Somers 1991), the default of 26 segments is usually satisfactory. Detrending of higher axes proceeds by a similar process.

One way to determine this relationship is to analyze the species data first by detrended correspondence analysis (DCA) and to examine the length of the maximum gradient. If the gradient exceeds 3 sd (sd¼standard deviation) (most of the species are replaced along the gradient), the data show unimodal response (Hill & Gauch, 1980). For example, in North East rangeland of Semnan, DCA axis 1 has an eigenvalue of 0.86 and a gradient length of 15.44. DCA axis 2 with an eigenvalue of 0.016 and a gradient length of 0.39 is less important. Fig 8 shows ordination diagram for vegetation types and soil variables. Table 5 shows the score classified site.

N NAME	AX1	AX2	AX3	RANKED 1		RANKED 2	
				EIG=0.861		EIG=0.017	
1 Ar.si-Er.ce	1714	23	10	1 Ar.si-Er.ce	1714	5 Ar.au-As.spp-B.to	39
2 Ha.sp	0	27	12	3 Ar.si-Zy.eu	1713	2Ha.st	27
3 Ar.si-Zy.eu	1713	8	0	5Ar.au-As.spp-B.to	1710	1 Ar.si-Er.ce	23
4 Zy.eu-Ar.si	1704	9	14	4Zy.eu-A.si	1704	4Zy.eu-A.si	9
5 Ar.au-As.spp-B.to	1710	12	12	6Se.ro	1694	3 Ar.si-Zy.eu	8
6 Se.ro	1694	0	15	2Ha.st	0	6Se.ro	

Table 7. Sample Scores- Weighted are weighted mean species scores (FIRST 6 EIGENVECTORS)

Figure 8 is an example of ordination plots showing the sites plotted on two axes. The ordination was a detrended correspondence analysis, and the sites with the same treatment level are outline for clarity.

One additional note, the different plots illustrate another common approach when using ordination: including only data on certain species thought to be more important as indicator species. This allows for different runs of the test to detect similarities or differences in composition based on a particular group.

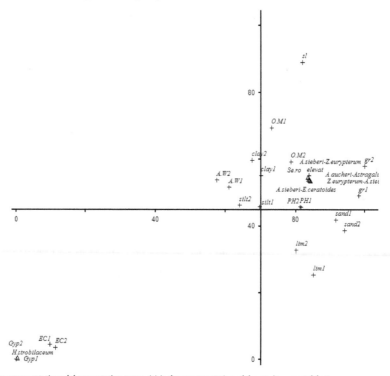

(Δ) is the representative of the vegetation types. (+) is the representative of the environmental factors.

Figure 10. DCA–ordination diagram of the environmental data. For vegetation types and variables abbreviations.

Nonmetric Multidimensional Scaling (NMS)

NMS actually refers to an entire related family of ordination techniques. These techniques use rank order information to identify similarity in a data set. NMS is a truly nonparametric ordination method which seeks to best reduce space portrayal of relationships. The verdict is still out on this type of ordination. Gauch (1982b) claims NMS is not worth the extra computational effort and that it gives effective results only for easy data sets with low diversity. Others hold NMS is extremely effective (Kenkel and Orloci, 1986, Bradfield and Kenkel, 1987).

DCA and NMDS are the two most popular methods for indirect gradient analysis. The reason they have remained side-by-side for so long is because, in part, they have different strengths and weaknesses. While the choice between the two is not always straightforward, it is worthwhile outlining a few of the key differences.

Some of the issues are relatively minor: for example, computation time is rarely an important consideration, except for the hugest data sets. Some issues are not entirely resolved: the degree to which noise affects NMDS, and the degree to which NMDS finds local rather than global options still need to be determined (Bakus, 2007).

Since NMDS is a distance-based method, all information about species identities is hidden once the distance matrix is created. For many, this is the biggest disadvantage of NMDS (Bakus, 2007).

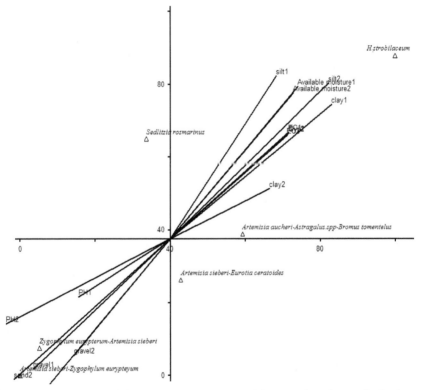

Figure 11. NMS ordination of plant species and environmental factors in along the rangelands of Semnan in Iran

DCA is based on an underlying model of species distributions, the unimodal model, while NMDS is not. Thus, DCA is closer to a theory of community ecology. However, NMDS may be a method of choice if species composition is determined by factors other than position along a gradient: For example, the species present on islands may have more to do with vicariance biogeography and chance extinction events than with environmental preferences

– and for such a system, NMDS would be a better *a priori* choice. As De'ath (1999) points out, there are two classes of ordination methods - 'species composition restoration' (e.g. NMDS) and 'gradient analysis' (e.g. DCA). The choice between the methods should ultimately be governed by this philosophical distinction.

Non-metric multidimensional scaling (NMS) (PC-ORD v. 4.25, 1999) was used to identify environmental variables correlated with plant species composition. A random starting location and Sorensen's distance measurement were used with the NMS autopilot slow and thorough method. Stepwise multiple linear regression (S-PLUS, 2000) was used to select models correlating vegetation cover and structure with environmental factors. Environmental explanatory factors that were not significant contributors (as determined from using stepwise selection at $\alpha = 0.05$) were excluded from the final model (Davies et al, 2007).

A Monte Carlo test of 30 runs with randomized data indicated the minimum stress of the 2 axes NMS ordination were lower than would be expected by chance ($p = 0.0968$). The final stress and instability of the 2-D solution were 23.71 and 0.00001, respectively. The first ordination axis (NMS1) captured 41.9% of the variability in the dataset and the second (NMS2) captured 31.8%, leading a cumulative 73.7% of variance in dataset explained (Fig.11).

5. Conclusion

Multivariate statistical analysis techniques were used to establish the relationships between plant diversity, Topography and soil factors. Plant community, structure and biodiversity have been shown to have a high degree of spatial variability that is controlled by both abiotic and biotic factors (Fu et al, 2004).

CCA is the constrained form of CA, and therefore is preferred for most ecological data sets (since unimodality is common). CCA also is appropriate under a linear model, as long as one is interested in species composition rather than absolute abundances (ter Braak and Šmilauer 1998). Correspondence analysis (CA) and canonical correspondence analysis (CCA) are widely used to obtain unconstrained unconstrained or constrained ordinations of species abundance data tables and the corresponding biplots or triplots which are extremely useful for ecological interpretation CA provided a good approximation for species with unimodal distributions along a single environmental gradient. There is a problem with this metric, however: a difference between abundance values for a common species contributes less to the distance than the same difference for a rare species, so that rare species may have an unduly large influence on the analysis (Greig-Smith 1983; ter Braak and Smilauer 1998; Legendre and Legendre 1998).

The most other general ordination technique, nonmetric multidimensional scaling (NMDS), which is based on the rankings of distances between points (Shepard, 1962), circumvents the linearity assumption of metric ordination methods. This method, used in ecological investigations (Kenkel and Orloci, 1986), Comparative studies of ordination techniques have, moreover, demonstrated the superiority of NMDS, and some authors have re commended its use, notwithstanding the computational burden.

The NMDS approach can in fact be tested each time measures of re semblance or dissimilarity are used to classify OTUs, whatever the causes and origins of arrangements found (Guiller et al, 1998).

In the biplots, where only the first two axes were used, all methods based upon PCA gave a fair representation of the relative numerical importance of the rare species. The weights in CCA are given by a diagonal matrix containing the square roots of the row sums of the species data table. This means that a site where many individuals have been observed contributes more to the regression than a site with few individuals. CCA should only be used when the sites have approximately the same number of individuals, or when one explicitly wants to give high weight to the richest sites. This problem of CCA was one of our incentives for looking for alternative methods for canonical ordination of community composition data.

For the analysis of sites representing short gradients, PCA may be suitable. For longer gradients, many species are replaced by others along the gradient and this generates many zeros in the species data table. Community ecologists have repeatedly argued that the Euclidean distance (and thus PCA) is inappropriate for raw species abundance data involving null abundances (e.g. Orlóci 1978; Wolda 1981; Legendre and Legendre 1998). For that reason, CCA is often the method favoured by researchers who are analysing compositional data, despite the problem posed by rare species.

De-trended correspondence analysis (DCA) is perhaps the most widely used method of indirect vegetation ordination. But direct ordination of vegetation and environment is achieved with canonical correspondence analysis (CCA). CCA is a relatively new method in which the axes of a vegetative ordination are restricted to linear groups of environmental variables (Zhang et al, 2006)

DCA and CA analyses should be run with the 'downweight rare species' option selected. We generally do not recommend NMS with the Euclidean distance measure; it performed the worst empirically, and has no advantages over the other methods (Culman et al, 2008)

Among the widely used ordination techniques for the plant community analysis Canonical Correspondence (CA) has shown to be superior to others such as PCA (Gauch, 1982). Most community data sets are heterogeneous and contain one or more gradients with lengths of at least two or three half-changes, which makes CA results ordinarily superior to PCA results. However, with relatively homogenous data sets with short gradients, PCA maybe better (Palmer, 1993). Despite the considerable superiority of the CA over PCA, CA is not superior to DCA, which corrects its two major faults such as "arch effect" and "compression of end of first axis" (Gauch, 1982; Kent & Coker, 1992).

For complex and heterogeneous data sets, DCA is distinctive in its effectiveness androbustness (Gauch, 1982). Comparative tests of different indirect ordination techniques have shown that DCA provides a good result (Cazzier & Penny, 2002). This study found that DCA provides better results than CA results (Malik & Husein, 2006).

For example all ordination techniques, used in North East rangeland of Semnan, clearly indicated that gypsum, EC, slope are the most important factors for the distribution of the vegetation pattern.

In the present study, combination of CCA, DCA and RA results showed that *Ar.aucheri-As.spp-Br.to, Artemisia sieberi-Erotia ceratoides, Ar.sieberi-Zy. eurypterum and Zy. eurypterum -Ar. sieberi* types correlated with A.W2, gr2, O.M2 and clay1 factors and clay in 0-20 depth indicates *Ar.aucheri-As.spp-Br.to* type. *H.strobilaceum* type has strong relationship with soil salinity and heavy texture. This species showed a trend to high soluble rate, salinity and clay percent. S. rosmarinus types indicate soils with light texture and this type directly related to pH and lime percentage while St.barbata-A.aucheri type shows an inverse relation with these factors.

I fact, analysis with DCA gave results similar to CCA, suggesting that there is a relatively strong correspondence between vegetation and environmental factors; with the difference that the DCA is less isolated the site. CCA better shows differences between types. RA shows relationship between sites and factors, like the CCA analysis. RA axis 1 has an eigenvalue of 0.86. RA axis 2 with an eigenvalue of 0.017 is less important. Total variance (inertia) in the species data is 0.8887.In this method eigenvalue of RA axis1 was higher than CCA and DCA axis1. This study reflects that a spatial approach dealing with the most distinctive species of vegetation communities can yield similar results to those obtained with costly physico-chemical analysis and based on complex matrices of plant communities.

Similarity as this study, also Jafari et al (2003) in their study in Hoz-e-Soltan Reigion of Qom Province, showed that PCA analysis indicates that Halocnemum strobilaceum type has direct relationship with Salinity, Lime, pH and Loam.

May this series of papers serve to enhance the understanding and the proper and creative use of ordination methods in community ecology. Finally, understanding relationships between environmental variables and vegetation distribution in each area helps us to apply these findings in management, reclamation, and development of arid and semi-arid grassland ecosystems (Alisauskas, 1998). The ability to factor out covariables and to test for statistical significance further extends the utility of CCA.

Understanding the relationships between ecological variables and distribution of plant communities can provide guidance to sustainable management, reclamation and development of this and similar regions. In this sense, these results increase our understanding of distribution patterns of desert vegetation and related major environmental factors in the North East of Semnan. The results will also provide a theoretical base for the restoration of degenerated vegetation in this area. Understanding the indicator of environmental factors of a given site leads us to recommend adaptable species for reclamation and improvement of that site and similar sites (Zhang et al, 2005)

Appendix

Artemisia sieberi-Erotia ceratoides.   *A.sieberi-E.ceratoides*
Halocnemum strobilaceum   *H. strobilaceum*
Artemisia sieberi–Zygophylom eurypoides.   *A.sieberi-Z.eurypterum*

Zygophylom eurypterum- Artemisia sieberi.	*Z.eurypterum –A.sieberi*
Artemisia aucheri-Astragalus spp.-Bromus tomentellus	*A.aucheri-As.sp.-Br.tomentellus*
Seidlitzia rosmarinus.	*S.rosmarinus*
Slope (%)	slope
Gravel (%)	gr
Clay (%)	clay
Silt (%)	silt
Sand (%)	sand
Available moisture (%)	A.W
Gypsum (%)	gyp
Lime (%)	Lim
PH(acidity)	pH
Electrical conductivity (ds/m)	EC
Organic matter (%)	O.M
Elevation (meter)	elevate

Code 1 is related to the soil characteristics were measured in the first layer (0–20 cm) Code 2 is related to the soil characteristics were measured in the second layer (20–80 cm)

Author details

Mohammad Ali Zare Chahouki
Associate Professor, Department of Rehabilitation of Arid and Mountainous Regions,
Natural Resources Faculty, University of Tehran, Iran

6. References

[1] Alisauskas, R. T. 1998. Winter range expansion and relationships between landscape and morphometrics of midcontinent Lesser Snow Geese. Auk 115(4):851-862.

[2] Anderson, M.J. & Ter Braak, C.J.F. (2002): Permutation tests for multi-factorial analysis of variance. Journal of Statistical Computation and Simulation (in press)

[3] Bakus Gerald J, 2007. Quantitative Analysis of Marine Biological Communities Field Biology and Environment. WILEY-INTERSCIENCE, A John Wiley & Sons, Inc., Publication,453p

[4] Beals, E. W. 1984. Bray-Curtis ordination: an effective strategy for analysis of multivariate ecological data. Adv. Ecol. Res. 14:1-55

[5] Bradfield, G.E. and Kenkel, N.C. 1987. Nonlinear ordination using flexible shortest path adjustment of ecological distances. Ecology 68: 750–753.

[6] Bray, J. R., and J. T. Curtis. 1957. An ordination of the upland forest communities of southern Wisconsin. Ecol. Mon. 27:325-49

[7] Causton, D. R. 1988. An introduction to vegetation analysis. Unwin Hyman, London.

[8] Curtis, J. T., and R. P. McIntosh. 1951. An upland forest continuum in the prairie-forest border region of Wisconsin. Ecology 32:476-96

[9] Culman, S.W. H.G. Gauch, C.B., Blackwood & J.E, Thies, 2008. Analysis of T-RFLP data using analysis of variance and ordination methods: A comparative study. Journal of Microbiological Methods 75 (2008) 55–63

[10] Daviesa, K.W., J.D, Batesa, R.F, Millerb,2007. Environmental and vegetation relationships of the Artemisia tridentata spp. wyomingensis alliance. Journal of Arid Environments 70 (2007) 478–494

[11] De'ath, G. 1999. Principal curves: a new technique for indirect and direct gradient analysis. Ecology 80:2237-53

[12] Dı´ez, I., A. Santolaria, J.M. Gorostiaga, 2003. The relationship of environmental factors to the structure and distribution of subtidal seaweed vegetation of the western Basque coast (N Spain). Estuarine, Coastal and Shelf Science 56 (2003) 1041–1054

[13] Dunn, C. P., and F. Stearns. 1987. Relationship of vegetation layers to soils in southeastern Wisconsin forested wetlands. Am. Midl. Nat. 118:366-74.

[14] Feoli, E. and Orl'oci, L. 1979. Analysis of concentration and detection of underying factors in structured tables. Vegetatio 40: 49–54.

[15] Gauch, H. G., Jr. 1982a. Multivariate Analysis and Community Structure. Cambridge University Press, Cambridge.

[16] Gauch, H. G., Jr. 1982b. Noise reduction by eigenvalue ordinations. Ecology 63:1643-9

[17] Gittins, R. (1985). Canonical analysis. A review with applications in ecology. Berlin: Springer-Verlag.

[18] Guiller, A., A, Bellido & L, Madec,1998. Genet ic Distances and Ordinat ion : The Land Sna il He lix aspe rsa in Nor th Afr ica as a Test Ca se. Syst . Biol . 47(2) : 208- 227

[19] Goodall, D. W. 1954. Objective methods for the classification of vegetation. III. An essay in the use of factor analysis. Austral. J. Bot. 1:39-63

[20] Green, R.H. 1979. Sampling design and statistical methods for environmental biologists. Wiley-Interscience, New York, Chichester, Brisbane, Toronto.

[21] Greig-Smith P (1983) Quantitative plant ecology, 3rd edn. Blackwell, London

[22] Hill, M. O. 1979. TWINSPAN - A FORTRAN programme for arranging multivariate data in an ordered two-way table by classification of individuals and attributes. Cornell University, Ithaca, New York.

[23] Hill, M.O., Bunce, R.G.H. & Shaw, M.V. (1975): Indicator species analysis, a divisive polythetic method of classification, and its application to survey of native pinewoods in Scotland. Journal of Ecology, 63: 597–613

[24] Hill, M. O. 1973. Reciprocal averaging: an eigenvector method of ordination. J. Ecol. 61:237-49

[25] Hill, M. O. and Gauch, H. G. 1980. Deterended correspondence analysis, an improved ordination technique. Vegetatio 42:47-58.

[26] Fu, B.J., S.L, Liu, K.M,Ma1 & Y.G, Zhu,2004. Relationships between soil characteristics, topography and plant diversity in a heterogeneous deciduous broad-leaved forest near Beijing, China. Plant and Soil 261: 47–54,

[27] Jafari, M., M.A, Zare Chahouki., A, Tavili & H, Azarnivand, 2003.Soil-Vegetation Rellationships in Hoz-e-Soltan Region of Qom Province, Iran. Pkistan Journal of Nutrition 2(6):329-334

[28] Jongman, R. H. G., ter Braak, C. J. F. & van Tongeren, O. F. R. (1987). Data analysis in community and landscape ecology. Wageningen: Pudoc [new edition: 1994, Cambridge: Cambridge University Press].

[29] Kendall, M.A., Widdicombe, S., 1999. Small scale patterns in the structure of macrofaunal assemblages of shallow soft sediments. J. Exp. Mar. Biol. Ecol. 237, 127–140.

[30] Kenkel, N. C., and L. Orloci. 1986. Applying metric and nonmetric multidimensional scaling to ecological studies: some new results. Ecology 67:919-928.

[31] Kent, M., and P. Coker. 1992. Vegetation description and analysis: a practical approach. Belhaven Press, London.

[32] Kent, M. (2006) Numerical classification and ordination methods in biogeography. Progress in Physical Geography 30, 399-408

[33] Krebs, Ch.J. 1999. Ecological methodology. Addison-Welsey educational publishers. 620pp

[34] Legendre, P., and L. Legendre. 1998. Numerical Ecology, 2nd English Edition. Elsevier, Amsterdam.

[35] Legendre, P & E.D, Gallagher, 2001. Ecologically meaningful transformations for ordination of species data. Oecologia :129:271

[36] Lep`s, J. and ˇ Smilauer, P. 2003. Multivariate Analysis of Ecological Data using CANOCO. Cambridge University Press, Cambridge.

[37] Malik, R.N., & S.Z, Husain, 2006. Classification and Ordination of vegetation communities of the lohibehr reserve forest and its surrounding areas. Rawalpini. Pak. J. Bot., 38(3). 543 558.

[38] Mucina, L. 1997. Classification of vegetation: past, present and future. J. Veg. Sci. 8: 751–760.

[39] McCune, B. and M.J. Mefford. 1999. PCORD. Multivariate Analysis of Ecological Data, Version 4. MjM Software Design, Gleneden Beach, Oregon, USA.

[40] McCune, B., Grace J.B. and D.L. Urban. 2002. Analysis of Ecological Communities. MjM Software Design, Gleneden Beach, Oregon.

[41] McIntosh, R. P. 1985. The Background of Ecology. Cambridge University Press, Cambridge, Great Britain.

[42] Orl'oci, L. 1978. Multivariate Analysis in Vegetation Research. 2nd ed. Junk, The Hague.

[43] Palmer, M. W. 1986. Pattern in corticolous bryophyte communities of the North Carolina piedmont: Do mosses see the forest or the trees? Bryologist 89:59-65

[44] Palmer, M. W. 1993. Putting things in even better order: the advantages of canonical correspondence analysis. Ecology 74:2215-30

[45] Peet, R. K. 1980. Ordination as a tool for analyzing complex data sets. Vegetatio 42:171-4

[46] Pielou, E. C. 1984. The Interpretation of Ecological Data: A Primer on Classification and Ordination. Wiley, New York.

[47] Prentice, I. C. 1977. Non-metric ordination methods in ecology. J. Ecol. 65:85-94

[48] Pritchard, N.M & J.B, Anderson, 1971. Observations on the use of Cluster analysis in botany with an ecological example. Journal of Ecology,Vol. 59,No.3, pp.727-747

[49] Shepard, R.N. (1962): The analysis of proximities: multidimensional scaling with an unknown distance function. Psychometrika, 27: 125–139

[50] Swan, J.M.A. 1970. An examination of some ordination problems by use of simulated vegetational data. Ecology 51: 89–102.

[51] Tavili, A. & Jafari, M., 2009. Interrelations Between Plants and Environmental Variables. Int. J. Environ. Res., 3(2):239-246

[52] ter Braak, C. J. F. 1985. CANOCO - A FORTRAN program for canonical correspondence analysis and detrended correspondence analysis. IWIS-TNO, Wageningen, The Netherlands.

[53] ter Braak, C. J. F. 1986. Canonical correspondence analysis: a new eigenvector technique for multivariate direct gradient analysis. Ecology 67:1167-79

[54] ter Braak, C. J. F., and C. W. N. Looman. 1987. Regression. Pages 29-77 in R. H. G. Jongman, C. J. F. ter Braak and O. F. R. van Tongeren, editors. Data Analysis in Community and Landscape Ecology. Pudoc, Wageningen, The Netherlands.

[55] ter Braak, C. J. F., and C. W. N. Looman. 1986. Weighted averaging, logistic regression and the Gaussian response model. Vegetatio 65:3-11

[56] ter Braak, C. J. F., and I. C. Prentice. 1988. A theory of gradient analysis. Adv. Ecol. Res. 18:271-313

[57] ter Braak, C. J. F., and P. Šmilauer. 1998. CANOCO reference manual and User's guide to Canoco for Windows: Software for Canonical Community Ordination (version 4). Microcomputer Power, Ithaca.

[58] Van der Maarel E.,1979. Transformation of cover-abundance values in phytosociology and its effect on community similarity. - Vegetatio, 38: 97 – 114

[59] Van der Meer, J. (1991). Exploring macrobenthos-environment relationship by canonical correlation analysis. Journal of Experimental Marine Biology and Ecology, 148, 105-120.

[60] Varis, O. (1991). Associations between lake phytoplankton community and growth factors – a canonical correlation analysis. Hydrobiologia, 210, 209-216.

[61] Whittaker, R. H. 1967. Gradient analysis of vegetation. Biol. Rev. 42:207-64

[62] Whittaker, R. H. 1969. Evolution of diversity in plant communities. Brookhaven Symp. Biol. 22:178-95

[63] Wildi, O., 2010. Data analysis in vegetation ecology. A John Wiley & Sons, Ltd., Publication, 211pp

[64] Williams, WT. & Lambert, J.M. (1959). Multivariate methods in plant ecology.I, Association analysis in plant communities .J. Ecol.47,83-101.

[65] Wolda H (1981) Similarity indices, sample size and diversity. Oecologia 50:296–302

[66] Zare Chahouki, M.A., Khalasi Ahvazi, L. & Azarnivand, H.,2010. Environmental factors affecting distribution of vegetation communities in Iranian Rangelands. VEGETOS Journal, 23(2): 1-15.

[67] Zhang W H, Lu T, Ma KM, et al. Analysis on the environmental and spatial factors for plant community distribution in the arid valley in the upper reach of Minjiang River. Acta Ecologica Sinica, 2004, 24(3): 532–559

[68] Zhang, Y.M., Y.N. Chen, B.R. Pan, 2005. Distribution and floristics of desert plant communities in the lower reaches of Tarim River, southern Xinjiang, People's Republic of China. Journal of Arid Environments 63 (2005) 772–784

[69] Zhang ,B, Valentine,I, Kemp,P, Lambert,G, 2006. Predictive modelling of hill-pasture productivity: integration of a decision tree and a geographical information system. Agricultural Systems 87 (2006) 1–17.

Chapter 10

Ageing and Deterioration of Materials in the Environment – Application of Multivariate Data Analysis

E. Smidt, M. Schwanninger, J. Tintner and K. Böhm

Additional information is available at the end of the chapter

1. Introduction

Ageing and deterioration of materials are key processes within the perpetual conversion of organic and inorganic matter. As far as natural cycles of organic substances are concerned a balance between syntheses, metabolic products, degradation and recycling can be expected. With respect to inorganic materials, weathering is the dominant natural process of ageing. It comprises transformation of chemical compounds and is caused by abiotic and biotic factors. The formation of new mineral phases closes the loop. Anthropogenic activities influence the well-balanced metabolism due to the increased consumption of resources and the inherent accelerated turnover rate. This development is paralleled by a relevant environmental impact caused by increasing concentrations of metabolic products. Especially greenhouse gases have become a crucial topic due to their global effect and the contribution to climate change. The fate of carbon, a key element in the global cycle, therefore attracts much attention [1-4]. Carbon sequestration and minimisation of gaseous emissions such as CO_2 and methane are promoted to decelerate the turnover. Deterioration and degradation are not only paralleled in many cases by the release of harmful substances but also by the loss of valuable resources. Prevention of negative environmental effects and careful use of resources therefore require a responsible management of products, substances and elements. Several elements such as nitrogen, phosphorus and sulphur that are released as different compounds during degradation of organic matter are in the focus of interest [5]. The ambivalence being both nutrient and pollutant has led to several techniques of resource recovery [6].

Ageing of materials or products implies changes of the original state, but it does not necessarily only comprise deterioration or degradation. Ageing can also mean formation of new substances and stabilisation. In some cases this effect is desirable. Ageing of incineration ash and slag leads to carbonation [7, 8]. With respect to organic matter humic substances are built up resulting in a stable organic fraction with low turnover rates. These natural processes that come along with material ageing were adopted for technical applications, e.g. humification in the course of composting.

On the one hand natural processes serve as a model for anthropogenic activities with regard to the closed loop of material recycling, especially in the field of organic substances [9]. On the other hand every endeavour is made to prevent or retard the natural ageing, deterioration and degradation process of materials and to maintain a constant quality of products by adequate measures. There are several options to achieve this objective: modification of biogenic materials, treatment of the surface and application of chemical substances against microbial deterioration and ageing by abiotic factors. Although abiotic factors play a relevant role for ageing and deterioration of organic materials, biological processes dominate. Inorganic materials are primarily affected by chemical and physical attacks, but some specialised microbial communities are capable of promoting the ageing process of inorganic components. The environmental milieu plays a crucial role as it determines both biological and chemical reactions. Historical and archaeological finds owe their preservation to conditions that prevented or delayed deterioration.

This study reports on natural ageing and degradation processes of organic matter and ageing of inorganic materials over weeks, years, decades and centuries. The questions to be answered focus on two main aspects: the environmental impact by ageing and deterioration of organic and inorganic matter and the proof of resistance of organic materials against biological degradation which is a main concern in material sciences to maintain the quality of products [10-12]. Ageing and deterioration can be described by many parameters. They focus on chemical and physical changes of the material by which the process is paralleled. In some cases, especially for product control, a single parameter might be sufficient to verify the ageing of materials [13]. For an overall characterisation of the state of deterioration those analytical methods are advantageous that provide a "fingerprint" of the material. FT-IR spectroscopy and STA were applied to reveal material characteristics and their changes over time under different environmental conditions.

FT-IR spectroscopy is based on the interaction of infrared radiation with matter. Infrared radiation provides the energy for molecule vibrations that become visible as absorption bands. The plot of wavenumbers (energy) within a defined range vs. band intensities results in the spectrum. Infrared spectra describe materials by the unique pattern and provide information on material chemistry. Band intensities depend on the concentration of the compound and the molar decadic absorption coefficient that is reflected in the spectrum and on individual properties of the functional group. Most molecules are infrared active and represented by diverse bands due to different types of molecule vibrations. They are characterised by a typical energy level and are therefore found at defined wavenumbers. The molecule skeleton and other functional groups influence the band position and can cause a band shift. Whereas pure substances show distinct bands that can be attributed to functional groups, complex materials feature broad and overlapping bands that are often not assignable. However, the material shows a "fingerprint". The information of underlying features can be extracted by multivariate data analysis. Spectroscopic methods are widely used due to many advantages, e.g. easy handling, robustness, complex information. Multivariate data analysis is an indispensable tool for data evaluation in practice.

The thermal behaviour of any substance depends on chemical and physical properties. Complex materials contribute with all components to a specific thermal pattern. STA comprises thermogravimetry (TG) and differential scanning calorimetry (DSC). Additionally the released gaseous compounds are recorded in the coupled mass spectrometer. With TG the mass loss of the material is measured during combustion. DSC measurements result in a heat flow curve indicating exothermic and endothermic reactions of the material during combustion. The enthalpy can be calculated by integration of the area below the heat flow profile and a baseline. The variation of combustion parameters regarding temperature range, heating rate, isothermal heating and gas flow, oxidative or pyrolytic conditions leads to different information about the sample. In material sciences thermal analysis is widely used for quality control. In general, distinct temperatures are in the focus of interest, e.g. melting and crystallisation temperature. The application of thermal analysis has been extended during the last decade. TG- and DSC-profiles also lead to comprehensive information as spectra do. Both FT-IR spectroscopy and STA have proven to be adequate tools for the characterisation and quality assessment of complex materials such as waste and soils [14-20]. The extensive use of these methods in this field is also a merit of multivariate data analysis. Based on this approach much information can be extracted from a huge data pool generated by FT-IR spectroscopy and STA.

2. Methods

2.1. FT-IR spectroscopy and simultaneous thermal analysis

FT-IR spectra of landfill samples were recorded by a Bruker Alpha® (Bruker, Germany) instrument in the mid infrared area (4000 cm^{-1} to 400 cm^{-1}) in the attenuated total reflection mode (ATR). For the milled lignocellulosic materials the ATR-FT-IR spectra were collected by a Bruker Vertex® with a Pike MIRacle™ ATR device in the wavenumber range from 4000 cm^{-1} to 600 cm^{-1}, at 4 cm^{-1} resolution averaging 32 scans. The milled sample was homogenised and directly applied on the ATR reflection module with a diamond crystal providing a measuring area of approximately 4 mm^2 and a pressure applicator. Twenty four scans per spectrum were collected at a resolution of 4 cm^{-1} and corrected against ambient air as background. The average of four spectra (maximum deviation of the four spectra from the average spectrum < 5%) was vector normalised prior to multivariate data analysis. Spectra treatment and data evaluation were carried out using the OPUS software.

Thermal analyses were carried out with a STA 409 CD Skimmer instrument (Netzsch GmbH) in an Al$_2$O$_3$ pan with the following combustion parameters: temperature range 30 – 950 °C, heating rate 10 °C·min^{-1}, gas flow 150 ml·min^{-1} (80% He and 20% O$_2$), sample amount 16.00 mg. The pyrolysis of wood powder was carried out at different temperatures (200, 300, 350, and 600 °C) under oxygen-free conditions (100% He) with a heating rate of 10 °C·min^{-1} and isothermal treatment for 20 min. After oxidative combustion of the pyrolysed wood powder the enthalpy was calculated by integration of the area below the heat flow curve and a horizontal baseline from 30 to 650 °C, starting at 30 °C.

For data evaluation the heat flow profiles and the temperature resolved curve of the CO_2 ion current extracted from the mass spectrum were used. For data evaluation the integrated software PROTEUS was used.

The sample sets that were subjected to multivariate data analysis are mentioned in the text. Depending on the material and the question to be answered different multivariate evaluation methods were applied using The Unscrambler® 9.2 and 10.0 respectively (Camo®).

2.2. Multivariate data analysis

A large number of multivariate data analysis techniques are available. Depending on the questions to be answered the adequate method is applied. The methods presented here either belong to the group of "pattern recognition" or to the group of "multivariate calibration methods". The group of "pattern recognition" comprises exploratory data evaluation such as principal component analysis (PCA) and classification methods (SIMCA). The PCA visualises the inherent data structure in the scores matrix and thus reveals hidden phenomena. The influence of variables on the data structure is illustrated by the loadings plot. Classification aims at separation of groups of data. It is a prerequisite for classification that class characteristics have to be known prior to analysis. Therefore classification is called a "supervised method" compared to a non-supervised method by which groups of data are distinguished after the data analysis without previous knowledge. From supervised methods a model can be derived in order to discriminate between the groups [21]. Thus classification is a predictive method based on category variables, e.g. material types, age, degree of degradation. A library of spectra or thermograms provides the opportunity of data evaluation according to different aspects that are expressed by category variables and allows a multiple evaluation of spectra and thermograms. Soft independent modelling of class analogy (SIMCA) is a classification procedure based on PCA class modelling. "Soft modelling" that is often used in chemical pattern recognition means that two classes can overlap. Thus it is possible that samples have characteristics of both defined classes, or of neither of the defined classes. Samples are assigned to a defined class if they show similar characteristics. Similarity in this context means a particular class pattern. This approach allows the samples to have their individual properties besides common features of the class that are the decisive factor for the membership. In order to find out to which degree the class models really differ, the model (class) distance is determined by fitting members from two defined classes to their own model as well as to the other model. It is calculated on the basis of pooled residual standard deviations. The distance from a model to itself is 1. According to Esbensen [21] distances of more than 3 indicate a significant segregation between the defined classes. The results obtained can be visualised by the Coomans plot. The crossing horizontal and vertical lines that divide the area into four quadrants indicate the significance level. In two quadrants the defined classes are located. If samples feature properties of both classes they are assigned to the overlapping quadrant ("both"). New samples outside the limits do not belong to the model. They are located in the quadrant "neither - nor". The 5% significance level means that 95% of the samples in the corresponding quadrants truly belong to the defined classes. New samples in these quadrants are therefore identified as members of the classes.

Partial Least Squares-Discriminant Analysis (PLS-DA) is based on PLS regression to model the differences between classes. For the separation of two classes the PLS algorithm is used with the dummy variable (e.g. -1/+1) to distinguish the two defined groups.

Methods of the "calibration" group allow models to be developed for parameter prediction if the parameter is adequately reflected by the collected data, in this study by the spectral and thermal patterns. Contrary to classification models by which class assignment according to defined properties is performed, the prediction model provides distinct values of the parameter in question. Prediction models focus on the determination of dependent Y-variables for new samples that were characterised by independent X-variables. Based on an established validated X-Y model the Y-variable can be derived from X-variables. Due to this relationship only X-measurements are necessary. This procedure can be advantageous if expensive and time-consuming methods for the determination of Y-variables are replaced by superior methods.

3. Application of multivariate data analysis

3.1. Deterioration of organic matter in dumps and landfills

Degradation of organic matter is a natural necessary process in the environment. On the one hand degradability is an inherent property of materials that depends on both chemistry and structure and on the other hand it is mainly influenced by environmental conditions that determine the velocity of this process. The balance between synthesis, transformation and degradation is a criterion of sustainability. Organic matter in mixed waste consists of native biomolecules, modified biomolecules or organic substances that are exclusively based on chemical syntheses. Modification means chemical and physical diversification. Modification of biomolecules, e.g. wood or cellulose is necessary to enhance the stability against microbial attacks. For biological degradation chemical or physical modification represents a barrier to some degree. Wood modification for instance such as acetylation and thermal treatment can increase the lifetime of a product, but pose a problem for degradation [22-24]. Microbial degradation of synthetics hardly takes place. Ageing by oxygen and UV exposure in the forefront can contribute to a certain bioavailability of molecule moieties. Due to the heterogeneity of materials and conditions in old landfills and dumps the turnover and the emissions are hardly predictable. This fact and the long aftercare phase led to the European "multi-barrier" concept that provides the pre-treatment of municipal solid waste prior to landfilling. This procedure ensures extensive degradation within a limited period of time under controlled aerobic conditions. Nevertheless, landfill sites from the past are still a current topic. Investigations of the solid waste focus on the assessment of the current stage, and the potential of future emissions can consequently be derived. Ageing of the landfill also comprises the attenuation of hazardous substances in the leachate that are released due to degradation of organic matter via the liquid path. The duration of the emission process is mainly influenced by sorption and desorption processes of the landfill. Degradation has taken place in the past, but due to manifold interactions with the mineral matrix the release of mineralisation products is delayed and requires monitoring over a long period of time [25].

Within the scope of a landfill risk assessment regarding the remaining emission potential characterisation of an old landfill (AL) was carried out using FT-IR spectroscopy and thermal analyses besides bio-indication by vegetation, biological tests and conventional parameters. The objective of these investigations was to decide on additional measures for landfill restoration, e.g. *in situ* aeration, if natural attenuation had been insufficient. The landfill originated from the 1970s and 1980s. For the risk assessment 70 old landfill (AL) samples were classified. Additionally 15 samples from a reactor landfill, where municipal solid waste was deposited without pre-treatment until 2007, were integrated in the research programme for comparison and were classified as well. The SIMCA models [21] comprised 110 samples originating from different old landfills ("LF") with very low gas forming potential and 190 mechanically-biologically treated ("MBT") waste samples representing all stages of degradation and diverse reactivity. Besides samples from the old landfill (AL) to be assessed, 130 landfill samples (115 samples from old landfills + 15 reactor landfill samples) with low, middle and high gas forming potential were used for the total organic carbon (TOC) prediction model by means of PLS-R. Table 1 compiles the sample set used for SIMCA (section 3.1.1) and PLS-R (section 3.1.2).

Sample origin	Sample number (SIMCA)	Sample number (PLS-R)
Old landfill (AL)	70	70
Old landfills (LF)	110	115
Reactor landfill	15	15
MBT	190	-

Table 1. Origin and number of samples used for SIMCA and PLS-R

3.1.1. The degree of degradation - Assessment by classification

The degree of organic matter degradation is a key parameter for the verification of efficient waste pre-treatment and safe disposal. With respect to the assessment of old deposits it decides on additional measures for landfill sanitation, e.g. *in situ* aeration. Gaseous emissions such as methane and nitrous oxide should be minimised due to their contribution to global warming. The microbial activity and the gas forming potential of the solid waste are usually determined on the basis of time-consuming biological tests. Both FT-IR spectroscopy and STA are useful alternative methods. Different approaches are possible to evaluate spectral and thermal data to reveal the emission potential: prediction of reactivity parameters based on infrared spectra and PLS-R or classification (SIMCA) of unreactive and reactive samples according to their spectral pattern. Prediction of the required parameters "respiration activity" and "gas generation potential" by FT-IR spectroscopy replaces time-consuming and expensive parameters if a model is available. This approach was realised for mechanically-biologically treated municipal solid waste and composts [26, 27]. For old landfill materials prediction did not lead to reliable results because chemical (spectral) characteristics do not adequately reflect the biological behaviour at low reactivity levels [4]. Mineral components affect the biological behaviour although biodegradable substances are still present and visible in the spectrum. Moreover, the biological tests are error-prone at low values. It should also be emphasised that the C-H vibrations of the aliphatic methylene group that are an essential indicator of decomposing biomolecules in fresh waste materials are rather assigned to plastics in old landfill materials which was confirmed by thermal analysis [4]. Due to these reasons classification by SIMCA was applied. It was based on mid-infrared spectra over the whole wavenumber range from 4000 cm^{-1} to 400 cm^{-1}. As mentioned above SIMCA does not lead to parameter values as PLS-R does, but provides information on specific properties of interest via classification. For the comparison with distinct limit values of the Landfill Ordinance [28] this might be a difficulty. However, the basis for the category variable can be distinct parameter values as illustrated in the following example. Two classes were defined: old landfills ("LF") with the reactivity level clearly below the limit values of the Austrian Landfill Ordinance [28] and biologically treated waste ("MBT") comprising all stages of degradation after mechanical pre-treatment. The limit values are defined for respiration activity to be 7 mg O_2 per gram dry matter over a 4-day-period and 20 NL (NL = norm litre) gas per kg dry matter over a 21-day-period. Samples used for the "LF" class cover a wide range of unreactive materials from different Austrian and German old landfills. Samples used for the "MBT" class originated from the sixteen Austrian treatment plants. Each class was modelled by a separate PCA. By means of SIMCA landfill (AL) and reactor landfill samples were classified. For the class "LF" very low reactivity is the common class property. The class "MBT" represents different degradation

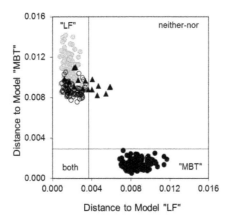

Figure 1. Classification of old landfill (AL) spectra (black circles) and reactor landfill spectra (black triangles) by means of the SIMCA model visualised by the Coomans plot; grey dots = "LF" class, black dots = "MBT" class

stages of municipal solid waste after the mechanical pre-treatment. The model distance was determined to be 42, which indicates a significant segregation between the class "LF" and the class "MBT". The results obtained were visualised by the Coomans plot (Figure 1). The assigned landfill (AL) samples (black circles) were identified as members of the "LF" class (grey dots). The chosen significance level of 5% indicates that 95% truly belong to unreactive landfills. The classification result of the investigated landfill samples reveals that ageing and degradation has taken place to a large degree and no risk is expected regarding the emission potential which is in accordance to the reactivity parameters that were determined for control. By contrast, the younger reactor landfill (black triangles) where degradation had progressed less, showed several reactive samples that are located in the quadrant "neither – nor" as they do not comply with the stability criteria that specify the "LF" class nor with characteristics of the MBT" class.

The question why reactive samples are not assigned to the "MBT" class that covers all stages of degradation can be answered by the different composition and different metabolic products under aerobic and anaerobic conditions. The different composition mainly results from resource recovery and mechanical pre-treatment.

3.1.2. The degree of degradation - assessment by parameter prediction

The compliance with the limit values according to the Austrian Landfill Ordinance [28] is a prerequisite for landfilling of waste materials in Austria. The TOC is a key criterion for the assessment of organic matter as it is the source of potential emissions. Due to degradation of organic matter the TOC content decreases continuously to a low level. The remaining organic carbon can be assigned to recalcitrant components such as wood, waxes, cork, natural rubber, chitin, humified matter, modified biomolecules and synthetics. A low value therefore indicates extensive degradation of biodegradable substances. Apart from the special regulation for biologically treated municipal solid waste a limit value of 5% for the TOC was stipulated by the Austrian Landfill Ordinance [28]. Within the scope of the risk assessment of the old landfill (AL) the TOC contents of the 70 samples were determined together with different landfill materials (Table 1) using the carbon-nitrogen-sulphur (CNS) analyser. The thermal behaviour is strongly related to material composition and reflects physical and chemical properties. Biodegradation leads to substantial changes of material properties that can be revealed by thermal analysis. The content of organic carbon mainly influences the thermal behaviour. Therefore it can be expected that the TOC is adequately reflected by the thermal pattern of the material. Among different combustion parameters the heat flow profile, resulting from differential scanning calorimetry (DSC), was selected for the TOC prediction model by means of PLS-R. The TOC is the Y-variable being in demand and DSC data represent the X-variable. Figure 2A displays the heat flow profiles of two old landfill (AL) samples (A and B). Sample A contains a high portion of plastics that are revealed by sharp and distinct exothermic peaks in the heat flow profile. Figure 2B demonstrates the correlation between the predicted and the measured TOC values. Four PLS components were used to calculate the model.

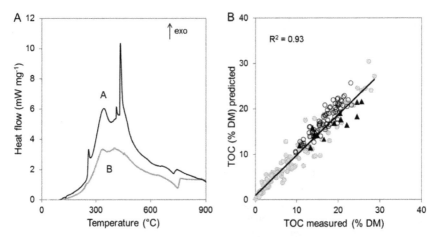

Figure 2. A-B: Heat flow profiles of two old landfill (AL) samples A and B (A); Correlation between the predicted and the measured TOC contents (B) based on heat flow profiles of old landfill samples (grey dots), old landfill (AL) samples (black circles), reactor landfill samples (black triangles) and PLS-R (n = 200, R^2 = 0.93, RMSECV = 1.95%); DM = dry matter

The root mean square error of cross validation (RMSECV) was found to be 1.95% and the coefficient of determination (R^2) 0.93. Despite the low reactivity the TOC values of the old landfill (AL) are relatively high and in the range of the reactor landfill. The TOC is a main parameter in the Austrian Landfill Ordinance [28] to describe the organic matter content. Landfilling criteria for all landfill types regarding organic matter contents are stipulated by the limit value of the TOC content. Only mechanically-biologically treated municipal solid waste of which landfilling criteria are defined by biological tests is an exception. The sum parameter does not differentiate organic substances that can considerably differ in the biological behaviour. This fact confirms the limited significance of the sum parameter, especially for the evaluation of old deposits where the high TOC is mainly caused by plastics and textiles that hardly contribute to emissions under anaerobic conditions.

3.2. Carbonation – ageing of incineration bottom ash deposits

Carbonates are relevant components in Austrian municipal solid waste (MSW). In the past construction waste was landfilled together with municipal solid waste which is still recognised by the high portion of carbonates in old deposits. The separation of construction waste has become a legal request in order to meet the target of material recycling, to improve the biological treatment of municipal solid waste and to comply with the limit values of the demolition waste landfill. Nevertheless, carbonates are always part of municipal solid waste. Residues of construction materials are the main source of carbonates. During waste combustion carbonate decay takes place at temperatures above 650 °C which is paralleled by CO_2 release and the formation of the corresponding oxides, e.g. CaO. The uptake of water leads to hydroxides and high pH-values between 12 and 13 of MSW incineration bottom ash. During the natural ageing process of the deposited material CO_2 from air causes the inverse reaction in that carbonates are built up again. The velocity of the process in the environment depends on available surfaces where carbonation takes place. It can be accelerated by the increase of the surface and artificial CO_2 supply. Carbonation causes the pH-value to decrease which leads to the stabilisation of the system and immobilisation of heavy metals [29, 30].

Fresh incineration bottom ash was compared to ashes aged under laboratory conditions. Laboratory conditions mean that the material is crushed < 20 mm and CO_2 is continuously supplied until saturation is reached and no additional CO_2 is adsorbed. Thermal analysis is an appropriate method for carbonate determination [31]. It was applied in combination with PLS-DA to find out whether artificially aged bottom ash could be clearly distinguished from fresh bottom ash. Additionally several samples of naturally aged incineration bottom ash that had been stored in a pile over decades and partially exposed to air were included to reveal the progress of carbonation under environmental conditions. The content of carbonates is reflected by both the mass loss (thermogravimetry) due to CO_2 release and by the peak intensity of the heat flow profile caused by the endothermic reaction of the carbonate decay above 650 °C. Moreover, the CO_2 ion current was recorded by the coupled mass spectrometer. It is evident (Figure 3A, curve A) that carbonates are also found in fresh bottom ash as the carbonation reaction starts immediately after contact of fresh bottom ash with air. Curve B displays a peak at around 450 °C. As the material does not contain organic compounds (TOC below the limit of determination) it can be assumed that CO_2 is adsorbed to a certain degree and is removed within this temperature range. The temperature resolved CO_2 ion current curves (Figure 3A) were used for data evaluation and subjected to PLS-DA. The dummy variable (-1) was assigned to fresh incineration bottom ash, the dummy variable (+1) to bottom ash with advanced carbonation. Figure 3B displays the result of the PLS-DA.

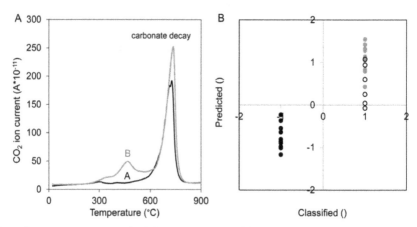

Figure 3. A-B: Temperature resolved CO_2 ion current (A) of fresh (black line A) and aged (grey line B) bottom ash; Discriminant analysis (PLS-DA) of the temperature resolved CO_2 ion current (B) of fresh (black dots) and aged bottom ash (artificial CO_2 supply = grey dots, natural ageing = black circles)

Despite the long lasting storage of incineration bottom ash in the environment carbonation was less efficient (black circles) and the discrimination from fresh ash is not as distinct which can be due to greater particle sizes and inhibited CO_2 supply in the pile. Minor carbonate contents are not the reason as more construction waste was usually deposited with municipal solid waste several decades ago.

3.3. Compost application on soils – Degradation and enrichment of organic matter

The loss of organic carbon in agricultural soils is caused by several factors. It is mainly influenced by tillage and application of mineral fertilisers. Climate change and increasing temperatures might support this development. The supply of organic matter is an indispensable measure to maintain relevant soil functions such as water and nutrient holding capacity and aggregate stability. Composting is one option to stabilise organic materials, especially by humification which corresponds to the natural process in soils. Although there are many questions to be answered how humification of composts can be improved, this procedure is a relevant contribution to carbon sequestration despite the benefits for soils. Composting is a process of degradation and stabilisation at once. Ageing does not only result in deterioration, but also in stable organic matter synthesis as it is the case for humic substances with a very low turnover rate. Depending on the input material the ageing process takes place in different ways. Some mixtures of organic materials are rather mineralised and deterioration dominates. A well-balanced mixture of organic residues containing a variety of biogenic materials with different biodegradability provides favourable conditions for humification and higher contents of humic substances are obtained. FT-IR spectra of different biogenic materials were recorded. They include several stages of decomposition and stabilisation from fresh to composted materials. The PCA result in Figure 4 shows the grouping of different biogenic materials. Group A (grey triangles = sewage sludge compost) comprises sewage sludge, paper sludge and bulk materials, group B (grey and black dots = biowaste composts from two composting plants) contains garden waste, kitchen waste and bulk materials. In order to track the humification process the relevant wavenumber regions (1745-1685 cm^{-1} and 1610-1567 cm^{-1}) according to Meissl et al. [27], where humic acids are reflected were selected for the PCA. The calculation was performed with four principal components (PC). The first PC explains 94% of the variance and the second PC 3%. Marginal humification took place in the sewage sludge mixture during composting [32]. Group B featured a relevant increase of humic acids to 40% of organic dry matter, as confirmed by chemical analyses.

Humic substances in composts are young compared to soil humic substances. It can be hypothesised that the process of ageing which includes further degradation, mineralisation and additional stabilisation of compost organic matter is continued after compost application to soils and influenced by many factors [33]. Several long-term experiments provide information on how soil parameters change and develop by fertiliser application and amelioration measures [34, 35]. Plaggen soils represent an example of anthropogenic soils generated by compost application over centuries which resulted in higher organic matter contents compared to the surrounding poor soils [36, 37]. The higher organic matter

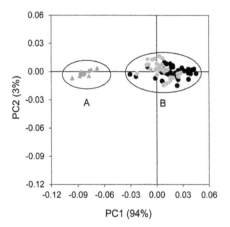

Figure 4. Scores plot of the PCA of hardly (A = grey triangles, sewage sludge compost) and well (B = grey and black dots, biowaste composts) humified composts based on the infrared spectral regions 1745-1685 cm^{-1} and 1610-1567 cm^{-1}

content is a typical feature of this soil type although it has considerably decreased if the level of the original compost serves as a rating scale. According to climate conditions the organic matter content develops towards the corresponding equilibrium over long periods of time. The interactions of compost organic matter with soil organic matter and mineral components under specific climatic conditions are hardly investigated, especially the influence of compost quality on dynamics of biodegradation [32]. Quality in this context focuses on the degree of organic matter stabilisation. Long-term monitoring systems will be necessary in the future to collect a comprehensive data set for statistical evaluation to find out which compost can efficiently compensate for organic matter losses. The multivariate approach enables identifying different factors that influence the ageing process, e.g. soil type, mineral matrix, degree of compost humification and climate.

A long-term project was started in 2010 to find out the development of organic matter contents in agricultural soils by application of well humified compost. The data represent the first two years of the long-term monitoring programme. Compost was applied on three different test plots (10 m x 10 m) in an agricultural region in Eastern Styria, Austria. A plot of the corresponding agricultural soil (10 m x 10 m) without compost application served as a reference. The composition of the soils differed in the clay content. Samples originating from the trial fields with compost application and samples from the reference plot were collected after the first and the second year of compost application and characterised by means of thermal analysis. All plots were represented by 4 composite samples, each one consisting of 10 individual samples. The material was taken from a depth up to 30 cm. Particles of organic matter (roots, leaves, stalks, vegetable residues etc.) were carefully separated in order to analyse only degraded organic matter. Thermal analysis is an appropriate method to describe complex matrices. Water in interface layers of clay minerals in soils can pretend higher organic matter contents if this parameter is determined via the mass loss caused by

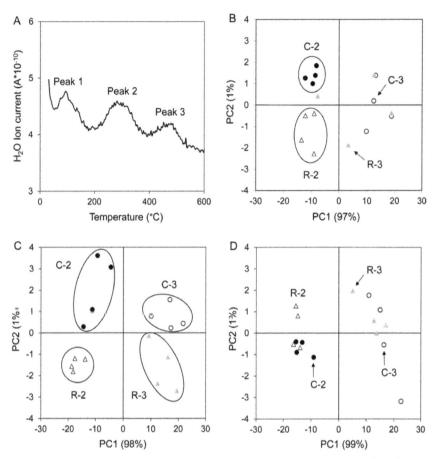

Figure 5. A-D: Temperature resolved H₂O ion current of combustion gases (A); Scores plots of the PCA based on the DSC profiles of samples from the three (B-D) test plots; sampling after one and two years with (C-2, C-3) and without (R-2, R-3) compost application

combustion in the muffle furnace. Figure 5A confirms this assumption by the temperature resolved ion current of water (m/z = 18) extracted from the mass spectrum of combustion gases. Peak 1 is assigned to residual water of the air-dried sample, peak 2 results from the oxidative combustion of organic matter and peak 3 can be attributed to water from interface layers of clay minerals. The PCAs were based on the heat flow (DSC) profiles. The heat flow pattern reflects the exothermic reaction of organic matter combustion and is therefore an adequate method to evaluate the development of organic matter in soils. Figures 5B-D display the scores plots of the PCAs calculated for the three test plots with compost (C) and the corresponding reference plots (R) after one (C-2, R-2) and two years (C-3, R-3). The different sampling times can be clearly distinguished (left and right areas in the scores plot of the PCA). Apart from the test plot shown in Figure 5C the influence of compost application on soil organic matter is not detectable after 2 years. Differences between the two sampling times are caused by other effects. It is evident that the process of organic matter deterioration is also affected by the soil matrix and local conditions. The interference by other effects implies long-term observations in order to unambiguously verify an increase of organic matter, especially if carbon sequestration is assessed and CO_2 balances are derived.

3.4. Ageing of charcoal

Carbonaceous residues from combustion processes in the environment have become a field of increasing interest. Incomplete combustion of organic materials under oxygen-free or - poor conditions is a common feature of carbonaceous materials. Depending on the material and the pyrolysis process several terms are in use for the resulting products: biochar, charcoal, chars, and soot carbon. All types of these products are subsumed under the terms "black, charred or pyrogenic carbon". Charcoals are ubiquitous in terrestrial and aquatic environments. They are found in many areas due to forest fires and in urban soils where anthropogenic activities or fire disasters have left their marks. Charcoal production has a long tradition in the context of early technical processes where heat and energy were needed. Residues of charcoal are found at historical sites of charcoal burning in connection with ore mining and metallurgical processes, glass production and lime kilns. The traditional production of charcoal has been abandoned in most cases. It is only found in a few areas on a diminished scale nowadays as cultural heritage. Charcoal is currently produced in closed systems, not least because of organic pollutants generated during pyrolysis.

Carbonaceous residues rank among the fraction of recalcitrant organic matter in soils. In the context of climate change its relevance in the carbon cycle and the contribution to carbon sequestration has become a crucial topic during the last decades [38, 39]. With the emerging scientific interest in "Terra preta" soils where charcoal is thought to play an important role in the amelioration of physical and chemical properties of tropical soils [40-42], additional benefits are attributed to pyrolysis products. The particular capillary structure of charcoals leads to enhanced water und nutrient retention and might explain their favourable impact to soils.

Due to its recalcitrance charcoal is a witness of anthropogenic activities in the past as revealed by excavations at archaeological sites [43, 44]. Besides historical, cultural and technological aspects, questions about the long-term behaviour of charcoals in the environment, carbon release, effects on soil and vegetation arise. Historical charcoals enable us to track the ageing process of a recalcitrant carbon fraction, to discover chemical and physical changes and to identify the significance of their environmental impact. Historical charcoals that trace back to the Middle Ages and the Modern period were investigated using thermal analysis and compared to recent charcoals that were produced according to the ancient technology in rectangular charcoal mounds. The historical charcoals were produced in rectangular mounds, but also in charcoal pits or charcoal platforms. Depending on the region and the availability different kinds of wood were used. The sample set used for these investigations was dominated by the following species *Picea abies, Pinus sylvestris* and *Fagus sylvatica*.

Thermal analysis is an appropriate method to characterise these materials [45]. The influence of pyrolysis temperature and wood species on the thermal behaviour was investigated in several experiments in order to support data interpretation. Figure 6A (left side) displays the enthalpy of charcoal that was produced from wood powder at different pyrolysis temperatures (200, 300, 350, and 600 °C) under laboratory conditions. The grey bars indicate the enthalpy referring to dry matter (DM) and the black bars the enthalpy referring to organic dry matter (oDM). It is evident that increasing pyrolysis temperatures result in higher enthalpies of the charcoal. Figure 6A (right side) additionally shows the enthalpy of charcoals (left pair of bars) produced at 350 °C from different wood species (Pa = *Picea abies*, Ps = *Pinus sylvestris*, Fs = *Fagus sylvatica*) under laboratory conditions and the enthalpy of the corresponding untreated wood (right pair of bars). The enthalpy of wood is low compared to its pyrolysis product. According to preliminary results the pyrolysis temperature has a stronger effect on enthalpies than the wood species. Further analyses will be performed to reveal more details about the impact of wood species, pyrolysis time and applied historical technologies. For multivariate data evaluation every influencing factor requires an adequate number of samples.

Due to the long exposure time in the environment historical charcoals are contaminated by different substances. In order to minimise the portion of adhesive mineral components from the surrounding soil, only charcoal particles were collected at historical sites. The surface of

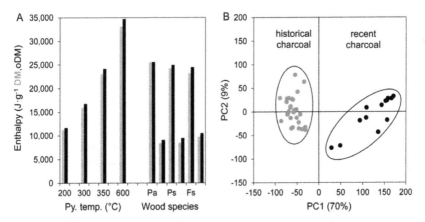

Figure 6. A-B: Left side (A): Enthalpies of charcoals from wood powder (pyrolysis temperatures 200, 300, 350, and 600 °C), right side (A): enthalpies of charcoals (pyrolysis temperature 350 °C) from different wood species and corresponding non treated wood (Pa = *Picea abies*, Ps = *Pinus sylvestris*, Fs = *Fagus sylvatica*, grey bars referring to DM, black bars referring to oDM); PCA based on DSC profiles of historical and recent charcoals (B).

the particle was removed and the core was used for sample preparation. However, mineral particles were also found in the capillaries of historical charcoals. Their presence was confirmed by the higher percentage of inorganic matter. It can be assumed that other unknown chemical compounds were adsorbed at the surfaces of charcoal capillaries. The inclusion of non-charcoal compounds was considered as an intrinsic factor of the ageing process and therefore the whole sample was taken as "historical" charcoal. Figure 6B displays a PCA result based on DSC profiles of historical and recent charcoals. Historical and recent charcoals are clearly segregated. The first PC explains 70% of the variance.

3.5. Lignocellulosic materials

Wood or lignocellulosic materials in general are ubiquitous in the environment and are therefore involved in many degradation processes of material mixtures such as municipal solid waste, landfill materials or soils. In the previous sections lignocellulosic material was often part of waste organic matter and evaluated together with other components. Although the degradation behaviour of the mixture can be or is different from those of single constituents, the knowledge of their composition, of differences and physico-chemical properties are useful for a better understanding of the behaviour of lignocellulosic material. The main structural wood polymers - cellulose, hemicelluloses, and lignin - are the most abundant biopolymers of the Earth's carbon cycle. These polymers form the lignocellulose complex in all woody tissues. The highly ordered structure of cellulose microfibril aggregates embedded in a matrix of hemicelluloses and lignin provides the basis for its mechanical strength [46] and for the resistance to microbial attack [47], to which also low molecular mass extractives contribute [48].

3.5.1. Wood types / species and their composition

The two wood types - hardwood and softwood – can be identified by FT-IR due to their different chemical composition. A PCA based on the fingerprint region (1800 cm^{-1} to 700 cm^{-1}) of ATR-FT-IR spectra of different wood species belonging to hardwood (Poplar - *Populus × canadensis*, Beech - *Fagus sylvatica*, Birch - *Betula pendula*) or softwood (Pine - *Pinus sylvestris*, Spruce - *Picea abies*) shows their separation in the scores plot along PC1 (Figure 7A), which accounts for 77% of the spectral variation. The loadings plot of the first principal component (PC1) (Figure 7C) shows the variables (wavenumbers) that are responsible for the separation, describing the differences due to different contents or numbers of functional groups representing chemical compounds. A positive loading means that the samples with positive values in the scores plot have a higher number of the functional group represented by this wavenumber, e.g. hardwoods have a higher number of acetyl groups (C=O stretching vibration of the acetyl group at 1735 cm^{-1}) than softwoods (Figure 7C) or vice versa softwoods have a lower number of acetyl groups. The acetyl groups derive from the acetic acid esters attached to the hemicelluloses. Comprehensive lists for the assignment of bands found in the infrared spectra of wood and acetylated wood can be found elsewhere [49-51]. The band at 1235 cm^{-1} corresponds to the C-O vibration of this acetyl ester. Three further remarkable bands at 1593 cm^{-1}, 1510 cm^{-1}, and 1268 cm^{-1} represent lignin. The lignin content and composition of hardwoods and softwoods are different. Softwood has higher lignin contents than hardwood which is represented in PC1 by the negative loading of the band at 1510 cm^{-1}. Softwood lignin consists mainly of G-lignin (guaiacyl units) and hardwood lignin mainly of S-lignin (syringyl units). Besides small differences of the wavenumber at which the maxima of the bands appear the latter has a stronger band at 1593 cm^{-1}. Therefore the loading of this band is positive (Figure 7C, PC1).

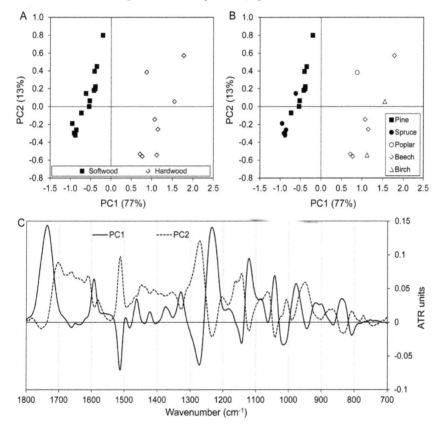

Figure 7. A-C: PCA based on the fingerprint region (1800 cm^{-1} to 700 cm^{-1}) of the baseline-corrected and minimum-maximum normalised ATR-FT-IR spectra of different wood species (Pine - *Pinus sylvestris*, Spruce - *Picea abies*, Poplar - *Populus × canadensis*, Beech - *Fagus sylvatica*, Birch - *Betula pendula*); Scores plots of the first two principal components labelled according to wood type (A) and species (B) and their loading spectra (C)

The band at 1268 cm^{-1} typical for G-lignin shows negative loadings and scores, because more G-lignin is found in softwoods. The separation along PC2 (13%) is mainly due to different lignin contents of the different species. For further interpretation of the differences the reader is pointed to additional literature [49-52].

Lignin content and lignin composition are important wood parameters. Their fast and reliable determination is therefore of interest and was studied with infrared spectroscopic methods using both ranges the near infrared (NIR) [53-59] and the mid infrared (MIR) [56, 60] leading to many PLS-R models. Simple linear regressions between the ratio of bands heights (H_{1510} / H_{897}) [60] and the lignin content (Figure 8A) result in prediction models with similar precision as those obtained form PLS-R models for MIR (Figure 8B) and NIR [58, 59].

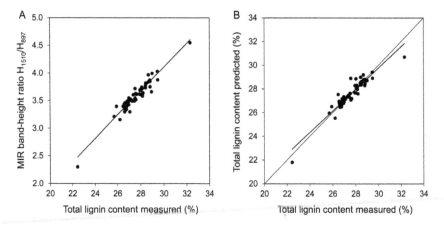

Figure 8. A-B: Calibration with a good correlation (r = 0.965) between band-heights ratios H_{1510} / H_{897} from MIR spectra and lignin contents (A); Cross-validation result of the PLS-R model for the total lignin content determination (B) using the minimum - maximum normalised MIR spectra in the wavenumber range from 1745 cm^{-1} to 790 cm^{-1} with 4 PLS components, R^2 = 0.89, and a RMSECV of 0.43%

3.5.2. Degradation of wood

Ageing and deterioration of wood is caused by light [61], temperature [62], moisture, microorganism [10], fungi [47, 63], and others, which influence physical and chemical properties.

Wood is a remarkably durable material. In nature, only higher fungi have developed biochemical systems to degrade the lignocellulose complex and perform the conversion and mineralisation of wood to carbon dioxide and water. Most of these fungi belong to basidiomycetes. Although they are phylogenetically closely related [64] their strategies of degrading wood are diverse: While brown-rot fungi degrade primarily the wood polysaccharides and leave behind a polymeric but highly modified lignin, simultaneous white-rot fungi degrade all polymeric wood constituents at similar rates. Selective white-rot fungi, which lack the ability to degrade cellulose efficiently, cause extensive delignification of wood. Ascomycetes and Deuteromycetes may cause soft-rot decay that leads to softening of wet wood. Cavity formations in wood cell walls are most characteristic for this decay type. Extensive reviews on decay pattern, chemistry, and biochemistry of microbial wood degradation are available [47, 63, 65].

NIR [60, 66-72] and MIR [73, 74] spectroscopy have been used since about three decades to follow the chemical changes due to fungal decay. How less invasive spectroscopic and microspectroscopic methods contribute to understand fungal wood decay has been reviewed recently [75].

The result of fungal decay of wood which has been exposed for a longer period can normally be seen at once. From the practical point of view when e.g. construction wood in service has to be evaluated the early degradation stages which cannot be seen are of special interest because the mechanical properties of wood are strongly influenced. Therefore spruce wood (*Picea abies* L. (Karst.)) was incubated with three strains of the selective white-rot fungi *Ceriporiopsis subvermispora* (namely FPL 90.031, FPL 105.752 and CBS 347.63) for 14 days (details in [60]). The PC1 – PC2 scores plot (Figure 9A) of a PCA, based on the second derivatives of the MIR spectra from 1800 cm^{-1} to 1490 cm^{-1}, shows that the time course can be followed along PC1. From the loadings spectra (not shown here but in [60]) it is known that the lignin content decreases with increasing incubation time. Along PC3 (Figure 9B) a kind of clustering of the three strains was obtained. This means that the PCA also allowed separation of the three strains and as a consequence from the loading spectra (cp. Figure 2e in [60]) information about the different behaviour of the three strains can be gained. Besides small differences in oxidation products and water adsorption properties the number of acetyl ester groups is different, which points to slightly different decay pattern of hemicelluloses. A better separation of the three strains was obtained using NIR spectra [60].

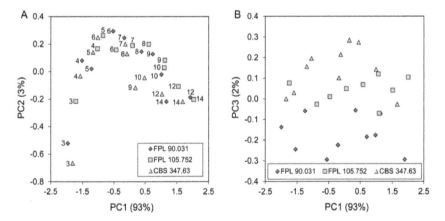

Figure 9. A-B: PCA results of the second derivatives of the MIR spectra from 1800 cm^{-1} to 1490 cm^{-1}: (A) scores plot PC1 – PC2; (B) scores plot PC1 – PC3; Adapted from [60] with the permission from IM Publications

The degradation of wood exposed for a longer period, was investigated using three types of pine wood (*Pinus sylvestris*) samples: a) recent, b) strongly degraded in a forest, and c) subfossil wood. The latter one, which was found in the sediment of a lake in Finland, was dated dendrochronologically to be 4000 – 5000 years-old [76].

The results of a PCA based on the fingerprint region (1800 cm^{-1} to 700 cm^{-1}) of the ATR-FT-IR spectra of pine wood (*Pinus sylvestris*) of varying degradation stages are shown in Figure 10. The scores plot of the first two principal components (Figure 10A) reveals that the two strongly degraded samples are far from the other ones along both axes. The loadings plot of PC2 (Figure 10C – PC2 A) shows that mainly polysaccharides, preferably hemicelluloses have been degraded. This conclusion is confirmed by the loss of the acetyl-ester band at 1735 cm^{-1}.

The loading spectrum of PC1 (Figure 10C – PC1 A) shows that the strongly degraded sample consists almost exclusively of lignin. A comparison of this spectrum with a milled wood lignin spectrum confirmed this (not shown). Therefore it can be concluded that this

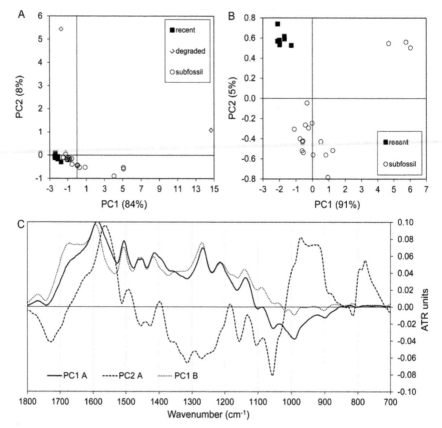

Figure 10. A-C: PCA based on the fingerprint region (1800 cm^{-1} to 700 cm^{-1}) of the baseline-corrected and minimum - maximum normalised ATR-FT-IR spectra of pine wood (*Pinus sylvestris* L.) of varying degradation stages; Scores plots of the first two principal components labelled according to degradation stage with (A) and without the samples labelled "degraded" (B) and their loading spectra (C), whereas A refers to the PCA in (A) and B to the PCA shown in (B)

sample was degraded by brown-rot fungi. The loading spectrum of PC1 (PC1 B) of the PCA shown in Figure 10B shows similarity with the previous one. This means that the difference between the recent samples and the subfossil samples is an increase in the lignin content. In his thesis Stich [76] reviewed possible degradation types and mechanisms including the preservation of organic matter in subfossil and fossil samples [77]. Based on his spectroscopic and chemical results he concluded that a slow *in situ* hydrolysis had taken place in these subfossil samples.

3.5.3. Natural durability of wood - Preventing wood from degradation

The service life of wood for outdoor use such as for windows, doors, balcony, roofs, bridges, and other applications should be as high as possible. Wood is a remarkably naturally durable material. This natural durability in terms of decay resistance against fungi, varies in a wide range between species and even within species [78-80] and can also be predicted by infrared spectroscopy [78, 81, 82]. The natural durability of wood mainly depends on the extractives composition [79, 83] but also on the extractives content [79] and is in general higher in hardwoods than in softwoods. Besides the natural durability and biological control of wood decay against fungal infection [84] thermal treatment of wood has shown to improve the service life [62, 85, 86] as well as chemical modification of wood such as acetylation [86-91], butyrylation [92] or furfurylation [93]. Traditional wood protection methods employ chemicals [94-99] that are considered toxic and can adversely affect human health and the environment [100]. Serious efforts are made globally to develop alternative protection methods based on natural products with little or no toxicity. The implementation of these technologies progresses slowly because of certain limitations, including discrepancies between laboratory and field performance of natural products, variability in their efficacy related to exposure/environmental conditions, and legislation difficulties due to disagreements on setting standards defining the quality of their performance and use. However, information on those natural compounds that have shown promise for wood protection is available under defined interactive categories [100].

4. Conclusions

Ageing and deterioration of different complex materials in the environment were characterised using FT-IR spectroscopy and thermal analysis. Due to large data pools generated by these analyses multivariate statistical methods were applied for data evaluation. Several examples of practical application and basic research were selected. Several samples originate from current investigations (section 3.3 and 3.4). The sample sets will be extended to elucidate the processes of ageing and deterioration. For compost application on soils the question of remaining organic matter in the long-term under the given climatic and soil conditions will be relevant. The contribution of different environmental factors should be revealed by multivariate data analysis. With regard to charcoals more historical samples from different regions are necessary to find out the contribution of pyrolysis temperature and time, wood species, applied technology and environmental conditions. Based on the collected data sets evaluation can be performed under diverse aspects by means of adequate multivariate methods.

Author details

E. Smidt and J. Tintner
Institute of Wood Science and Technology, University of Natural Resources and Life Sciences, Vienna, Austria

M. Schwanninger
Department of Chemistry, University of Natural Resources and Life Sciences, Vienna, Austria

K. Böhm
Institute of Waste Management, University of Natural Resources and Life Sciences, Vienna, Austria

Acknowledgement

M.S. thanks Leo Stich and Barbara Hinterstoisser, University of Natural Resources and Life Sciences, Vienna, Austria for providing the subfossil pine samples.

5. References

[1] Bogner J, Spokas K, Burton E, Sweeney R, Corona V (1995) Landfills as atmospheric methane sources and sinks. Chemosphere 31: 4119-4130.

[2] Manfredi S, Tonini D, Christensen TH, Scharff H (2009) Landfilling of waste: Accounting of greenhouse gases and global warming contributions. Waste Manage. Res. 27: 825-836.

[3] Tesar M, Prantl R, Lechner P (2007) Application of FT-IR for assessment of the biological stability of landfilled municipal solid waste (MSW) during in situ aeration. J. Environ. Monitor. 9: 110-118.

[4] Tintner J, Smidt E, Böhm K, Matiasch L (2012) Risk assessment of an old landfill regarding the potential of gaseous emissions - A case study based on bioindication, FT-IR spectroscopy and thermal analysis. Waste Manage. in press: 10.1016/j.wasman.2012.1007.1022.

[5] Neset TSS, Cordell D (2012) Global phosphorus scarcity: Identifying synergies for a sustainable future. J. Sci. Food Agr. 92: 2-6.

[6] Zhao QL, Ding J (2011) Nutrient removal and recovery from nitrogen- and phosphorus-laden waste streams in the form of struvite. Water Practice and Technology 6: DOI: 10.2166/wpt.2011.0072.

[7] Baciocchi R, Costa G, Lategano E, Marini C, Polettini A, Pomi R, et al. (2010) Accelerated carbonation of different size fractions of bottom ash from RDF incineration. Waste Manage. 30: 1310-1317.

[8] Dabo D, Badreddine R, De Windt L, Drouadaine I (2009) Ten-year chemical evolution of leachate and municipal solid waste incineration bottom ash used in a test road site. J. Hazard. Mater. 172: 904-913.

[9] Lehmann S (2011) Resource recovery and materials flow in the city: Zero waste and sustainable consumption as paradigm in urban development. J. Green Build. 6: 88-105.

[10] Schmidt O (2006) Wood and Tree Fungi: Biology, Damage, Protection, and Use. Berlin Heidelberg, Germany: Springer-Verlag. 334 p.

[11] Hon DN-S (2001) Weathering and Photochemistry of Wood. In: Hon DN-SaN, Shiraishi, editor. Wood and celllosic chemistry. New York: Marcel Dekker, Inc. p. 513-546.

[12] Hon DN-S, Minemura N (2001) Color and Discoloration. In: Hon DN-SaN, Shiraishi, editor. Wood and celllosic chemistry. New York: Marcel Dekker, Inc. p. 385-442.

[13] Chernev BS, Eder GC (2011) Spectroscopic characterization of the oligomeric surface structures on polyamide materials formed during accelerated aging. Appl. Spectrosc. 65: 1133-1144.

[14] Dell'Abate MT, Benedetti A, Sequi P (2000) Thermal methods of organic matter maturation monitoring during a composting process. J. Therm. Anal. Calorim. 61: 389-396.

[15] Leifeld J, Franko U, Schulz E (2006) Thermal stability responses of soil organic matter to long-term fertilization practices. Biogeosciences 3: 371-374.

[16] Provenzano MR, Ouatmane A, Hafidi M, Senesi N (2000) Differential scanning calorimetric analysis of composted materials from different sources. J. Therm. Anal. Calorim. 61: 607-614.

[17] Provenzano MR, Senesi N, Piccone G (1998) Thermal and spectroscopic characterization of composts from municipal solid wastes. Compost Sci. Util 6: 67-73.

[18] Smidt E, Böhm K, Tintner J (2010) Evaluation of old landfills - A thermoanalytical and spectroscopic approach. J. Environ. Monitor. 13: 362-369.

[19] Smidt E, Meissl K (2007) The applicability of Fourier Transform Infrared (FT-IR) spectroscopy in waste management. Waste Manage. 27: 268-276.

[20] Smidt E, Schwanninger M (2005) Characterization of waste materials using FTIR spectroscopy: Process monitoring and quality assessment. Spectrosc. Lett. 38: 247-270.

[21] Esbensen K (2002) Multivariate Data Analysis - in practice. Esbjerg: Alborg University. 598 p.

[22] Bryne LE, Lausmaa J, Ernstsson M, Englund F, Wälinder MEP (2010) Ageing of modified wood. Part 2: Determination of surface composition of acetylated, furfurylated, and thermally modified wood by XPS and ToF-SIMS. Holzforschung 64: 305-313.

[23] Hill CAS (2009) Why does acetylation protect wood from microbiological attack? Wood mater. sci. eng. 4: 37-45.

[24] Mohebby B, Militz H (2010) Microbial attack of acetylated wood in field soil trials. Int. Biodeterior. Biodegrad. 64: 41-50.

[25] Scharff H, Van Zomeren A, Van Der Sloot HA (2011) Landfill sustainability and aftercare completion criteria. Waste Manage. Res. 29: 30-40.

[26] Böhm K, Smidt E, Binner E, Schwanninger M, Tintner J, Lechner P (2010) Determination of MBT-waste reactivity - An infrared spectroscopic and multivariate statistical approach to identify and avoid failures of biological tests. Waste Manage. 30: 583-590.

[27] Meissl K, Smidt E, Schwanninger M (2007) Prediction of humic acid content and respiration activity of biogenic waste by means of Fourier transform infrared (FTIR) spectra and partial least squares regression (PLS-R) models. Talanta 72: 791-799.

[28] Verordnung des Bundesministers für Land- und Forstwirtschaft, Umwelt und Wasserwirtschaft über Deponien (Deponieverordnung 2008), BGBl. Nr. II 39/2008 (2008).

[29] Hyks J, Astrup T (2009) Influence of operational conditions, waste input and ageing on contaminant leaching from waste incinerator bottom ash: A full-scale study. Chemosphere 76: 1178-1184.

[30] Wei Y, Shimaoka T, Saffarzadeh A, Takahashi F (2011) Mineralogical characterization of municipal solid waste incineration bottom ash with an emphasis on heavy metal-bearing phases. J. Hazard. Mater. 187: 534-543.

[31] Smidt E, Meissl K, Tintner J, Ottner F (2010) Interferences of carbonate quantification in municipal solid waste incinerator bottom ash: Evaluation of different methods. Environ. Chem. Lett. 8: 217-222.

[32] Nicolàs C, Masciandaro G, Hernández T, Garcia C (2012) Chemical-Structural Changes of Organic Matter in a Semi-Arid Soil After Organic Amendment. Pedosphere 22: 283-293.

[33] Pérez-Lomas AL, Delgado G, Párraga J, Delgado R, Almendros G, Aranda V (2010) Evolution of organic matter fractions after application of co-compost of sewage sludge with pruning waste to four Mediterranean agricultural soils. A soil microcosm experiment. Waste Manage. 30: 1957-1965.

[34] Heitkamp F, Wendland M, Offenberger K, Gerold G (2012) Implications of input estimation, residue quality and carbon saturation on the predictive power of the Rothamsted Carbon Model. Geoderma 170: 168-175.

[35] Jandl G, Leinweber P, Schulten HR (2007) Origin and fate of soil lipids in a Phaeozem under rye and maize monoculture in central Germany. Biol. Fert. Soils 43: 321-332.

[36] Conry MJ (1974) Plaggen soils - A review of man-made raised soils. Soils & Fertilizers 37: 319-326.

[37] Hubbe A, Chertov O, Kalinina O, Nadporozhskaya M, Tolksdorf-Lienemann E, Giani L (2007) Evidence of plaggen soils in European North Russia (Arkhangelsk region). J. Plant Nutr. Soil Sc. 170: 329-334.

[38] Knicker H (2007) How does fire affect the nature and stability of soil organic nitrogen and carbon? A review. Biogeochemistry 85: 91-118.

[39] Kuhlbusch TAJ, Crutzen PJ (1995) Toward a global estimate of black carbon in residues of vegetation fires representing a sink of atmospheric CO_2 and a source of O_2. Global Biogeochem. Cy. 9: 491-501.

[40] Glaser B, Haumaier L, Guggenberger G, Zech W (2001) The 'Terra Preta' phenomenon: A model for sustainable agriculture in the humid tropics. Naturwissenschaften 88: 37-41.

[41] Glaser B, Lehmann J, Zech W (2002) Ameliorating physical and chemical properties of highly weathered soils in the tropics with charcoal - A review. Biol. Fert. Soils 35: 219-230.

[42] Steiner C, Glaser B, Teixeira WG, Lehmann J, Blum WEH, Zech W (2008) Nitrogen retention and plant uptake on a highly weathered central Amazonian Ferralsol amended with compost and charcoal. J. Plant Nutr. Soil Sc. 171: 893-899.

[43] Klemm S (2003) Montanarchäologie in den Eisenerzer Alpen, Steiermark. Archäologische und naturwissenschaftliche Untersuchungen zum prähistorischen Kupferbergbau in der Eisenerzer Ramsau. VÖAW. Available: http://www.verlag.oeaw.ac.at. 205 p.

[44] Klemm S (2005) Interdisziplinäre Untersuchungen von Kohlstätten aus Mittelalter und Neuzeit in der Eisenerzer Ramsau, Steiermark. Arch. Austr. 89: 269–329.

[45] Leifeld J (2007) Thermal stability of black carbon characterised by oxidative differential scanning calorimetry. Org. Geochem. 38: 112-127.

[46] Salmén L, Burgert I (2009) Cell wall features with regard to mechanical performance. A review. Holzforschung 63: 121-129.

[47] Daniel G (2003) Microview of Wood under Degradation by Bacteria and Fungi. In: Goodell B, Nicholas DD, Schultz TP, editors. Wood Deterioration and Degradation. Advances in Our Changing World: ACS Symposium Series. p. 34 - 72.

[48] Zabel RA, Morrell JJ (1992) Wood Microbiology - Decay and its Prevention. San Diego. 476 p.

[49] Schwanninger M, Rodrigues J, Pereira H, Hinterstoisser B (2004) Effects of short-time vibratory ball milling on the shape of FT-IR spectra of wood and cellulose. Vib. Spectrosc. 36: 23-40.

[50] Stefke B, Windeisen E, Schwanninger M, Hinterstoisser B (2008) Determination of the weight percentage gain and of the acetyl group content of acetylated wood by means of different infrared spectroscopic methods. Anal. Chem. 80. 1272 1279.

[51] Schwanninger M, Stefke B, Hinterstoisser B (2011) Qualitative assessment of acetylated wood with infrared spectroscopic methods. J. Near Infrared Spectrosc. 19: 349-357.

[52] Fengel D, Wegener G (2003) Wood: chemistry, ultrastructure, reactions.: Kessel, Norbert, reprint of the original published by Walter de Gruyter & Co., Berlin. 613 p.

[53] Alves A, Simoes R, Stackpole DJ, Vaillancourt RE, Potts BM, Schwanninger M, et al. (2011) Determination of the syringyl/guaiacyl ratio of Eucalyptus globulus wood lignin by near infrared-based partial least squares regression models using analytical pyrolysis as the reference method. J. Near Infrared Spectrosc. 19: 343-348.

[54] Tsuchikawa S (2007) A review of recent near infrared research for wood and paper. Appl. Spectrosc. Rev. 42: 43-71.

[55] Tsuchikawa S, Schwanninger M (2012) A review of recent near infrared research for wood and paper (Part 2). Appl. Spectrosc. Rev. in press DOI: 10.1080/05704928.05702011.05621079.

[56] Fackler K, Schwanninger M, Gradinger C, Hinterstoisser B, Messner K (2007) Qualitative and quantitative changes of beech wood degraded by wood rotting basidiomycetes monitored by Fourier transform infrared spectroscopic methods and multivariate data analysis. FEMS Microbiol. Lett. 271: 162-169.

[57] Schwanninger M, Rodrigues JC, Fackler K (2011) A review of band assignments in near infrared spectra of wood and wood components. J. Near Infrared Spectrosc. 19: 287-308.

[58] Schwanninger M, Rodrigues JC, Gierlinger N, Hinterstoisser B (2011) Determination of lignin content in Norway spruce wood by Fourier transformed near infrared

spectroscopy and partial least squares regression. Part 1: Wavenumber selection and evaluation of the selected range. J. Near Infrared Spectrosc. 19: 319-329.

[59] Schwanninger M, Rodrigues JC, Gierlinger N, Hinterstoisser B (2011) Determination of lignin content in Norway spruce wood by Fourier transformed near infrared spectroscopy and partial least squares regression analysis. Part 2: Development and evaluation of the final model. J. Near Infrared Spectrosc. 19: 331-341.

[60] Schwanninger M, Hinterstoisser B, Gradinger C, Messner K, Fackler K (2004) Examination of spruce wood biodegraded by *Ceriporiopsis subvermispora* using near and mid infrared spectroscopy. J. Near Infrared Spectrosc. 12: 397-409.

[61] Müller U, Rätzsch M, Schwanninger M, Steiner M, Zobl H (2003) Yellowing and IR-changes of spruce wood as result of UV-irradiation. J. Photochem. Photobiol. B-Biol. 69: 97-105.

[62] Esteves BM, Pereira HM (2009) Wood modification by heat treatment: A review. Bioresources 4: 370-404.

[63] Eriksson K-EL, Blanchette RA, Ander P (1990) Microbial and Enzymatic Degradation of Wood and Wood Components. Berlin: Springer. 313 p.

[64] Binder M, Hibbett DS (2002) Higher-level phylogenetic relationships of homobasidiomycetes (mushroom-forming fungi) inferred from four rDNA regions. Mol. Phylogenet. Evol. 22: 76-90.

[65] Goodell B (2003) Brown-Rot Fungal Degradation of Wood: Our Evolving View. In: Goodell B, Nicholas DD, Schultz TP, editors. Wood Deterioration and Degradation. Advances in Our Changing World: ACS Symposium Series. p. 97-118.

[66] Fackler K, Gradinger C, Hinterstoisser B, Messner K, Schwanninger M (2006) Lignin degradation by white rot fungi on spruce wood shavings during short-time solid-state fermentations monitored by near infrared spectroscopy. Enzyme Microb. Technol. 39: 1476-1483.

[67] Fackler K, Gradinger C, Schmutzer M, Tavzes C, Burgert I, Schwanninger M, et al. (2007) Biotechnological wood modification with selective white-rot fungi and its molecular mechanisms. Food Technol. Biotechnol. 45: 269-276.

[68] Fackler K, Schmutzer M, Manoch L, Schwanninger M, Hinterstoisser B, Ters T, et al. (2007) Evaluation of the selectivity of white rot isolates using near infrared spectroscopic techniques. Enzyme Microb. Technol. 41: 881-887.

[69] Fackler K, Schwanninger M (2011) Accessibility of hydroxyl groups of brown-rot degraded spruce wood to heavy water. J. Near Infrared Spectrosc. 19: 359-368.

[70] Fackler K, Schwanninger M (2010) Polysaccharide degradation and lignin modification during brown rot of spruce wood: a polarised Fourier transform near infrared study. J. Near Infrared Spectrosc. 18: 403-416.

[71] Krongtaew C, Messner K, Ters T, Fackler K (2010) Characterization of key parameters for biotechnological lignocellulose conversion assessed by FT-NIR spectroscopy. Part I: Qualitative analysis of pretreated straw. Bioresources 5: 2063-2080.

[72] Krongtaew C, Messner K, Ters T, Fackler K (2010) Characterization of key parameters for biotechnological lignocellulose conversion assessed by FT-NIR spectroscopy. Part II: Quantitative analysis by Partial Least Squares Regression. Bioresources 5: 2081-2096.

[73] Fackler K, Stevanic JS, Ters T, Hinterstoisser B, Schwanninger M, Salmen L (2011) FT-IR imaging microscopy to localise and characterise simultaneous and selective white-rot decay within spruce wood cells. Holzforschung 65: 411-420.

[74] Fackler K, Stevanic JS, Ters T, Hinterstoisser B, Schwanninger M, Salmen L (2010) Localisation and characterisation of incipient brown-rot decay within spruce wood cell walls using FT-IR imaging microscopy. Enzyme Microb. Technol. 47: 257-267.

[75] Fackler K, Schwanninger M (2012) How less invasive spectroscopic and microspectroscopic methods contribute to understand fungal wood decay. Appl. Microbiol. Biotechnol. accepted.

[76] Stich L. *Pinus sylvestris* L. Chemische Charakterisierung von rezentem und subfossilem Kiefernholz [Diploma]. Vienna: Universität für Bodenkultur; 2006.

[77] Jacomet S, Kreuz A (1999) Archäobotanik: Aufgaben, Methoden und Ergebnisse vegetations- und agrargeschichtlicher Forschung. Stuttgart: Ulmer; UTB. 368 p.

[78] Sykacek E, Gierlinger N, Wimmer R, Schwanninger M (2006) Prediction of natural durability of commercial available European and Siberian larch by near-infrared spectroscopy. Holzforschung 60: 643-647.

[79] Gierlinger N, Jacques D, Schwanninger M, Wimmer R, Pâques LE (2004) Heartwood extractives and lignin content of different larch species (*Larix* sp.) and relationships to brown-rot decay-resistance. Trees-Struct. Funct. 18: 230-236.

[80] Curnel Y, Jacques D, Gierlinger N, Pâques LE (2008) Variation in the decay resistance of larch to fungi. Ann. For. Sci. 65: 810.

[81] Gierlinger N, Jacques D, Schwanninger M, Wimmer R, Hinterstoisser B, Pâques LE (2003) Rapid prediction of natural durability of larch heartwood using Fourier transform near-infrared spectroscopy. Can. J. For. Res.-Rev. Can. Rech. For. 33: 1727-1736.

[82] Gierlinger N, Schwanninger M, Hinterstoisser B, Wimmer R (2002) Rapid determination of heartwood extractives in Larix sp. by means of Fourier transform near infrared spectroscopy. J. Near Infrared Spectrosc. 10: 203-214.

[83] Windeisen E, Wegener G, Lesnino G, Schumacher P (2002) Investigation of the correlation between extractives content and natural durability in 20 cultivated larch trees. Holz Roh- Werkst. 60: 373-374.

[84] Susi P, Aktuganov G, Himanen J, Korpela T (2011) Biological control of wood decay against fungal infection. J. Environ. Manage. 92: 1681-1689.

[85] Esteves BM, Domingos IJ, Pereira HM (2008) Pine wood modification by heat treatment in air. Bioresources 3: 142-154.

[86] Menezzi CHSD, Souza RQd, Thompson RM, Teixeira DE, Okino EYA, Costa AFd (2008) Properties after weathering and decay resistance of a thermally modified wood structural board. Int. Biodeterior. Biodegrad. 62: 448-454.

[87] Brelid PL, Simonson R, Bergman O, Nilsson T (2000) Resistance of acetylated wood to biological degradation. Holz Roh- Werkst. 58: 331-337.

[88] Evans PD, Wallis AFA, Owen NL (2000) Weathering of chemically modified wood surfaces. Natural weathering of Scots pine acetylated to different weight gains. Wood Sci. Technol. 34: 151-165.

[89] Hadi YS, Darma IGKT, Febrianto F, Herliyana EN (1995) Acetylated rubberwood flakeboard resistance to bio-deterioration. Forest Prod. J. 45: 64-66.

[90] Hill CAS, Forster SC, Farahani MRM, Hale MDC, Ormondroyd GA, Williams GR (2005) An investigation of cell wall micropore blocking as a possible mechanism for the decay resistance of anhydride modified wood. Int. Biodeterior. Biodegrad. 55: 69-76.

[91] Papadopoulos AN (2010) Chemical Modification of Solid Wood and Wood Raw Material for Composites Production with Linear Chain Carboxylic Acid Anhydrides: A Brief Review. Bioresources 5: 499-506.

[92] Chang S-T, Chang H-T (2001) Inhibition of the photodiscoloration of wood by butyrylation. Holzforschung 55: 255-259.

[93] Esteves B, Nunes L, Pereira H (2011) Properties of furfurylated wood (*Pinus pinaster*). Eur. J. Wood Wood Prod. 69: 521-525.

[94] Ahmed BM, French JR, Vinden P (2004) Review of remedial and preventative methods to protect timber in service from attack by subterranean termites in Australia. Sociobiology 44: 297-312.

[95] Bigelow J, Lebow S, Clausen CA, Greimann L, Wipf TJ (2009) Preservation treatment for wood bridge application. Transp. Res. Record 2108: 77-85.

[96] de Meijer M (2001) Review on the durability of exterior wood coatings with reduced VOC-content. Prog. Org. Coat. 43: 217-225.

[97] Katz SA, Salem H (2005) Chemistry and toxicology of building timbers pressure-treated with chromated copper arsenate: a review. J. Appl. Toxicol. 25: 1-7.

[98] Obanda DN, Shupe TF, Barnes HM (2008) Reducing leaching of boron-based wood preservatives - A review of research. Bioresour. Technol. 99: 7312-7322.

[99] Seiler JP (1991) Pentachlorophenol. Mutat. Res. 257: 27-47.

[100] Singh T, Singh AP (2012) A review on natural products as wood protectant. Wood Sci. Technol. 46: 851-870.

Chapter 11

Multivariate Analysis for Fourier Transform Infrared Spectra of Complex Biological Systems and Processes

Diletta Ami, Paolo Mereghetti and Silvia Maria Doglia

Additional information is available at the end of the chapter

1. Introduction

Fourier transform infrared (FTIR) spectroscopy is a label-free and non invasive technique that exerts an enormous attraction in biology and medicine, since it allows to obtain in a rapid way a biochemical fingerprint of the sample under investigation, giving information on its main biomolecule content. This spectroscopic tool is successfully applied not only to the study of the structural properties of isolated biomolecules, such as proteins, nucleic acids, lipids, and carbohydrates, but also to the characterization of complex biological systems, for instance intact cells, tissues, and whole model organisms.

In particular, FTIR microspectroscopy, obtained by the coupling of an infrared microscope to a FTIR spectrometer, makes it possible to collect the IR spectrum from a selected sample area down to ~ 20 microns x 20 microns when conventional IR source and detector are employed, and down to of a few micrometers when more specialized and sensitive detectors and the highly brilliant synchrotron light source are used. In this way, FTIR microspectroscopy provides detailed information on several biological processes in situ, among which stem cell differentiation [1-5], somatic cell reprogramming [6], cell maturation [7, 8], amyloid aggregation [9-12] and cancer onset and progression [13-15], making it possible to disclose the infrared response not only from single cells, but also from subcellular compartments [8, 16, 17].

The FTIR spectra of biological systems are very complex since they consist of the overlapping absorption of the main biomolecules; for this reason, to pull out the significant and non-redundant information contained in the spectra it is necessary to apply an appropriate multivariate analysis, able to process very high-dimensional data. This is even more crucial when time-dependent biological processes, such as cell maturation or differentiation, are studied. Indeed, in this case it is fundamental to be able to extract from the spectral data the relevant information of the process you are investigating [18-21].

In Figure 1 we schematized the procedure that should be followed to successfully tackle the FTIR characterization of complex biological systems.

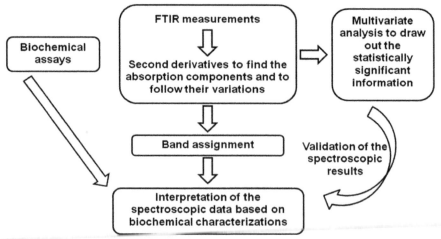

Figure 1. Scheme of the FTIR approach to study complex biological systems. The IR absorption spectra are analysed by resolution enhancement approaches (e.g. second derivatives) to resolve the overlapped absorption components and to monitor their variations during the process under investigation. The spectroscopic results are validated by an appropriate multivariate analysis approach, to identify firstly specific marker bands of the studied process. The interpretation of the spectroscopic data should be then confirmed by standard biochemical assays.

Several multivariate analysis approaches exist and for the scope of this book they can be divided into two main categories: regression and classification techniques. In the first category fall all methods that allow to derive a model describing the relationship between two sets of variables. The second category includes techniques to split observations into groups or classes.

In this chapter, we will firstly introduce the most widely used multivariate analysis approaches in the field of spectroscopy.

We will then illustrate the basic principles and experimental details for the application of principal component - linear discriminant analysis (PCA-LDA) to the analysis of FTIR spectral data of complex biological systems. The potential of these combined tools will be described on illustrative examples of cell biological process studies. In particular, we will discuss in details its application on our FTIR study of murine oocytes characterized by two different types of chromatin organisation around the nucleolus, strongly affecting their development after fertilization. In this case, PCA-LDA analysis made it possible to identify not only the maturation stage in which the fate separation between the two kinds of oocytes occurred, but also to disclose the most significant cellular processes responsible for the different oocyte destiny, thus validating the visual inspection of the infrared spectra [7].

2. FTIR microspectroscopy of complex biological systems

Fourier transform infrared (FTIR) microspectroscopy is a powerful technique that allows to obtain a molecular fingerprint of the sample under investigation in a rapid and non-invasive way. In the case of complex biological systems it provides simultaneously, in a single measurement, information on the main biomolecules, such as lipids, proteins, nucleic acids, and carbohydrates, requiring also a very limited amount of sample. For these reasons, it became recently a very attracting tool for biomedical research [20, 22-24], being successfully employed for the study of several biological systems, from intact cells [6, 7, 25] to tissues [11, 26, 27] and whole model organisms (i.e. the nematode *Caenorhabditis elegans*) [9, 28].

As an example, in Figure 2 it is reported the FTIR absorption spectrum of a single intact murine oocyte. As shown, its IR response is very complex, being due to the absorption of the main biomolecules. In particular, between 3050 - 2800 cm^{-1} and 1500 - 1350 cm^{-1} the absorption of the lipid acyl chains occurs, while around 1740 cm^{-1} the ester carbonyl absorbs [29]. Moreover, the amide I and amide II bands - mainly due to the C=O stretching and the NH bending of the peptide bond respectively - give information on the protein secondary structure [30], while the spectral range between 1000 and 800 cm^{-1} is very informative on nucleic acid absorption, since it is due in particular to sugar vibrations sensitive to their conformation and to backbone vibrational modes [31, 32]. Finally, we should also mention the very complex spectral range between 1250 - 1000 cm^{-1}, mainly due to phosphodiester groups of nucleic acids and phospholipids and to the C-O absorption of glycogen and other carbohydrates [31, 33, 34].

Making it possible to obtain a sample biochemical fingerprint in a rapid and non destructive way, FTIR microspectroscopy is widely applied to the in situ characterization of cellular processes, such as cell maturation, differentiation, and reprogramming [3, 5-7, 25, 35], and to the detection of several diseases, as, for instance, cancer [13-15] and neurodegenerative disorders [10, 11], whose onset is accompanied by changes in the composition and structure of several biomolecules.

Since water has a strong absorption in the mid-infrared spectral range, samples have to be dried rapidly before IR measurements, in particular when working in transmission mode (see for details the following paragraph). The suitability of such "dry-fixing" has been proved by Raman spectroscopy, a vibrational tool complementary to FTIR, whose response is not affected by water. In particular, Raman measurements performed on differentiating human embryonic stem cells, hydrated and dry-fixed, demonstrated that the rapid desiccation didn't affect the spectroscopic response of the main biomolecules. Indeed, in both cases the same temporal pattern of the differentiation marker bands - due to tryptophan, nucleic acid backbone and base vibrations - was observed during the biological process under investigation [36].

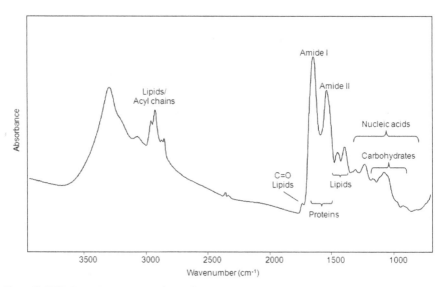

Figure 2. FTIR absorption spectrum of a single intact murine oocyte. The measured absorption spectrum of a single intact murine oocyte (surrounded nucleolus, MI 10 H) is reported without any corrections. The oocyte - deposited on a BaF₂ window - was measured in transmission by the IR microscope UMA 500, coupled to the FTIR spectrometer FTS 40A (both from Digilab), at a resolution of 2 cm⁻¹. The absorption regions of the main biomolecules are indicated.

We should add that to obtain reliable results on the studied process it is crucial to standardize firstly the sample preparation, since - for instance - metabolic changes due to cell aging could result in significant spectral changes that could, in turn, hide the IR response specifically due to the process of interest, as it has been recently reported in the literature [37]. For these reasons, it is fundamental to check accurately the stage of cell growth in culture before performing spectroscopic measurements.

We should also briefly mention that, before spectral analyses, the measured IR spectra could require some corrections due to artifacts that can interfere with the spectroscopic response. For instance, single cells, or subcellular compartments, or particles of the size of the same order of that of the incident infrared light (≈3-10 microns) could give rise to Mie scattering, that significantly distorts the measured spectrum, causing misinterpretation of the results. For this reason, before further analyses, it is strongly recommended to correct the measured spectra with opportune algorithms specifically developed to this aim [38].

Since the IR spectra of complex biological systems are due to the overlapping spectral features of multiple components, their analysis requires often the employment of resolution enhancement procedures to better resolve their absorption bands, an essential prerequisite for the identification of peak positions and their assignment to the vibrational modes of the different molecules. Among these, second derivative analysis is widely applied, as described in [39]. Since second derivative band intensity is inversely proportional to the square of the original band half-width, this procedure introduces an enhancement of sharp lines, as those due to vapour and noise. For this reason, this analysis requires spectral data free of vapour absorption and with excellent signal to noise ratio.

Furthermore, due to the intrinsic complexity of biological systems, their spectral analysis requires the support of appropriate multivariate analysis approaches able to tackle the study of high-dimensional data, to verify firstly the reproducibility of the results and then to extract the most significant spectral information [18-21] (see for details paragraph 4).

3. FTIR microspectroscopy: Technical considerations

FTIR microspectroscopy is realized coupling to a FTIR spectrometer an infrared microscope characterized by an all reflecting optics, since typical lenses and condensers of visible microscopy - being made of glass, not transparent to the IR radiation - cannot be employed.

The main advantage of FTIR microspectroscopy is that it offers the possibility to study selected areas of the sample under investigation, resulting particularly useful in the case of systems characterized by an intrinsic heterogeneity, such as biological systems.

Two main types of IR microscopy exist, depending on the detector employed, and both equipped with an IR thermal source (globar), whose spatial resolution is diffraction-limited.

The first, conventional, generally equipped with a nitrogen cooled mercury cadmium telluride (MCT) detector, makes it possible to measure IR absorption spectra from a microvolume within the sample, selected by a variable aperture of the microscope, whose side can be adjusted down to a few tens of microns.

The second type of IR microscope, more advanced, is equipped with a focal plane array (FPA), consisting of an array of infrared detector elements, that enables not only to collect the IR absorption spectrum of the sample, but also an IR chemical imaging, where the image contrast is given by the response of selected sample regions to particular IR wavenumbers. Depending mainly on the detection array, the spatial resolution in this kind of microscopy is approximately between 20 and 5 microns, making it possible to reach, therefore, a resolution near to the diffraction limit.

We should, however, add that the use of a synchrotron IR light source, with a brightness of at least two orders of magnitude higher than that of a conventional thermal source, makes it possible to achieve diffraction-limited spatial resolution with enhanced signal-to-noise ratio. In this way, synchrotron light could allow to explore the IR spectra at the subcellular level.

A final remark should be done concerning the spectral acquisition mode. Indeed, infrared measurements can be mainly performed in transmission, reflectance or attenuated total reflection (ATR) mode. Typically, measurements on complex biological systems are performed in transmission mode, using appropriate IR transparent supports for the deposition of the sample, such as BaF_2, CaF_2, ZnSe. In this case, the IR beam goes through the sample, that - depending mainly on its molar extinction coefficient - should have a uniform thickness, not exceeding 15-20 microns.

Moreover, in reflectance mode - where the sample is placed onto proper reflective slides - the IR beam passes the sample, is reflected by the slide, and passes the sample again. In particular, the sample slides reflect mid-infrared radiation almost completely and usually are also transparent to visible light, allowing sample inspection by a conventional light microscope. This approach is, for instance, useful for tissue characterizations.

Finally, in the ATR approach, where the sample is placed into contact with a higher refractive index and an IR transparent element (mainly germanium and diamond), samples with higher thickness than in transmission can be processed. In particular, the IR beam reaches the interface between the ATR support and the sample at an angle larger than that corresponding to the total reflection. In this way the beam is totally reflected by the interface and penetrates into the sample as an evanescent wave, where it can be absorbed. The beam penetration depth is of the order of the IR wavelength (a few micrometers) and depends on the wavelength, the incident angle, as well as on the refractive indices of the sample and of the ATR element. Furthermore, it should be noted that this kind of approach makes it possible to measure also samples not necessarily deposited onto an IR transparent support, as in ATR measurements it is only required that the sample be in close contact with the ATR element.

For a review of the technical aspects of FTIR microspectroscopy, see [40-42].

4. Multivariate analyses

4.1. Introduction to multivariate analysis

Several phenomena can only be described or explained by taking into account several variables at the same time. These cases represent the realm of the Multivariate statistical analysis (MVA).

We now define the structure of our data that will be kept throughout the text for all described techniques. For a given phenomenon we perform a certain measurement and store the value in a uni- or multivariate variable called $\mathbf{y} = \left(y_1, y_2, ..., y_m\right)^T$, where m is the number of independent variables. The same measurement can be repeated several times on the same sample or on different samples. We then define a group as a collection of two or more replica of the same experiment and we also define the term instance or observation to refer to a specific experiment within one group.

Each instance associated to the variable $\mathbf{y}$ is stored in a matrix $\mathbf{Y}$ composed of n rows (the observations) and m columns (the independent variables).

$$\mathbf{Y} = \begin{pmatrix} y_{11} & y_{12} & \cdots & y_{1m} \\ \vdots & \vdots & \vdots & \vdots \\ y_{n1} & y_{n1} & \cdots & y_{nm} \end{pmatrix} = \left(\mathbf{y}_1, \mathbf{y}_2, ..., \mathbf{y}_n\right)^T \tag{1}$$

Each element of matrix $\mathbf{Y}$ can be indicated as y_{ij} where i indicate the observation and j is an independent variable. In some cases we want to find or explain the relationship between the independent variables **Y** and another set of uni- or multivariate variables **Z**. Similarly to the **Y** matrix, the matrix **Z** has n rows, one for each observation and m columns, the dependent variables.

$$\mathbf{Z} = \begin{pmatrix} z_{11} & z_{12} & \cdots & z_{1m} \\ \vdots & \vdots & \vdots & \vdots \\ z_{n1} & z_{n1} & \cdots & z_{nm} \end{pmatrix} = \left(\mathbf{z}_1, \mathbf{z}_2, ..., \mathbf{z}_n \right)^T \tag{2}$$

The matrix **Y** (composed of the independent variables y) represents the only input for several multivariate techniques described here; in some other cases the matrices **Y** and **Z** (composed of the dependent variables z) are both required.

In the following part, we will make a distinction between regression and classification techniques. However, it should be clear that the separation between these two domains is not always sharp and the same technique can be either used for regression or for classification purposes.

4.2. Multivariate regression techniques

4.2.1 Linear Multivariate Regression (LMVR)

LMVR (or MLR) can be used to model linear relationships between one or more z (dependent variable) and one or more y (independent variable). In the most general case, we have n independent multivariate variables y represented by the matrix **Y** and the corresponding response multivariate variable z, stored in the matrix **Z**.

The LMVR is based, as many other statistical techniques, on the generalized linear model: $\mathbf{Z} = \beta\mathbf{Y} + \varepsilon$ where β is a matrix containing the parameters to be estimated, and ε is a matrix which models the errors or noise. The coefficients β are usually estimated using the ordinary least square, which consists of minimizing the sum of the square differences of the n observed y's from their modeled values. Mathematically, the optimal values of β are obtained by $\beta = \left(\mathbf{Y}^T\mathbf{Y} \right)^{-1} \mathbf{Y}^T\mathbf{Z}$. To apply the least square method we must have $n - 1 > m$ (e.g. the number of observation must be larger than the number of variables, which is often not the case), otherwise the matrix $\mathbf{Y}^T\mathbf{Y}$ is singular and cannot be inverted. Another common problem is the correlation between variables; more specifically, none of the independent variables must be a linear combination of any other. This phenomenon is called "multicollinearity" [43, 44] and it will be explained in more details in section 4.2.3.

4.2.2. Non-Linear Multivariate Regression (NLMVR)

In some cases linear models cannot be used and one could try to apply non-linear models.

Common models which frequently apply to natural phenomena are the exponentials (which, indeed, is a transformed linear model. A linear model can be applied upon on the logarithm of the data), logistic models or power law models.The regressed model has the general form of $Z = \beta f(Y) + \varepsilon$, where $f(Y)$ can be any non-linear function.

The optimal values for the coefficients β can be obtained using deterministic optimization algorithm such as the conjugate gradients [45] or the Levenberg-Marquard method [46, 47], or stochastic algorithm such as genetic algorithms [48].

4.2.3. The multicollinearity problem

When the number of observations is smaller than the number of variables (as it often happens for spectral data), the matrix $Y^T Y$ is singular and is not invertible. This rules out the possibility of using standard linear multivariate techniques (LMVR) based on the least square criterion, as the solution will not be unique.

Increasing the number of observations (above the number of variables) will not always solve the problem. This is due to the so-called near-multicollinearity which means that some variables can be written approximately as linear functions of other variables. This problem is often found among spectral measurements. Even if the solution will be mathematically unique, it may be unstable and lead to poor prediction performances.

Linearly correlated or quasi-linearly correlated variables have to be removed prior to apply a regression method. In the following sections, we will describe two methods that are frequently used to remove correlations among variables, namely principal component analysis (PCA) and partial least squares (PLS).

4.2.3.1. Principal Component Analysis (PCA)

We should first recall the structure of the data. Suppose that we have n observations, each one defined by a vector y_i composed of m variables, where $i=1,2,...,n$ stands for the i-th observation. The matrix of the original data Y is then composed by n rows (the observations) and m columns (the variables).

By using PCA, our intent is to develop a smaller number of uncorrelated artificial variables, called principal components (PC), that will account for most of the variance in the observed variables. The new uncorrelated variables are obtained as linear combination of the original data as $T = AY$. Correlation among variables can be measured using the covariance matrix.

Given the sample mean of the m-dimensional vector y_i, $\langle y \rangle = \dfrac{1}{n}\sum_{i=1}^{n} y_i$, an unbiased estimator of the sample covariance matrix is $S = \dfrac{1}{n-1}\sum_{i=1}^{n}(y_i - \langle y \rangle)(y_i - \langle y \rangle)^T$.

For uncorrelated variables, the off-diagonal values of the sample covariance matrix are zero, that is, S is diagonal. The covariance of linearly transformed variables $T = AY$ is equal to $S_T = ASA^T$, where S is the sample covariance of the original data Y [49].

Thus, we want to find the matrix $\mathbf{A}$ such that the covariance matrix of the transformed data, $\mathbf{S}_T$, is diagonal, which corresponds to find the eigenvectors of the covariance matrix and the corresponding eigenvalues.

The eigenvalues, which coincide with the matrix $\mathbf{S}_T$, are the sample variance of the principal components $\mathbf{T}$ and are ranked according to their magnitude. The first principal component is then the linear combination with maximal variance (the largest eigenvalue). The second principal component is the linear combination with the maximal variance along a direction orthogonal to the first component, and so on [44].

The number of eigenvalues is equal to the number of original variables; however, since the eigenvalues are equal to the variance of the principal components and they are sorted in a decreasing order, the first k eigenvalues can account for a large portion of the variance of the data.

Hence, to describe our original dataset we can use only the first k uncorrelated principal components, instead of the complete set of redundant m variables. In matrix notation this can be written as $\mathbf{T}_k = \mathbf{A}_k \mathbf{Y}$, where $\mathbf{A}_k$ is the eigenvector matrix truncated to the k-th eigenvector, and $\mathbf{T}_k$ is the matrix of the first k principal components, also called score matrix [50].

Choosing which and the number of principal components that should be retained in order to summarize our data is a task that can be solved using several strategies [43, 49]. For example, one way commonly used is to retain the first k principal components that explain a given total percentage of the variance, e.g. 90% [43, 44]. Another rule is to plot the eigenvalues in decreasing order. Moving from left to right, the eigenvalues usually have an initial steep drop followed by a slow decrease. All the components after the elbow between the steep and the flat part of the curve should be discarded. This test is called screen plot.

Alternatively, one can select the principal components that can be associated to a physical meaning related to the studied system. For example, following the differentiations of a cell line growing in different experimental conditions, one principal component may represents the different conditions, while another PC may describe the maturation stage of the cells. None of the above methods are better than the other; usually more than one test should be done and the results compared.

The principal component analysis allows to obtain uncorrelated variables and then to remove the multicollinearity problem.

4.2.3.2. Principal Component Regression (PCR): multivariate regression following PCA

Once a set of k principal components has been obtained using the PCA method, they can be used as input variables for a multivariate regression analysis instead of the original data. The regression equation $\mathbf{Z} = \beta \mathbf{Y} + \varepsilon$, shown in section 4.2.1, can be written as $\mathbf{Z} = \beta \mathbf{T}_k + \varepsilon$, where $\mathbf{T}_k$ is the matrix of the principal components (scores matrix) and the regression coefficients β can be estimated by least squares. When the number of principal components is equal to the number of variables, this method becomes equivalent to the LMVR. By removing correlations in the original data, the PCR method allows to perform linear regression on a multicollinear dataset.

4.2.3.3. Partial Least Squares (PLS)

Another way to face the multicollinearity problem is to use PLS. The goal of PLS regression is to predict **Z** from **Y** and to describe their common structure [50].

In the PCR method described above, the principal components are selected based on their ability of explaining the variance of the **Y** matrix (the dependent variable matrix). By contrast, PLS regression finds components from **Y** that are also relevant for **Z**. Specifically, PLS regression searches for a set of components that performs a simultaneous decomposition of **Y** and **Z**, with the constraint that these components explain as much as possible the covariance between **Y** and **Z**. In this way, compared to the PCR, the principal components contain more information about the relationship between predictors and dependent variables [50]. For categorical dependent variables, the PLS method takes the name of partial least square discriminant analysis (PLS-DA) [43].

4.3. Multivariate classification techniques

Classification methods can be divided into two main categories, supervised and unsupervised. Supervised techniques require the knowledge of the group membership of the observations and can be used to understand the structure of the data, e.g. why certain observations belong to a given group. Moreover, once the classification model is calibrated on a "training" dataset, it can be used in a predictive way to group observations whose group membership is unknown.

On the other hand, unsupervised methods try to group the observations without any knowledge of the group membership.

In the following paragraph, we will describe the main multivariate classification approaches.

4.3.1. Discriminant Analysis (DA)

Discriminant analysis is mainly a supervised technique which was originally developed by Ronald Fisher as a way to subdivide a set of taxonomic observations into two groups based on some measured features [51]. Later, DA was extended to treat cases where there are more than two groups, the so-called "multiclass discriminant analysis" [49, 52, 53].

DA can have mainly two objectives. First, it can be used in a supervised way to describe and explain the differences among the groups. As we will see later, mathematically DA finds the optimal hyperplane that separates the groups among each other. Or, in other words, it finds the optimal linear combination of the original variables that maximizes the distance among the groups. The transformed observations are called discriminant functions.

The use of a linear combination implies that each original variable is weighted by a coefficient which can be used to study the relative importance of the variable in the separation among the groups. A second possible role of DA is to classify observations into groups. An observation, which has to be assigned to a group, is evaluated by a discriminant function (already calibrated on another dataset) and it is assigned to one of the groups at which most likely it belongs [43, 44, 49]; in this view DA is used as an unsupervised method.

When only linear transformations are applied to the variables used as DA input, the discriminant analysis is called linear discriminant analysis (LDA).

In some cases, LDA alone is not suitable and the original variables can be mapped to a new space via any non-linear function. Then, the LDA is applied in this non-linear space (which is equivalent to non-linear classification in the original space). This procedure can be seen under several names such as "non-linear DA" (NLDA) or "kernel Fisher discriminant analysis" (KFD) or "generalized discriminant analysis".

In the following sections we will focus on LDA, first describing the descriptive approach and subsequently the classification approach.

4.3.1.1. Linear DA (LDA) as a descriptive method

The initial dataset is an ensemble of multivariate observations partitioned into G distinct groups (e.g. different experimental treatments, times or conditions). Each of the G groups contains n_g observations, where g runs from 1 to G and refers to the g-th group. The multivariate observation vectors can be written as $\mathbf{y}_{gj}$ where g is the g-th group and j is the j-th observation. The vector has size m, which corresponds to the number of variables.

Our goal in LDA is to search for the linear combination that optimally separates our multivariate observation into G groups.

The linear transformation of $\mathbf{y}_{gj}$ is written as

$$z_{gj} = \mathbf{w}^T \mathbf{y}_{gj} \tag{3}$$

Since z_{gj} is a linear transformation of $\mathbf{y}_{gj}$, the mean of the group g of the transformed data can be written as

$$\langle z_g \rangle = \mathbf{w}^T \langle \mathbf{y}_g \rangle \tag{4}$$

where $\mathbf{y}_g$ is the mean, of the observations within a group, obtained as

$$\langle \mathbf{y}_g \rangle = \sum_{j=1}^{n_g} \mathbf{y}_{gj} / n_g$$

We now introduce the between groups sum of squares $\mathbf{B}$ in equation 5 (measure of the dispersion among the groups) and the within-group sum of squares $\mathbf{E}$ in equation 6 (measure of the dispersion within one group). First, we define them for the uni-dimensional case relatively to the untransformed data:

$$\mathbf{B}(y) = \sum_{g=1}^{G}\left(\left\langle y_g\right\rangle - \left\langle y\right\rangle\right)^2 \tag{5}$$

and

$$\mathbf{E}(y) = \sum_{g=1}^{G}\sum_{j=1}^{n_g}\left(y_{gj} - \left\langle y_g\right\rangle\right)^2 \tag{6}$$

where $\left\langle y\right\rangle = \dfrac{1}{G}\sum_{g=1}^{G}\dfrac{1}{n_g}\sum_{j=1}^{n_g}y_{gj}$ is the total average of the data.

Analogously, in the multivariate case (where each observation is constituted by m variables) we have the two matrices:

$$\mathbf{B}(\mathbf{y}) = \sum_{g=1}^{G}n_g\left(\left\langle \mathbf{y}_g\right\rangle - \left\langle \mathbf{y}\right\rangle\right)\left(\left\langle \mathbf{y}_g\right\rangle - \left\langle \mathbf{y}\right\rangle\right)^T \tag{7}$$

and

$$\mathbf{E}(\mathbf{y}) = \sum_{g=1}^{G}n_g\sum_{j=1}^{n_g}\left(\left\langle \mathbf{y}_{gj}\right\rangle - \left\langle \mathbf{y}_g\right\rangle\right)\left(\left\langle \mathbf{y}_{gj}\right\rangle - \left\langle \mathbf{y}_g\right\rangle\right)^T \tag{8}$$

Finding the optimal linear combination that separates our multivariate observations into k groups means to find the vector w which maximizes the rate between the between-groups sum of squares over the within-groups sum of squares. Using the equations for the transformed data (equations 3 and 4) into the equations 7 and 8, we can write:

$$\lambda = \frac{\mathbf{w}^T\mathbf{B}(\mathbf{y})\mathbf{w}}{\mathbf{w}^T\mathbf{E}(\mathbf{y})\mathbf{w}} = \frac{\mathbf{B}(\mathbf{z})}{\mathbf{E}(\mathbf{z})} \tag{9}$$

We want to find w such that λ is maximized.

Equation 9 can be rewritten in the form $\mathbf{w}^T\left(\mathbf{Bw} - \lambda\mathbf{Ew}\right) = 0$; then we search for all the non trivial ($\mathbf{w}^T = 0$ is excluded) solutions of this equation and we choose the one which gives the maximum value of λ. This means to solve the eigenvalue problem $\mathbf{Bw} - \lambda\mathbf{Ew} = 0$ that can be written in the usual form:

$$\left(\mathbf{A} - \lambda\mathbf{I}\right)\mathbf{w} = 0 \tag{10}$$

where $\mathbf{A} = \mathbf{E}^{-1}\mathbf{B}$.

The solutions of equation 10 are the eigenvalues $\lambda_1, \lambda_2, ..., \lambda_m$ associated to the eigenvectors $w_1, w_2, ..., w_m$. The solutions are ranked for the eigenvalues $\lambda_1 > \lambda_2 > ... > \lambda_m$. Hence, the first eigenvalue λ_1 corresponds to the maximum value of equation 9.

The discriminant functions are then obtained considering only the first s positive eigenvalues and multiplying the original data by the eigenvectors $z_1 = w_1^T Y, z_2 = w_2^T Y, ..., z_s = w_s^T Y$.

Discriminant functions are uncorrelated but not orthogonal since the matrix $A = E^{-1}B$ is not symmetric.

In many cases the first two or three discriminant functions account for most of $\lambda_1 + \lambda_2 + ... + \lambda_s$. This allows to represent the multivariate observations as 2 or 3 dimensional points which can be plotted on a scatter plot. These plots are particularly helpful to visualize the separation of our observations into the different groups. Moreover, we can deduce, looking at the scatter plot, the meaning of a given discriminant function, i.e. we can associate the discriminant function to a given property of the analyzed system.

The weighting vectors $w_1, w_2, ... w_s$ are called unstandardized discriminant function coefficients and give the weight associated to each variable on every discriminant function.

If the variables are on very different scales and with different variance, to assess the importance of each variable in the group separation the standardized discriminant functions can be used. The standardization is done by multiplying the unstandardized coefficients by the square root of the diagonal element of the within-group covariance matrix.

Another way to assess the variable importance is to look at the correlation between each variable and the discriminant function. These correlations are called structure or loading coefficients. However, it has been shown that these parameters are intrinsically univariate and they only show how a single variable contributes to the separation among groups, without taking into account the presence of the other variables [49].

4.3.1.2. Linear as a classification method

After a set of discriminant functions are calibrated as described in the previous section, the discriminant analysis can be applied to classify new observations into the most probable groups. From this point of view, the linear discriminant analysis becomes a predictive tool, since it is able to classify observations whose group membership is unknown [43, 49]. The discrimination ability of our LDA model can be tested by a procedure called "re-substitution" [49]. This method consists of producing an LDA model using our dataset (i.e. finding the optimal w). Then, each observation vector is re-submitted to the classification function ($z_{gj} = w^T y_{gj}$) and assigned to a group. Since we know the group membership of the submitted vector, we can count the number of observations correctly classified and the number of observations misclassified. To measure the classification accuracy we can count the number of observations correctly classified and the number of observations misclassified. Then, we can estimate the classification rate as the number of correctly classified observations over the total number of observations. In general, in evaluating the accuracy of a model, we have then to distinguish between two types of accuracy: the fitting accuracy and the prediction accuracy [43, 54].

The fitting accuracy is the ability to reproduce the data, namely how the model is able to reproduce the data that were used to build the model (the training set). This corresponds to the apparent classification rate and it is obtained using the re-substitution procedure.

The prediction accuracy is the ability to predict the value or the class of an observation, that was not included in the construction of the model. This kind of accuracy is often referred to as the ability of the model to generalize. The data used to measure this accuracy are called "test set". The prediction accuracy can be called "actual classification rate". This is mainly used in settings where the goal is prediction, and one wants to estimate how accurately a predictive model will perform in practice. To have an estimation of the actual classification rate, two main procedures can be applied: the hold-out and cross-validation [43].

In the hold-out, the dataset is divided into two partitions: one partition is used to develop the model (e.g. the discriminant functions) and the second partition is given as input to the model. The first partition is usually called "training set" or "calibration set", while the second partition is the validation set [54].

When the number of observations is small, the cross-validation is usually preferred over the hold-out. The basic idea of the cross-validation procedure is to divide the entire dataset into L disjoint sets. L-1 sets are used to develop the model (i.e. the calibration set on which the discriminant functions are computed) and the omitted portion is used to test the model (i.e. the validation set given as input to the model). This is repeated for all the L sets and an average result is obtained.

Apparent or actual classification accuracies can be summarized in a confusion matrix. As an example, total N observations, n_1 , belong to the group 1 and n_2 belong to the group 2. C_{11} is the total number of observations correctly classified in group 1 and C_{12} is the total number of data misclassified in group 2. Similarly, C_{22} is the total number of observations correctly classified in group 2 and C_{21} is the number of misclassified in group 1.

The confusion matrix becomes then:

	Actual group	Predicted group
	1	2
1	C_{11}	C_{12}
2	C_{21}	C_{22}

and the accuracy (the actual or apparent classification rate (acr)) is computed as:

$$acr = \frac{C_{11} + C_{22}}{n_1 + n_2}$$

4.3.2. PCA-LDA

A powerful analysis tool is the combination of the principal component analysis with the linear discriminant analysis [52]. This is particularly helpful when the number of variables is large. In particular, if the number of observations (N) is less than the number of variables (m) - specifically $N-1<m$ - the covariance matrix is singular and cannot be inverted (see section 4.2.3.). We then need to find a way to reduce the number of variables, for example using the PCA [49, 55]. This procedure has been widely used for several problems in different fields [35, 52, 56-60]. The condition $N-1<m$ almost always appears in spectroscopy, where the number of observations (N) is usually 10^2 and the number of variables (m) is typically within 10^2 to 10^3.

Let's take into account the same situation described for the many group linear discriminant analysis. The original dataset is an ensemble of multivariate observations which is partitioned into k distinct groups. Again, we want to find the discriminant functions which optimally separate our multivariate observation into the k groups. Then, the discriminant functions can be used to identify the most important variables in terms of ability of distinguishing among the groups. Thus, first the original dataset is submitted to the PCA to reduce the number of variables; subsequently, the reduced dataset is analyzed using the LDA.

Another way that can be used instead of PCA is to perform the PLS.

4.3.3. PLS-LDA

In a way analogous to the PCA-LDA procedure, here we first apply the PLS algorithm to the original data and then the LDA on the selected principal components [61].

Given that the PLS searches for a set of components that performs a simultaneous decomposition of the dependent and independent datasets, the main difference with PCA-LDA is that the principal components resulting as output of PLS better describe the relationship between independent and dependent variables. This does not necessarily mean that this method is better in general. Indeed, applying PCA or PLS on the same dataset often leads to similar results [62, 63] and the classification accuracy or the descriptive ability is mostly determined by the underlying structure of the data which can make one of the two methods more suitable than the other.

4.3.4. Cluster Analysis (CA)

The goal of cluster analysis is to find the best grouping of the multivariate observations such that the clusters are dissimilar to each other but the observations within a cluster are similar [44].

CA is an unsupervised technique, that is, the group membership of the observations (and often the number of groups) is not known in advance.

At first we have to define a measure of similarity or dissimilarity also called distance functions. The most common distance functions are: i) the Euclidean distance; ii) the Manatthan distance; iii) the Mahalanobis distance; iv) the maximum norm.

Based on the procedure they use, clustering algorithms can be divided into three main groups: hierarchical, partitional and density-based clustering. None of the following algorithms is better than the other. The choice of the clustering method strongly depends on the structure of the data and on which kind of results one would expect.

Hierarchical clustering algorithms can be again subdivided into agglomerative or divisive. The agglomerative clustering starts with all observations placed in different clusters and in each step an observation or a cluster of observations is merged into another cluster. The most commonly employed agglomerative clustering strategies are complete-linkage, average-linkage, single-linkage, centroid-linkage. The drawback of the agglomerative clustering algorithms is that observations cannot be moved among the clusters once a cluster is made.

The divisive method starts with one single cluster containing all observations and then it divides the cluster into two sub-clusters at each step. Divisive methods have the same drawback of the agglomerative clustering, that is, once a cluster is made, an observation cannot be moved to another cluster. Divisive methods are suited when large clusters are searched for.

The partitional algorithm assigns the observations to a set of clusters without using hierarchical approaches. One of the most used non-hierarchical approach is the k-means clustering.

The density-based clustering seeks to search for regions of high density without any assumption about the shape of the cluster.

4.4. Artificial Neural Networks (ANN)

The artificial neural networks are mathematical models that were developed in analogy to a network of biological neurons [64]. Mathematically, a neuron can be modeled as a switch that receives, as input, a series of values and produces an output consisting of a weighted sum of the input eventually transformed by a function f. Many neurons can be combined to create more complex networks. Depending on the type of neurons and on how the neurons are connected to each others, different kinds of neural networks can be created. The most common type of neural network is the feed-forward neural network, in which neurons are grouped into layers, each neuron of a layer is connected to all the neurons of the next layer and the information flows from the input to the output without loops. For a comprehensive description of neural networks and their applications see [54, 65].

5. Applications of multivariate analysis to spectroscopic data of complex biological systems

In the following, we will provide a few selected examples of the application of FTIR microspectroscopy coupled with multivariate analysis for biomedical relevant studies, with the aim to highlight the importance of linking the two approaches to extract the most significant spectral information from highly informative systems.

In some cases, PCA alone represents a powerful method for the analysis of multidimensional FTIR spectra. Indeed, several interesting works are reported in the literature, in which this approach is employed to support the spectroscopic investigation of complex biological systems and processes. For instance, synchrotron based FTIR microspectroscopy coupled with PCA has been applied to the characterization of human corneal stem cells [27, 66], in cancer research for the screening of cervical cancer [14], as well as to disclose the effects induced by a surface glycoprotein in colon carcinoma cells [67].

For instance, Matthew German and colleagues [68] coupled high-resolution synchrotron radiation-based FTIR (SR-FTIR) microspectroscopy with PCA to investigate the characteristics of putative adult stem cell (SC), transiently amplified (TA) cell, and terminally differentiated (TD) cell populations of the corneal epithelium. Using PCA, each spectrum, composed by many variables (the wavenumbers), is reduced to a point in a low dimensional space. Then, each observation can be visualized in a two or three dimensional score plot. Choosing the appropriate principal components, the authors were able to clearly distinguish the three cell populations confirming the ability of SR-FTIR microspectroscopy to identify SC, TA cell, and TD cell populations.

PCA alone is extremely powerful to reduce the number of variables; however, it is not a clustering algorithm and the group into clusters must be done with other techniques.

For example, Tanthanuch and colleagues applied FTIR microspectroscopy-supported by PCA and unsupervised hierarchical cluster analysis (UHCA) to identify specific spectral markers of the differentiation of murine embryonic stem cell (mESCs) and to distinguish them into different neural cell types [25]. In particular, focal plane array (FPA) - FTIR and SR-FTIR microspectroscopy measurements - performed on cell clumps and single cells respectively - allowed to obtain a biochemical fingerprint of different mESC developmental stages, namely embryoid bodies (EBs), neural progenitor cells (NPCs) and embryonic stem-derived neural cells (ESNCs). Interestingly, it should be noted that the results obtained on cell clumps and on single cells were found to be comparable, corroborating the FPA-FTIR results on cell clumps. The analysis of second derivative spectra enabled to highlight important spectral changes occurring during ES cell differentiation, mainly in the lipid CH_2 and CH_3 stretching region and in the protein amide I band. Noteworthy, these results overall indicated that during neural differentiation the cell lipid content increased significantly, likely reflecting modifications in cell membranes, whose lipid content is known to have a key role in neural cell differentiation and signal transduction. Moreover, changes in the profile of amide I band, mainly involving the alpha-helix component around 1650-1652 cm^{-1}, indicated an increased expression of alpha-helix reach protein in ESNCs compared with their progenitor cells, a result that could reflect the expression of cytoskeleton protein, crucial for the establishment of neural structure and function. These results were then strongly supported by PCA, that made it possible to disclose regions of the IR spectrum which most contributed to the spectral variance, namely amide I band and C-H

· stretching region. Furthermore, the application of UHCA allowed to successfully discriminate and classify each stage of ESNCs differentiation, again considering the spectra in the spectral range mainly due to acyl chain vibrations and the extended region between 1750 and 900 cm^{-1}.

As discussed previously, PCA is frequently used for preliminary dimensionality reduction before further analyses, as LDA [21]. Indeed, a limit of using PCA alone is that it does not allow to obtain an unambiguous grouping of the data into clusters, requiring therefore the application of another analysis step able to reduce the intra-category variation while maximizing that inter-category [69]. The coupling, for instance, of PCA with LDA is a well established procedure which enables not only to classify the observations into groups but to quantify the importance of the single variables for this group separation. In this view, the advantage of LDA is that it makes it possible to reveal clusters, identifying objectively also the most contributory wavenumbers responsible for spectra discrimination [21, 58]. In particular, the application of PCA-LDA to spectroscopic investigation of complex biological systems proved to be a useful tool for the identification of spectral biomarkers of the process under investigation [7, 35, 69, 70, 71].

One outstanding work, worth to mention here, was done by Kelly and colleagues [70], where the authors showed how infrared spectroscopy and multivariate techniques can be used as a novel diagnostic approach for endometrial cancer screening. They first demonstrated how SR-FTIR microspectroscopy with subsequent PCA-LDA allows the clear segregation of different subtypes of endometrial carcinoma. However, the requirement of a particle accelerator impairs the use of endometrial spectroscopy as practical diagnostic application.

Recently, Taylor and colleagues applied ATR-FTIR spectroscopy supported by PCA-LDA analysis to interrogate endometrial tissues, employing in particular a conventional IR radiation source [72], showing that this approach, that can be applied directly to liquid or solid samples without further preparation, could provide a useful and simple objective test for endometrial cancer diagnosis.

Furthermore, in the work of Walsh and colleagues [69], ATR microspectroscopy has been successfully applied to the characterization of samples of exfoliative cervical cytology of different categories, with increasing severity of atypia. The spectral analysis was supported by PCA, with or without subsequent LDA, to verify if it was possible to discriminate among normal, low grade and high grade of exfoliative cytology. Indeed, important differences were found in the spectral range between 1500 and 1000 cm^{-1}, mainly due to proteins, glycoproteins, phosphates and carbohydrates. Noteworthy, the authors stressed that only the employment of the combined PCA-LDA allowed to maximize the inter-category variance, whilst reducing that intra-category. In particular, they found that the glycogen content strongly influenced the intra-category variance, while that inter-category resulted to be mainly due to protein and DNA conformational changes. In this view, FTIR microspectroscopy coupled with PCA-LDA could allow for an objective classification approach to class cervical cytology.

We should note that a delicate point of PCA-LDA is the choice of the principal components to be used as LDA input and, as described in the previous section about PCA, several ways have been developed to perform this task. Alternatively, the PLS method can be used instead of PCA [6, 73, 74]. For instance, Sandt and colleagues, using synchrotron infrared microspectroscopy coupled with PLS-DA, were able to characterize the metabolic fingerprint of induced pluripotent stem cells (iPSCs). In particular, they found that iPSCs are characterized by a chemical composition that leads to a spectral signature indistinguishable from that of embryonic stem cells (ESCs), but entirely different from that of the original somatic cells [6].

5.1. FTIR microspectroscopy supported by PCA-LDA for the characterization of SN and NSN murine oocytes

Recently, we applied FTIR microspectroscopy supported by PCA-LDA to the study of murine oocytes characterized by two different types of chromatin organization, namely surrounded nucleolus (SN) oocytes in which the chromatin is highly condensed and forms a ring around the nucleolus, and the not surrounded nucleolus (NSN) type where chromatin is dispersed and less condensed around the nucleolus [7, 75]. Interestingly, only SN oocytes are capable to complete the embryonic development after fertilization, while the NSN type, if fertilized, arrests at the two cell stage. To try to get new insights on the mechanisms that drive the different chromatin organization in the two kinds of oocytes, crucial for their embryonic development after fertilization, we studied the infrared absorption of single intact cells at different maturation stages, namely antral germinal vesicle (GV), metaphase I (MI, matured for 10 hours in vitro), and metaphase II (MII, matured for 20 hours in vitro).

Indeed, as we will show in the following, the FTIR spectra of the oocytes taken at the different maturation stages are very complex, since they provide information on different processes that were taking place simultaneously within the cells. For this reason, beside a fundamental visual inspection of the data, enabling the identification and assignment of the different spectral bands, it was crucial the application of PCA-LDA that made it possible to draw out the most significant spectral information responsible for the different cell behavior. Moreover, PCA-LDA allowed to identify the stage at which the separation between the SN and NSN oocytes took place, leading to their well distinct cell destinies.

As we discussed in paragraph 2, since the FTIR spectrum of cells is due to the overlapping contributes of the main biomolecules (see Figure 2), we analysed the second derivative spectra to identify the band peak positions and to assign them to the different biomolecule vibrational modes. The spectral analysis, strongly supported by PCA LDA, allowed us to disclose the most important spectral differences between the two types of oocytes, at each maturation stage, that were found to occur mainly in the lipid and nucleic acid absorption regions, as we will discuss below. For a full discussion of the results see [7].

5.1.1. Lipid analysis

5.1.1.1. NSN oocytes

The analysis between 3050 and 2800 cm^{-1}, mainly due to the lipid carbon-hydrogen stretching vibrations [29], disclosed significant variations in the lipid content of NSN oocytes during their maturation up to MII. Indeed, besides an increase of the CH$_2$ band intensity up to MII, respectively at 2922 cm^{-1} and 2852 cm^{-1}, important changes concerned mainly the unsaturated fatty acid composition, as indicated by variations of the band between 3020 and 3000 cm^{-1} due to the olefinic group absorption. Indeed, as shown in Figure 3A, a single peak around 3013 cm^{-1} was present at GV and MI stages, while a splitting in two components at ~ 3016 cm^{-1} and at ~ 3010 cm^{-1} characterized the MII stage (see the inset of Figure 3A). These results could reflect important changes in membrane fluidity, which in turn could confer to the oocyte a different division ability after fertilization [8].

5.1.1.2. SN oocytes

SN oocytes were found to be characterized - during maturation up to MII - by a significant increase of the 2937 cm^{-1} component that could be likely due to cholesterol and/or phospholipids (Figure 3B) [76, 77]. As discussed for NSN oocytes, the observed changes could reflect variations in the membrane properties, again highlighting the crucial role of lipids as markers of oocyte developmental competence [8, 78].

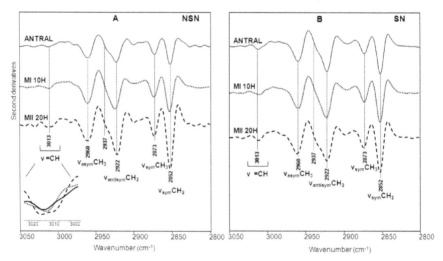

Figure 3. Second derivative absorption spectra of NSN (A) and SN (B) oocytes in the lipid absorption region. The second derivatives of the FTIR absorption spectra of single oocytes, measured at the antral (continuous line), MI 10 H (dotted line), and MII 20 H (dashed line) stages, are reported in the acyl chain absorption region, after normalization at the tyrosine peak (~1516 cm^{-1}). In the inset a magnification of the olefinic group band is shown.

5.1.1.3. PCA-LDA analysis

The results obtained by the direct inspection of second derivative spectra were confirmed by
PCA-LDA analysis performed on raw spectra. Firstly, the analysis was made on each type of
oocyte taken at the different maturation stages. For the SN oocytes, the component
carrying the highest discrimination weight resulted that at 2938 cm^{-1}, likely due to
cholesterol and / or phospholipids [76, 77], in agreement with what found by the direct
inspection of the spectra.

Concerning the NSN oocytes, on the other hand, the wavenumbers with the highest
discrimination weight were the 2922 cm^{-1}, due to the CH$_2$ stretching vibration, which
increases up to MII, and the 3018 cm^{-1}, assigned to the olefinic group =CH of
polyunsaturated fatty acids, whose absorption was observed to vary during the oocyte
maturation.

We, then, compared the two types of oocyte at each maturation stage - as illustrated in
Figure 4 - and we found that at the antral and MII stages the spectral components with the
highest discrimination weight were those due to cholesterol and /or phospholipids, while at
MI was that due to the olefinic group. Furthermore, to support the crucial role played by
lipids in determining at some extent the oocyte developmental capacity, we should add that
when we compared by PCA-LDA the spectra of the two oocyte types at the same
maturation stage in the 1800-1500 cm^{-1} spectral range, dominated by the amide I and amide
II absorption, the wavenumber with the highest discrimination weight was the 1739 cm^{-1},
due to the carbonyl stretching vibration of esters [7, 29].

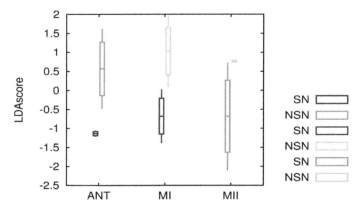

Figure 4. PCA-LDA analysis of SN and NSN oocytes in the lipid acyl chain absorption region (3050 –
2800 cm^{-1}). The separation between the two types of oocytes at each maturation stage is reported as
average of PCA-LDA scores. The height of the boxes and the whiskers corresponds to 1 and 1.5
standard deviations from the mean values, respectively. The analysis has been performed on the
measured spectra.

5.1.2. Nucleic acid analysis

5.1.2.1. NSN oocytes

We then analyzed the nucleic acid IR response of NSN and SN oocytes during their maturation, exploring the spectral region between 1000 and 800 cm^{-1}, where RNA and DNA vibrational modes mainly occur [31, 32].

We found that NSN oocytes maintain, in all the studied stages, an appreciable transcriptional activity as indicated mainly by the simultaneous presence of the RNA ribose component around 921 cm^{-1} and of the DNA deoxyribose between 895-898 cm^{-1} - indicative of a DNA/RNA hybrid - whose relative intensities were seen to vary during maturation (see Figure 5A). In particular, the intensity of these two components is higher at the antral stage, while it decreases at MI, to increase again up to MII. These results were also supported by the response of the complex band between 980-950 cm^{-1}, mainly due to the CC stretching vibration of DNA backbone. Indeed, the profile of this band varies depending on the DNA structure that, in turn, could reflect a different nucleic acid activity. In particular, for the NSN oocytes we found that at the antral stage DNA is mainly in A-form - with a triplet at 975 cm^{-1}, 966 cm^{-1} and 951 cm^{-1} - typical of the DNA/RNA hybrid during transcription. At MI, the reduction of the 975 cm^{-1} and 966 cm^{-1} bands and the appearance of that at 969 cm^{-1} indicate that DNA is mainly in the B-form, suggesting a sort of transcriptional "stand by state", further supported by the reduction extent of the DNA/RNA hybrid, as discussed above. From this "stand by state" NSN oocytes seem to resume their transcriptional activity at MII, where a coexistence of DNA A and B forms was observed, as indicated by the increase of the ~ 975 cm^{-1} band and again in agreement with the simultaneous increase of the ribose (921 cm^{-1}) and deoxyribose (898 cm^{-1}) components.

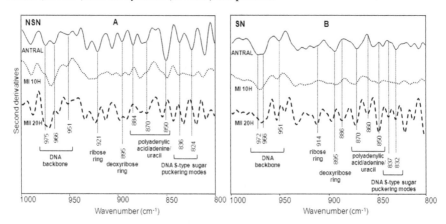

Figure 5. Second derivative absorption spectra of NSN (A) and SN (B) oocytes in the nucleic acid absorption region. The second derivatives of the FTIR absorption spectra of single oocytes, measured at the antral (continuous line), MI 10 H (dotted line), and MII 20 H (dashed line) stages, are reported in the 1000-800 cm^{-1} absorption region, after normalization at the tyrosine peak (~1516 cm^{-1}).

Furthermore, the analysis of the low frequency range, between 840-820 cm^{-1}, allowed us to obtain information on DNA methylation. In particular, in this spectral range, bands due to DNA S-type sugar puckering modes occur, which are sensitive to changes in the DNA sugar conformation induced by cytosine methylation [32]. The possibility to monitor changes in the profile of this spectral region in whole intact cells makes it possible, therefore, to obtain information on the variation of global DNA methylation in the CpG islands. In this way, we found that in the NSN oocytes DNA methylation was high at the antral stage, while it became very low, almost negligible at MII, in agreement with what found for the transcriptional activity pattern at the different maturation stages.

Finally, significant spectral differences were found between 890 and 850 cm^{-1}, where four different bands due to adenine and uracil vibrational modes occur (see Figure 5) [79]. Interestingly, the relative variation of these bands enables to monitor the mRNA polyadenylation extent, a crucial mechanism that regulates transcription. We found, in particular, that NSN oocytes were characterized during maturation by a low level of mRNA polyadenylation, being the polyadenylic acid band at 884 cm^{-1} absent at MII, while a new band at 854 cm^{-1} - likely due to adenine possibly not involved in polyA tail [80] – appeared. These results seem to suggest that an inadequate level of mRNA polyadenylation could preclude the possibility to resume meiosis, leaving the NSN oocytes in an unsuccessful transcriptional state

5.1.2.2. SN oocytes

The analysis of SN oocytes (Figure 5B) in the spectral range between 1000 and 800 cm^{-1} led to very different results compared to NSN oocytes (see Figure 5A). Briefly, during all the studied maturation stages, the SN oocyte transcriptional activity was found to be maintained at lower levels than NSN oocytes, as revealed by the analysis of the CC stretching of the DNA backbone (980-950 cm^{-1}) and the monitoring of the ribose (~ 922 cm^{-1}) and deoxyribose (895-898 cm^{-1}) vibrations. These results were supported by the temporal evolution of the DNA methylation bands that suggested a partial CpG methylation at the antral and MI stages, which dramatically increased at MII, contrary to what observed for NSN oocytes.

Noteworthy, while no evidence of mRNA polyadenylation was observed for SN oocytes at the antral stage - as indicated by the absence of the two polyadenylic acid bands around 884 cm^{-1} and 860 cm^{-1} - starting from MI the adenine and uracile bands at 870 cm^{-1} and 850 cm^{-1} appeared, to then dramatically increase up to MII. These findings likely indicate that SN MII oocytes are characterized by an adequate level of maternal polyadenylated mRNAs, making them ready to sustain a proper embryo development, contrary to NSN oocytes.

5.1.2.3. PCA-LDA analysis

The above results overall indicate that the IR spectra of oocytes at different maturation stages are very informative in the nucleic acid absorption region, allowing to obtain information on several cell processes simultaneously, including transcriptional activity, DNA methylation, and RNA polyadenylation. For this reason, PCA-LDA analysis was crucial to disclose the most significant spectral response, enabling to identify the marker bands able to discriminate between the two kinds of oocytes.

Firstly, we analyzed the different maturation stages of each kind of oocyte. In particular, NSN oocytes displayed a segregation into three separated clusters, each corresponding to a maturation stage, with a classification accuracy of about 80%. Noteworthy, the wavenumber with the highest weight (1.0) was that around 880 cm^{-1}, due to polyadenylic acid, that, as revealed by second derivative analysis, was present only at the antral stage and disappeared upon maturation up to MII.

On the other hand, PCA-LDA analysis of SN oocytes led to an excellent discrimination accuracy (97%), with the wavenumbers with the highest discrimination weight at 817 cm^{-1} (1.0) and 859 cm^{-1} (0.83). While this last component is due to polyadenylic acid, the assignment of the 817 cm^{-1} band is not unequivocal, being due to overlapping contributions of DNA and polyadenylic acid.

The above results were then confirmed by the PCA-LDA analysis performed between 1400-1000 cm^{-1}, where contributions due to nucleic acids, such as sugar-phosphate vibrations, also occur [31]. In particular, for the NSN oocytes the wavenumber with the highest discrimination weight (1.0) was the 1305 cm^{-1}, which is due to free adenine, possibly not involved in polyadenylation [79]. In agreement with the temporal pattern of the adenine band at 870 cm^{-1}, discussed previously, the 1305 cm^{-1} component displayed a higher intensity at MII, confirming that an inadequate mRNA polyadenylation could preclude NSN oocytes from a successful embryonic development (see Figure 6).

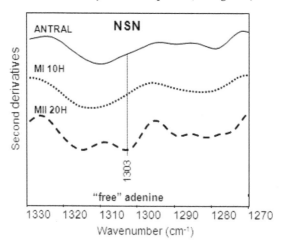

Figure 6. Second derivative absorption spectra of NSN oocytes in the absorption region of "free" adenine. The second derivatives of the FTIR absorption spectra of single NSN oocytes, measured at the antral (continuous line), MI 10 H (dotted line), and MII 20 H (dashed line) stages, are reported in the 1330-1270 cm^{-1} spectral range, where "free" adenine absorbs, after normalization at the tyrosine peak (~1516 cm^{-1}).

We then compared by PCA-LDA the two types of oocytes taken at the same maturation stage. As reported in Figure 7, we found the largest spectral distance at MI (92% classification accuracy), with the components carrying the highest discrimination weight due to A-DNA, likely reflecting differences in the transcriptional activity. In this view, MI stage could be considered a sort of crucial checkpoint, when some molecular rearrangements occur, deciding the oocyte fate.

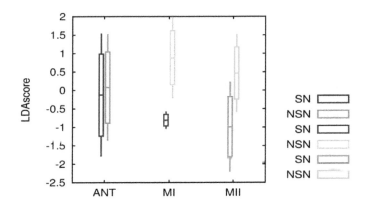

Figure 7. PCA-LDA analysis of SN and NSN oocytes in the nucleic acid absorption region (1000 - 800 cm⁻¹). The separation between the two types of oocytes at each maturation stage is reported as average of PCA-LDA scores. The height of the boxes and the whiskers corresponds to 1 and 1.5 standard deviations from the mean values, respectively. The analysis has been performed on the measured spectra.

These findings have been strongly supported by the comparison of the SN and NSN oocytes at each maturation stage, altogether. A very good discrimination accuracy (89%) was again found analyzing the nucleic acid absorption region, between 1000 and 800 cm⁻¹, that led to a clear cut separation into two groups (see Figure 8): one containing only the MII SN oocytes, and the other containing all the other SN and NSN stages. In particular, the wavenumbers carrying the highest discrimination weight were found at 926 cm⁻¹ (1.00), due to ribose vibration, and at 855 cm⁻¹ (0.97), assigned to adenine vibration, indicating again that differences in the temporal evolution and extent of transcription and polyadenylation play a crucial role in determining the different oocyte fate: the MII SN oocytes, with their proper content of maternal mRNAs polyadenylated, ready to support successfully the embryonic development; on the other hand, the MII NSN oocytes, with their mRNA lacking the appropriate polyadenylation, are kept in an unsuccessful transcriptional state.

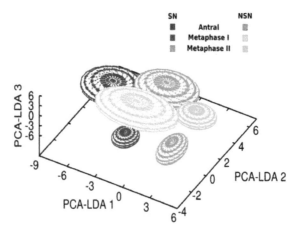

Figure 8. PCA–LDA analysis of SN and NSN oocytes in the nucleic acid absorption region. The PCA–LDA analysis has been carried out on measured FTIR absorption spectra obtained from SN and NSN oocytes at each maturation stage, between 1000 and 800 cm⁻¹. The semi-axes of ellipsoids in the 3D score plot correspond to two standard deviations of the data along each direction.

6. Conclusions

FTIR microspectroscopy has recently emerged as a powerful tool in biomedical research, thanks to the possibility of providing, in a non-invasive and rapid way, a chemical fingerprint of biological samples. In particular, being successfully applied to the study of complex biological systems, it makes it possible not only to characterize in situ biological processes, but also to provide a rapid diagnosis of several diseases, such as cancer and amyloid-based disorders.

We should, however, note that the intrinsic complexity of the IR response of biological systems - due to the overlapping absorption of the main biomolecules - requires the support of an appropriate multivariate analysis approach able to draw out the significant and non-redundant information contained in these highly dimensional data. Indeed, only a suitable combination of biospectroscopy and of multivariate analysis would provide robust and reliable results through the identification of specific biomarkers, an essential prerequisite for unbiased result interpretation [19, 20].

Author details

Diletta Ami* and Silvia Maria Doglia

Department of Biotechnology and Biosciences, University of Milano-Bicocca, Milano, Italy
Consorzio Nazionale Interuniversitario per le Scienze Fisiche della Materia (CNISM), UdR Milano-Bicocca, Milan, Italy

---

* Corresponding Author

Paolo Mereghetti
Center for Nanotechnology Innovation @NEST, Italian Institute of Technology (IIT), Pisa, Italy

Acknowledgement

D. A. is indebted to the University of Milano-Bicocca (I) for the supporting postdoctoral fellowship. P. M. acknowledges a postdoctoral fellowship from Italian Institute of Technology. S.M. D. acknowledges the financial support of the FAR (Fondo di Ateneo per la Ricerca) of the University of Milano-Bicocca (I).

The authors wish to thank Carlo Alberto Redi and his collaborators at the University of Pavia (I) for the collaboration on murine oocyte maturation, and Antonino Natalello of the University of Milano-Bicocca (I) for helpful discussions.

7. References

[1] Aksoy C, Severcan F. Role of Vibrational Spectroscopy in Stem Cell Research. Spectroscopy: An International Journal 2012; 27(3) 167-184.

[2] Ami D, Mereghetti P, Natalello A, Doglia SM. Fourier transform infrared microspectroscopy as a tool for embryonic stem cell studies. In: Atwood CS. (ed.) Stem Cells in Clinic and Research. Rijeka. InTech, 2011 p. 193-218.

[3] Heraud P, Nga ES, Caine S, Yu QC, Hirst C, Mayberry R, Bruce A, Wood BR, McNaughton D, Stanley EG, Elefanty AG. Fourier transform infrared microspectroscopy identifies early lineage commitment in differentiating human embryonic stem cells. Stem Cell Research 2010; 4(2) 140-147.

[4] Chan JW, Lieu DK. Label-free biochemical characterization of stem cells using vibrational spectroscopy. Journal of Biophotonics 2009; 2(11) 656-668.

[5] Walsh M J, Hammiche A, Fellous TG, Nicholson JM, Cotte M, Susini J, Fullwood NJ, Martin-Hirsch PL, Alison MR, Martin FL. Tracking the cell hierarchy in the human intestine using biochemical signatures derived by mid-infrared microspectroscopy. Stem Cell Research 2009; 3(1) 15-27.

[6] Sandt C, Féraud O, Oudrhiri N, Bonnet ML, Meunier MC, Valogne Y, Bertrand A, Raphaël M, Griscelli F, Turhan AG, Dumas P, Bennaceur-Griscelli A. Identification of spectral modifications occurring during reprogramming of somatic cells. PLoS ONE 2012; 7(4) e30743.

[7] Ami D, Mereghetti P, Natalello A, Doglia SM, Zanoni M, Redi CA, Monti M. FTIR spectral signatures of mouse antral oocytes: molecular markers of oocyte maturation and developmental competence. Biochimica et Biophysica Acta, 2011; 1813(6) 1220–1229.

[8] Wood BR, Chernenko T, Matthäus C, Diem M, Chong C, Bernhard U, Jene C, Brandli AA, McNaughton D, Tobin MJ, Trounson A, Lacham-Kaplan O. Shedding New Light on the Molecular Architecture of Oocytes Using a Combination of Synchrotron Fourier

Transform-Infrared and Raman Spectroscopic Mapping. Analytical Chemistry, 2008; 80(23) 9065-9072.

[9] Diomede L, Cassata G, Fiordaliso F, Salio M, Ami D, Natalello A, Doglia SM, De Luigi A, Salmona M. Tetracycline and its analogues protect Caenorhabditis elegans from β amyloid-induced toxicity by targeting oligomers. Neurobiology of Disease, 2010; 40(2) 424-431.

[10] Kuzyk A, Kastyak M, Agrawal V, Gallant M, Sivakumar G, Rak M, Del Bigio MR, Westaway D, Julian R, Gough KM. Association among amyloid plaque, lipid, and creatine in hippocampus of TgCRND8 mouse model for Alzheimer disease. The Journal of Biological Chemistry, 2010; 285(41) 31202-31207.

[11] Choo LP, Wetzel DL, Halliday WC, Jackson M, LeVine SM, Mantsch HH. In situ characterization of beta-amyloid in Alzheimer's diseased tissue by synchrotron Fourier transform infrared microspectroscopy. Biophysical Journal, 1996; 71(4) 1672-1679.

[12] Kneipp J, Miller LM, Joncic M, Kittel M, Lasch P, Beekes M, Naumann D. In situ identification of protein structural changes in prion-infected tissue. Biochimica et Biophysica Acta, 2003; 639(3) 152-158.

[13] Bellisola G, Sorio C. Infrared spectroscopy and microscopy in cancer research and diagnosis. American Journal of Cancer Research, 2012; 2(1) 1-21.

[14] Walsh MJ, German MJ, Singh M, Pollock HM, Hammiche A, Kyrgiou M, Stringfellow HF, Paraskevaidis E, Martin-Hirsch PL, Martin FL. IR microspectroscopy: potential applications in cervical cancer screening. Cancer Letters, 2007; 246(1-2) 1-11.

[15] Petibois C, Déléris G. Chemical mapping of tumor progression by FT-IR imaging: towards molecular histopathology. Trends in Biotechnology, 2006; 24(10) 455-462.

[16] Kastyak-Ibrahim MZ, Nasse MJ, Rak M, Hirschmugl C, Del Bigio MR, Albensi BC, Gough KM. Biochemical label-free tissue imaging with subcellular-resolution synchrotron FTIR with focal plane array detector. Neuroimage, 2012; 60(1) 376-383.

[17] Miller LM, Dumas P. From structure to cellular mechanism with infrared microspectroscopy. Current Opinion in Structural Biology, 2010; 20(5) 649-656.

[18] Trevisan J, Angelov PP, Carmichael PL, Scott AD, Martin FL. Extracting biological information with computational analysis of Fourier-transform infrared (FTIR) biospectroscopy datasets: current practices to future perspectives. The Analyst, 2012; 137(14) 3202-3215.

[19] Kelly JG, Trevisan J, Scott AD, Carmichael PL, Pollock HM, Martin-Hirsch PL, Martin FL. Biospectroscopy to metabolically profile biomolecular structure: a multistage approach linking computational analysis with biomarkers. Journal of Proteome Research, 2011; 10(4) 1437-1448.

[20] Wang L, Mizaikoff B. Application of multivariate data-analysis techniques to biomedical diagnostics based on mid-infrared spectroscopy. Analytical and Bioanalytical Chemistry, 2008; 391(5) 1641-1654.

[21] Martin FL, German MJ, Wit E, Fearn T, Ragavan N, Pollock HM. Identifying variables responsible for clustering in discriminant analysis of data from infrared microspectroscopy of a biological sample. Journal of Computational Biology, 2007; 14(9) 1176-1184.

[22] Heraud P, Tobin MJ. The emergence of biospectroscopy in stem cell research. Stem Cell Research, 2009; 3(1) 12-14.

[23] Kazarian SG, Chan KL. Applications of ATR-FTIR spectroscopic imaging to biomedical samples. Biochimica et Biophysica Acta, 2006; 1758(7) 858-867.

[24] Holman H-YN, Martin MC, McKinney WR. Tracking chemical changes in a live cell: Biomedical applications of SR-FTIR spectromicroscopy, 2003; 17 (2-3) 139-159.

[25] Tanthanuch W, Thumanu K, Lorthongpanich C, Parnpai R, Heraud P. Neural differentiation of mouse embryonic stem cells studied by FTIR spectroscopy. Journal of Molecular Structure, 2010; 967(1–3) 189–195.

[26] Caine S, Heraud P, Tobin MJ, McNaughton D, Bernard CC. The application of Fourier transform infrared microspectroscopy for the study of diseased central nervous system tissue. Neuroimage, 2012; 59(4) 3624-3640.

[27] Nakamura T, Kelly JG, Trevisan J, Cooper LJ, Bentley AJ, Carmichael PL, Scott AD, Cotte M, Susini J, Martin-Hirsch PL, Kinoshita S, Fullwood NJ, Martin FL. Microspectroscopy of spectral biomarkers associated with human corneal stem cells. Molecular Vision, 2010; 16 359-368.

[28] Ami D, Natalello A, Zullini A, Doglia SM. Fourier transform infrared microspectroscopy as a new tool for nematode studies. FEBS Letters, 2004; 576(3) 297-300.

[29] Casal HL, Mantsch HH. Polymorphic phase behaviour of phospholipid membranes studied by infrared spectroscopy. Biochimica et Biophysica Acta, 1984; 779(4) 381-401

[30] Barth A. Infrared spectroscopy of proteins. Biochimica et Biophysica Acta, 2007; 1767 (9) 1073–1101.

[31] Banyay M, Sarkar M, Gräslund A. A library of IR bands of nucleic acids in solution. Biophysical Chemistry, 2003; 104(2) 477-488.

[32] Banyay M, Gräslund A. Structural effects of cytosine methylation on DNA sugar pucker studied by FTIR. Journal of Molecular Biology, 2002; 324(4) 667-676.

[33] Kačuráková M, Mathlouthi M. FTIR and laser-Raman spectra of oligosaccharides in water: characterization of the glycosidic bond. Carbohydrate Research, 1996; 284 145-157.

[34] Wong PT, Wong RK, Caputo TA, Godwin TA, Rigas B. Infrared spectroscopy of exfoliated human cervical cells: evidence of extensive structural changes during carcinogenesis. Proceedings of the National Academy of Sciences USA, 1991; 88(24) 10988-10992.

[35] Ami D, Neri T, Natalello A, Mereghetti P, Doglia SM, Zanoni M, Zuccotti M, Garagna S, Redi CA. Embryonic stem cell differentiation studied by FT-IR spectroscopy. Biochimica et Biophysica Acta, 2008; 1783(1) 98-106.

[36] Konorov SO, Schulze HG, Caron NJ, Piret JM, Blades MW, Turner RFB. Raman microspectroscopic evidence that dry-fixing preserves the temporal pattern of non-specific differentiation in live human embryonic stem cells. Journal of Raman Spectroscopy, 2011; 42(4) 576–579.

[37] Zhao R, Quaroni L, Casson AG. Fourier transform infrared (FTIR) spectromicroscopic characterisation of stem-like cell populations in human esophageal normal and adenocarcinoma cell lines. The Analyst, 2010; 135(1) 53–61.

[38] Bassan P, Kohler A, Martens H, Lee J, Byrne HJ, Dumas P, Gazi E, Brown M, Clarke N, Gardner P. Resonant Mie scattering (RMieS) correction of infrared spectra from highly scattering biological samples. The Analyst, 2010; 135(2) 268-277.

[39] Susi H, Byler DM. Resolution-enhanced Fourier transform infrared spectroscopy of enzymes. Methods in Enzymology, 1986;130 290-311.

[40] Levin IW, Bhargava R. Fourier transform infrared vibrational spectroscopic imaging: integrating microscopy and molecular recognition. Annual Review of Physical Chemistry, 2005; 56 429-474.

[41] Dumas P, Miller L. The use of synchrotron infrared microspectroscopy in biological and biomedical investigations. Vibrational Spectroscopy, 2003; 32 3–21.

[42] Katon JE. Infrared Microspectroscopy. A Review of Fundamentals and Applications. Micron, 1996; 27(5) 303-314.

[43] Eriksson L, Johansson E, Kettaneh-Wold N, Trygg J, Wikstrom C, Wold S. Multivariate and Megavariate Data Analysis Basic Principles and Applications. San Jose: Umetrics Academy; 2006.

[44] Manly BFJ. Multivariate Statistical Methods. London: Chapman & Hall/CRC press; 2004.

[45] Hestenes MR, Stiefel E. Methods of Conjugate Gradients for Solving Linear Systems. Journal of Research of the National Bureau of Standards 1952;49: 409-436.

[46] Marquardt D. An Algorithm for Least-Squares Estimation of Nonlinear Parameters. SIAM Journal on Applied Mathematics 1963; 11(2) 431-441.

[47] Levenberg K. A Method for the Solution of Certain Non-Linear Problems in Least Squares. Quarterly of Applied Mathematics 1944; 2 164-168.

[48] Goldberg D E. Genetic Algorithms in Search Optimization and Machine Learning. Boston: Addison-Wesley Longman Publishing; 1969.

[49] Rencher A C. Methods of Multivariate Analysis. Hoboken: Wiley; 2002.

[50] Nas T, Isaksson T, Fearn T, Davies T. Multivariate Calibration and Classification. Chichester: NIR Publications; 2004.

[51] Fisher RA. The use of multiple measurements in taxonomic problems. Annals of Eugenics 1936; 7 179-188.

[52] Fearn, T. (2002). Discriminant analysis, In: Handbook of Vibrational Spectroscopy, Chalmers, J.M. & Griffiths, P.R. (eds.), New York: Wiley, p2086–2093.

[53] Fukunaga K. Introduction to Statistical Pattern Recognition. San Diego: Academic Press Professional Inc.; 1990.

[54] Bishop CM. Neural Networks for Pattern Recognition. New York: Oxford University Press; 1995.

[55] Jonathan P, McCarthy WV, Roberts MIA. Discriminant Analysis With Singular Covariance Matrices. A Method Incorporating Cross-Validation And Efficient Randomized Permutation Tests. Journal Of Chemometrics, 1996; 10(4) 189-213.

[56] Rezzi S, Giani I, Héberger K, Axelson DE, Moretti VM, Reniero F and Claude G. Classification of Gilthead Sea Bream (Sparus aurata) from 1H NMR Lipid Profiling Combined with Principal Component and Linear Discriminant Analysis. Journal of agricultural and food chemistry 2007; 55 9963-9968.

[57] Skrobot LS, Castro VRE, Pereira RCC, Pasa VMD and Fortes ICP. Use of Principal Component Analysis (PCA) and Linear Discriminant Analysis (LDA) in Gas Chromatographic (GC) Data in the Investigation of Gasoline Adulteration. Energy & Fuels 2007; 21 3394-3400.

[58] Walsh MJ, Singh MN, Pollock HM, Cooper LJ, German MJ, Stringfellow HF, Fullwood NJ, Paraskevaidis E, Martin-Hirsch PL, Martin FL. ATR microspectroscopy with multivariate analysis segregates grades of exfoliative cervical cytology. Biochemical and Biophysical Research Communications, 2007; 352(1) 213-219.

[59] Pereira RCC, Skrobot VL, Castro EVR, Fortes ICP, Pasa VMD. Determination of Gasoline Adulteration by Principal Components Analysis-Linear Discriminant Analysis Applied to FTIR Spectra. Energy & Fuels 2006; 20: 1097-1102.

[60] Héberger K, Csomós E andLivia S. Principal Component and Linear Discriminant Analyses of Free Amino Acids and Biogenic Amines in Hungarian Wines. Journal of Agricultural and Food Chemistry 2003; 51 8055-8060.

[61] Indahl UG, Liland KH, Naes T. Canonical partial least squares - a unified PLS approach to classification and regression problems Journal of Chemometrics 2009; 23 495–504.

[62] Rieppo L, Rieppo J, Jurvelin JS, Saarakkala S: Fourier transform infrared spectroscopic imaging and multivariate regression for prediction of proteoglycan content of articular cartilage. PloS ONE 2012, 7 e32344.

[63] Hemmateenejad B, Akhond M and Samari F. A comparative study between PCR and PLS in simultaneous spectrophotometric determination of diphenylamine, aniline, and phenol: Effect of wavelength selection, Spectrochimica Acta Part A: Molecular and Biomolecular Spectroscopy 2007; 67 958-965.

[64] Krogh A. What are artificial neural networks? Nature Biotechnology, 2008; 25(2) 195-197

[65] Haykin S. Neural Networks: A Comprehensive Foundation. Englewood Cliffs: Prentice Hall Inc.; 1999.

[66] Bentley AJ, Nakamura T, Hammiche A, Pollock HM, Martin FL, Kinoshita S, Fullwood NJ. Characterization of human corneal stem cells by synchrotron infrared micro-spectroscopy. Molecular Vision, 2007; 13 237-242.

[67] Yousef I, Bréard J, SidAhmed-Adrar N, Maâmer-Azzabi A, Marchal C, Dumas P, Le Naour F. Infrared spectral signatures of CDCP1-induced effects in colon carcinoma cells. The Analyst, 2011; 136(24) 5162-5168.

[68] German MJ, Hammiche A, Ragavan N, Tobin MJ, Cooper LJ, Matanhelia SS, Hindley AC, Nicholson CM, Fullwood NJ, Pollock HM, Martin FL. Infrared spectroscopy with multivariate analysis potentially facilitates the segregation of different types of prostate cell. Biophysical Journal, 2006; 90(10) 3783-3795.

[69] Walsh MJ, Singh MN, Stringfellow HF, Pollock HM, Hammiche A, Grude O, Fullwood NJ, Pitt MA, Martin-Hirsch PL, Martin FL. FTIR Microspectroscopy Coupled with Two-

Class Discrimination Segregates Markers Responsible for Inter- and Intra-Category Variance in Exfoliative Cervical Cytology. Biomarker Insights, 2008; 3 179–189.

[70] Kelly JG, Singh MN, Stringfellow HF, Walsh MJ, Nicholson JM, Bahrami F, Ashton KM, Pitt MA, Martin-Hirsch PL, Martin FL. Derivation of a subtype-specific biochemical signature of endometrial carcinoma using synchrotron-based Fourier-transform infrared microspectroscopy. Cancer Letters, 2009; 274(2) 208-217.

[71] Walsh MJ, Fellous TG, Hammiche A, Lin WR, Fullwood NJ, Grude O, Bahrami F, Nicholson JM, Cotte M, Susini J, Pollock HM, Brittan M, Martin-Hirsch PL, Alison MR, Martin FL. Fourier transform infrared microspectroscopy identifies symmetric PO(2)(-) modifications as a marker of the putative stem cell region of human intestinal crypts. Stem Cells, 2008; 26(1) 108-118.

[72] Taylor SE, Cheung KT, Patel II, Trevisan J, Stringfellow HF, Ashton KM, Wood NJ, Keating PJ, Martin-Hirsch PL, Martin FL. Infrared spectroscopy with multivariate analysis to interrogate endometrial tissue: a novel and objective diagnostic approach. British Journal of Cancer, 2011; 104(5) 790-797.

[73] Chonanant C, Jearanaikoon N, Leelayuwat C, Limpaiboon T, Tobin MJ, Jearanaikoon P, Heraud P. Characterisation of chondrogenic differentiation of human mesenchymal stem cells using synchrotron FTIR microspectroscopy. The Analyst, 2011; 136(12) 2542-2551.

[74] Thumanu K, Tanthanuch W, Danna Y, Anawat S, Chanchao L, Rangsun P, Philip H. Spectroscopic signature of mouse embryonic stem cell-derived hepatocytes using synchrotron Fourier transform infrared microspectroscopy. Journal of Biomedical Optics 2011; 16(5) 057005.

[75] Debey P, Szöllösi MS, Szöllösi D, Vautier D, Girousse A, Besombes D. Competent mouse oocytes isolated from antral follicles exhibit different chromatin organization and follow different maturation dynamics. Molecular Reproduction and Development, 1993; 36(1) 59-74.

[76] Marty R, N'soukpoé-Kossi CN, Charbonneau DM, Kreplak L, Tajmir-Riahi HA. Structural characterization of cationic lipid-tRNA complexes. Nucleic Acid Research, 2009; 37(15) 5197-5207.

[77] Liu J, Conboy JC. Structure of a gel phase lipid bilayer prepared by the Langmuir-Blodgett/Langmuir-Schaefer method characterized by sum-frequency vibrational spectroscopy. Langmuir, 2005; 21(20) 9091-9097.

[78] Gentile L, Monti M, Sebastiano V, Merico V, Nicolai R, Calvani M, Garagna S, Redi CA, Zuccotti M. Single-cell quantitative RT-PCR analysis of Cpt1b and Cpt2 gene expression in mouse antral oocytes and in preimplantation embryos. Cytogenetic and Genome Research, 2004; 105(2-4) 215-21.

[79] Zhizhina GP, Oleinik EF. Infrared spectroscopy of nucleic acids. Russian Chemical Reviews, 1972; 41(3) 258 -280.

[80] Ten GN, Baranov VI. Manifestation of intramolecular proton transfer in imidazole in the electronic-vibrational spectrum. Journal of Applied Spectroscopy, 2008; 75(2) 168-173.

Permissions

The contributors of this book come from diverse backgrounds, making this book a truly international effort. This book will bring forth new frontiers with its revolutionizing research information and detailed analysis of the nascent developments around the world.

We would like to thank Leandro Valim de Freitas and Ana Paula Barbosa Rodrigues de Freitas, for lending their expertise to make the book truly unique. They have played a crucial role in the development of this book. Without their invaluable contribution this book wouldn't have been possible. They have made vital efforts to compile up to date information on the varied aspects of this subject to make this book a valuable addition to the collection of many professionals and students.

This book was conceptualized with the vision of imparting up-to-date information and advanced data in this field. To ensure the same, a matchless editorial board was set up. Every individual on the board went through rigorous rounds of assessment to prove their worth. After which they invested a large part of their time researching and compiling the most relevant data for our readers. Conferences and sessions were held from time to time between the editorial board and the contributing authors to present the data in the most comprehensible form. The editorial team has worked tirelessly to provide valuable and valid information to help people across the globe.

Every chapter published in this book has been scrutinized by our experts. Their significance has been extensively debated. The topics covered herein carry significant findings which will fuel the growth of the discipline. They may even be implemented as practical applications or may be referred to as a beginning point for another development. Chapters in this book were first published by InTech; hereby published with permission under the Creative Commons Attribution License or equivalent.

The editorial board has been involved in producing this book since its inception. They have spent rigorous hours researching and exploring the diverse topics which have resulted in the successful publishing of this book. They have passed on their knowledge of decades through this book. To expedite this challenging task, the publisher supported the team at every step. A small team of assistant editors was also appointed to further simplify the editing procedure and attain best results for the readers.

Our editorial team has been hand-picked from every corner of the world. Their multi-ethnicity adds dynamic inputs to the discussions which result in innovative outcomes. These outcomes are then further discussed with the researchers and contributors who give their valuable feedback and opinion regarding the same. The feedback is then collaborated with the researches and they are edited in a comprehensive manner to aid the understanding of the subject.

Apart from the editorial board, the designing team has also invested a significant amount of their time in understanding the subject and creating the most relevant covers. They scrutinized every image to scout for the most suitable representation of the subject and create an appropriate cover for the book.

The publishing team has been involved in this book since its early stages. They were actively engaged in every process, be it collecting the data, connecting with the contributors or procuring relevant information. The team has been an ardent support to the editorial, designing and production team. Their endless efforts to recruit the best for this project, has resulted in the accomplishment of this book. They are a veteran in the field of academics and their pool of knowledge is as vast as their experience in printing. Their expertise and guidance has proved useful at every step. Their uncompromising quality standards have made this book an exceptional effort. Their encouragement from time to time has been an inspiration for everyone.

The publisher and the editorial board hope that this book will prove to be a valuable piece of knowledge for researchers, students, practitioners and scholars across the globe.

List of Contributors

Leandro Valim de Freitas
Petróleo Brasileiro SA (PETROBRAS), Brazil
São Paulo State University (UNESP), Brazil
Universidade Estadual Paulista "Júlio de Mesquita Filho", (UNESP), Guaratinguetá, SP, Brazil

Ana Paula Barbosa Rodrigues de Freitas and Messias Borges Silva
São Paulo State University (UNESP), Brazil
University of São Paulo (USP), Brazil

Fernando Augusto Silva Marins
São Paulo State University (UNESP), Brazil

Estéfano Vizconde Veraszto
Municipal College Franco Montoro Professor (FMPFM), Brazil
Campinas State University (UNICAMP), Brazil

José Tarcísio Franco de Camargo
Municipal College Franco Montoro Professor (FMPFM), Brazil
Centro Universitário Regional de Espírito Santo do Pinhal (UNIPINHAL), Esp. Sto do Pinhal, SP, Brazil

J. Paulo Davim
Aveiro University (UA), Portugal

Dirceu da Silva
Universidade Estadual de Campinas (UNICAMP), Campinas/SP, Brazil

K. Böhm
Institute of Waste Management, Department of Water, Atmosphere and Environment, University of
Natural Resources and Life Sciences, Vienna, Austria

E. Smidt and J. Tintner
Institute of Wood Science and Technology, Department of Material Sciences and Process Engineering, University of Natural Resources and Life Sciences, Vienna, Austria

Carla Cristina Almeida Loures
São Paulo State University (UNESP), Brazil

Carla Cristina Almeida Loures, Fatima Salman and Hilton Túlio Lima dos Santos
University of São Paulo (USP), Brazil

Gisella Lamas Samanamud
University of Texas at San Antonio (UTSA), USA

Silvia Cateni, Marco Vannucci, Marco Vannocci and Valentina Colla
Scuola Superiore S.Anna, TECIP - PERCRO Ghezzano, Pisa, Italy

Rosangela Villwock
Mathematics division, Western Paraná State University, Cascavel, Brazil
Maria Teresinha Arns Steiner, Andrea Sell Dyminski and Anselmo Chaves Neto
PPGMNE, Federal University of Paraná, Curitiba, Brazil

Hilton Túlio Lima dos Santos and Wagner Freitas
University of São Paulo (USP), Brazil

André Maurício de Oliveira
Federal Center of Technology – Minas Gerais (CEFET - MG), Brazil

Patrícia Gontijo de Melo
Federal University of Uberlândia (UFU), Brazil

John R. Castro-Suarez, William Ortiz-Rivera, Nataly Galan-Freyle, Amanda Figueroa-Navedo, Leonardo C. Pacheco-Londoño and Samuel P. Hernández-Rivera
ALERT DHS Center of Excellence, Department of Chemistry, University of Puerto Rico-Mayagüez, Mayagüez, PR

Mohammad Ali Zare Chahouki
Associate Professor, Department of Rehabilitation of Arid and Mountainous Regions, Natural Resources Faculty, University of Tehran, Iran

M. Schwanninger
Department of Chemistry, University of Natural Resources and Life Sciences, Vienna, Austria

Diletta Ami and Silvia Maria Doglia
Department of Biotechnology and Biosciences, University of Milano-Bicocca, Milano, Italy
Consorzio Nazionale Interuniversitario per le Scienze Fisiche della Materia (CNISM), UdR Milano- Bicocca, Milan, Italy

Paolo Mereghetti
Center for Nanotechnology Innovation @NEST, Italian Institute of Technology (IIT), Pisa, Italy

Printed in the USA
CPSIA information can be obtained
at www.ICGtesting.com
JSHW011814301024
72690JS00002B/84